POLITICS
and PROPHECY

Christa Reinach and
Alan J. Reinach, editors

Pacific Press® Publishing Association
Nampa, Idaho
Oshawa, Ontario, Canada
www.pacificpress.com

Copyright 2007 by Pacific Press® Publishing Association
Printed in the United States of America
All rights reserved

Cover design by Gerald Lee Monks
Cover design resources from dreamstime.com
Inside design by Steve Lanto

Library of Congress Cataloging-in-Publication Data

Politics and prophecy : the battle for religious liberty and the
authentic Gospel / Alan J. Reinach and Christa Reinach, editors.
p. cm.
ISBN-13: 978-0-8163-2227-5 (pbk.)
ISBN-10: 0-8163-2227-9 (pbk.)
1. Freedom of religion—United States. I. Reinach, Alan J., 1957-
II. Reinach, Christa, 1965-
BR516.P65 2008
261.7'20973—dc22
2007033287

You can obtain additional copies of this book by calling toll-free 1-800-765-6955
or by visiting http://www.adventistbookcenter.com.

07 08 09 10 11 • 5 4 3 2 1

Contents

Part II: Current Issues

Contributors

Barry W. Bussey is the general counsel and public affairs director for the Seventh-day Adventist Church in Canada. He has an M.A. in political science from Memorial University of Newfoundland, an LL.M. in constitutional law from Osgoode Hall Law School at York University, and is working toward a Ph.D. in law at Osgoode Hall Law School.

Jonathan Gallagher, Ph.D., is deputy secretary general of the International Religious Liberty Association (IRLA) and the United Nations representative of the Seventh-day Adventist Church.

John Graz, Ph.D., is director of the Department of Public Affairs and Religious Liberty for the General Conference of the Seventh-day Adventist Church. He is also secretary general of the International Religious Liberty Association, secretary general of the Conference of Secretaries of the World Christian Communions, and a member of the board of the International Academy of Religious Freedom. He is the general editor of *Building Bridges of Faith* and has authored and/or coauthored several other books—among them, *101 Questions Adventists Ask*—and numerous journal and magazine articles.

Nicholas P. Miller, Esq., an honors graduate of Columbia University Law School and director of the Andrews University International Religious Liberty Institute, is completing his Ph.D. work in American religious history, focusing on religious influences on the Constitution. He is the author of numerous scholarly and popular articles on church and state and has argued in defense of religious freedom to the United States Supreme Court.

Douglas Morgan, Ph.D., is professor of history and political studies at Columbia Union College in Takoma Park, Maryland. He is the author of *Adventism and the American Republic: The Public Involvement of a Major Apocalyptic Movement* (Knoxville, Tenn.: University of Tennessee Press, 2001) and editor of *The Peacemaking Remnant: Essays and Historic Documents* (Silver Spring, Md.: Adventist Peace Fellowship, 2005).

Michael D. Peabody, Esq., serves as executive director of the North American Religious Liberty Association—West, in Sacramento, California, and also as vice president of the Seventh-day Adventist Church State Council and legislative affairs director for the Pacific Union Conference of Seventh-day Adventists.

Alan J. Reinach, Esq., is director of the Department of Public Affairs and Religious Liberty of the Pacific Union Conference of Seventh-day Adventists. He also serves as president of the Seventh-day Adventist Church State Council and of the North American Religious Liberty Association—West. He is host of "Freedom's Ring," a nationally syndicated weekly radio show, has authored numerous legal and popular articles on church and state, and has argued in defense of religious freedom in the United States and California Supreme Courts.

James D. Standish, Esq., received his bachelor's degree from Newbold College in England, his MBA from the University of Virginia, and his juris doctor *cum laude* from Georgetown University, where he was president of the church-state law forum. Currently director of legislative affairs for the Seventh-day Adventist Church and executive director of the North American Religious Liberty Association, he also hosts the weekly television show "Global Faith & Freedom."

Timothy G. Standish, Ph.D., is a research scientist with a doctorate in biology and public policy who currently works at the Geoscience Research Institute of the General Conference of Seventh-day Adventists.

Alan J. Reinach

The Battle for the Gospel

For many Christians, the hot-button issues of the day include abortion, gay marriage, public schools perceived to be hostile to God, and the defense of liberty against its terrorist enemies. This book will consider several of these issues and others, including the teaching of origins in public schools, school prayer, the public display of the Ten Commandments, and attacks on the Supreme Court.

Many books have been written about these topics, but this book has a different premise. The issues identified above are certainly important, but they are only surface issues. The real battle is for the gospel of Jesus Christ.

The culture-war battles are symptomatic of a deep spiritual malaise afflicting our society. Conservatives blame these spiritual problems on secularizing trends and on liberals, humanists, atheists, and gays who seek to marginalize the role of religion in public life. It is true that some liberal activists are hostile to religion and would like to banish overtly religious ideology from public-policy debate. However, it is the secularization of the religious community that poses an even greater danger.

Religious conservatives have reacted to the secularizing trends in ways that have profound implications for the gospel. Politics has become the new gospel. Many Christian leaders are out to "save America" through political means. The church has forsaken her true source of power, her only real ability to transform culture—the power of the gospel of Jesus Christ. Ironically, the church's new emphasis on obtaining political power is itself a form of secularization.

Spiritual revival really can change history. It has happened repeatedly. The American Revolution would not have been possible without a powerful revival known as the First Great Awakening. This revival also laid the foundation for the First Amendment by creating such religious diversity and passion that it became impossible to sustain any state or federal religious establishment. Religion had to be cut loose from the state and granted full freedom.

In the nineteenth century, the Second Great Awakening laid the spiritual foundation for the abolitionist movement, which again transformed society and changed the constitutional order. The new constitutional amendments obligated the states to respect individual rights and liberties equally with the federal government. The Second Great Awakening also produced a new explosion of American religions, including the Seventh-day Adventist Church.

This book is based on the conviction that there is more to modern culture-war battles than can be understood merely through policy analysis or moral discourse—a conviction that a prophetic perspective is essential. It isn't enough for Christians to be socially or politically engaged and to seek a more righteous society, although doing so is valuable. The rule of the righteous has been tried before—in Calvin's Geneva and in Cromwell's England, for example. Each attempt has been a spectacular failure.

No, Christians are first and foremost "ambassadors for Christ" and serve the interests of the King and His kingdom. This kingdom, Jesus declared, "is not of this world." All of our efforts to establish God's kingdom as a temporal dominion are dangerous and heretical. Christians don't make the greatest impact on society by pursuing political power but by obtaining genuine spiritual power.

This book is not advocating a return to pietism. Pietism represents a misguided retreat from the world in which the church buries its head in the Bible, preaches spiritual truth, and ignores its social obligations. Both pietism and power politics are ditches to be avoided. They represent two extremes and are inconsistent with the biblical role of the church. Instead, the church is called to fulfill a prophetic function: to speak truth to power.

The church's prophetic role

In Bible times, the priests rarely if ever fulfilled this prophetic function. They couldn't speak truth to power because they were the powerful elite. They exercised power. On the other hand, the prophets—such as Amos, the shepherd—had no conflict of interest. They had no power to lose. They had no ties to the establishment. So they could proclaim the "word of the Lord" fearlessly. Today, the church has become part of the hierarchy of power. As David Kuo writes in *Tempting Faith,* groups like the Christian Coalition and the Family Research Council have moved from seeking a place at the table to sitting at the head of the table.[1]

The church's power play has been an utter failure. Even evangelical critics have observed that the church has mostly failed to achieve its important policy objectives and that instead, it has become subject to being manipulated by the politicians.[2] Even assuming that the church is far more successful in achieving its agenda in the near future, the biblical injunction will always hold true: "Do not put your trust in princes, nor in a son of man, in whom there is no help."[3] And again: "It is better to trust in the LORD than to put confidence in princes."[4] The prophet Jeremiah warned Israel not to drink of the waters of Egypt and Assyria. Isaiah declared, " 'Look! You are trusting in the staff of this broken reed, Egypt, on which if a man leans, it will go into his hand and pierce it. So is Pharaoh king of Egypt to all who trust in him.' "[5] The prophets did not recommend political alliances to the people of God. Their message was always to trust in the Lord, and to turn to the Lord, and to drink deeply at the wells of salvation.

The church's grasping for political power has profound eschatological implications. Today, popular prophetic scenarios have directed attention to the Middle East and the anticipation of war and rapture. Such scenarios are tragically wrong and dangerous. Meanwhile, the book of Revelation warns against the church becoming a harlot by her immoral, intimate association with the kings of the earth.[6] This is an uncannily accurate portrait of the modern American political scene.

This is not to criticize the church's political agenda. Several chapters of this book discuss issues that will resonate with religious conservatives. Barry W. Bussey brings considerable insight and perspective to his discussion of the collision between liberal and Christian values in the battle for marriage. Dr. Timothy G. Standish rightly criticizes the scientific community for turning Darwinism into the established dogma of the public schools; he contends for more balance in the approach to the study of origins. "Caught Between God and Mammon" examines the most critical religious liberty issue in America today: thousands of Americans are losing their jobs for no crime other than their determination to obey God and practice their faith.

However, other chapters sharply diverge from the rhetoric and policy of the Religious Right. "Can Johnny Pray in Public School?" is a ringing endorsement of the Supreme Court's embrace of official government neutrality toward religion. Dr. Douglas Morgan sharply criticizes American preemptive intervention in Iraq in light of Revelation 13. He notes that the United States is the subject of this critical prophecy, which says that this country's lamblike qualities will give way to a dragon's voice. Michael D. Peabody, Esq., exposes the dangerous efforts to undermine an independent judiciary that is the bulwark of American freedom. "The Battle for the Ten Commandments" examines some of the practical and theological problems of asking the state to assume responsibility for promoting and respecting this religious law.

An authentic prophetic voice does not toe the political party line. It must proclaim truth to power regardless of where that truth lines up politically. This volume contains chapters that will offend liberals, and others that will inflame conservatives. Those capable of setting aside their political convictions long enough to consider the spiritual perspectives will find gems of truth to be mined.

The opening chapters of the book lay a foundation for understanding the respective roles of church and state. These roles are distinct and must not be confused. "Liberty and the Gospel" was written by a theologian who is also a world leader in bringing government and faith leaders together to dialogue about critical religious freedom problems in the most difficult countries. Dr. John Graz brings a profoundly Christ-centered emphasis to the subject and establishes the principle of religious freedom squarely on the gospel itself, the foundation it must have. " 'Render Unto God' " will surprise many, for its analysis of the biblical evidence regarding the roles of church and state is fresh and insightful. " 'Render Unto Caesar' " takes a profoundly prophetic view of the roles of church and state. The insight offered in these opening chapters cannot readily be found in much of the literature on church and state relations.

Separation of church and state

The separation of church and state is of uniquely Protestant origin. Christian conservatives who attack this principle are no longer truly Protestant; indeed, they have largely embraced the Roman Catholic approach to church-state relations. Catholic theologians have taught that the Catholic Church is the repository of truth and that the state has an obligation to support and uphold the truth it proclaims.[7] Modern evangelicals behave in ways that suggest the same attitude. Indeed, American evangelicals have made common cause with Catholics in their quest to shape public policy.

This observation is not meant to suggest that religious ideas ought to be banished from policy debate, as some liberals contend. One cannot rule out restrictive abortion policies simply because they agree with a theological orientation. Neither is it legitimate to overturn the historic definition of marriage because it is rooted in religious tradition. What is missing from the public square is the understanding that the state has no role to play in advancing religion. All parties to the debate agree that the state may regulate marriage. It is legitimate, therefore, to debate the form such regulation should take. It is *not* legitimate for the state to regulate prayer or other forms of worship. The Supreme Court rightly criticized the New York State Board of Regents for requiring public-school students to recite its prayer. It is critical that Americans regain a sense of balance on these issues and understand the proper limits of both church and state. The preservation of American liberty depends on the preservation of proper limits on both church and state.

Liberty is a central concern of prophecy. It rises and falls with the gospel of Jesus Christ. This is why the real battle is for the gospel. When Israel lost its grip on the Lord and made alliances with surrounding nations, its power waned. When it returned to the Lord, its power increased.

Dr. Graz reminds us that the early church reached out to the civil power to coerce dissenters to accept its teachings. Apparently, it thought the power of the gospel inadequate to persuade and to save. According to prophecy, this history will be repeated; a spiritually powerless church will embrace the power of the state to advance the kingdom of God. Persecution is the inevitable result.[8]

Today, the gospel is mostly absent across the religious spectrum. What remains of it is greatly watered down. We are told that Jesus died for our sins but He doesn't require much from us. There are several variations of the same theme: only believe, only recite the sinner's prayer, only speak in tongues, only send a generous offering, only vote a certain way, and you are definitely "in." Once you're in, you're in for life. The theologian Dietrich Bonhoeffer called this "cheap grace." Modern American religious life has little of the deep repentance that characterized the historic revivals. There is little sorrow for sin and most definitely little turning from it. The statistical record bears this out.[9] Evangelicals, to their shame, are morally indistinguishable from the world around them. The lives they live reflect the secular norms of society. Too little attention has been paid to what has apparently caused this secularization of the church—the fact that the gospel has been stripped of its power.

Christians lament the moral and spiritual decline of the nation and blame these ills on all those whom God has never charged with building up its moral and spiritual foundations. Hollywood, Madison Avenue, and Washington, D.C., don't have a divine mandate to renew American spirituality; the church does. America's moral failures may be placed squarely at the door of the church. For generations, the American church has taught that the law of God was nailed to the cross and that believers are not "under law" but "under grace." This theology represents a false dichotomy between salvation and obedience. It has undermined public morals.

The Bible consistently rejects such a divide between grace and obedience. Jesus Himself declared, " 'If you love Me, keep My commandments.' "[10] The apostle John repeated this theme: "By this we know that we love the children of God, when we love God and keep His commandments. For this is the love of God, that we keep His commandments. And His commandments are not burdensome."[11]

America's best hope

The best hope for America is for its people to recover the authentic gospel. Indeed, the nation's survival depends on it. This is the theme of Revelation 14. In that chapter, God's final warning to the world is given by three angels. The first one calls the world to genuine repentance, to true worship of the Creator, and to recovery of the everlasting gospel of Jesus Christ. This call becomes urgent in light of the warnings of the second and third angels. The third angel warns about the danger of receiving the infamous mark of the beast and suffering the wrath of God. Revelation 13 declares that those who refuse the mark will be persecuted. Liberty will die. The second angel shows how liberty dies.

So, it is high time for the church to recover her authentically prophetic voice and function—speaking truth to power instead of grasping for power. The real battle is to recover the power of God, which Paul declared is found in the gospel of Jesus Christ: "I am not ashamed of the gospel of Christ, for it is the power of God to salvation for everyone who believes, for the Jew first and also for the Greek. For in it the righteousness of God is revealed from faith to faith; as it is written, *'The just shall live by faith.' "*[12]

The book of Revelation defines the central issue in the final conflict as worship. In chapter 13, the church-state union enforces worship of the beast and imposes the mark of the beast on dissenters. In Revelation 14, the first angel calls the world to the true worship of the Creator. One's eternal destiny will be determined on the basis of one's choice of worship.

Many Christians wrongly assume that "the beast" that seeks worship will be a religious form readily distinguished from Christianity. Such a scenario wouldn't deceive Bible believers because it would be so obviously "anti-Christ." In reaching such a conclusion, those who believe this fail to consider Jesus' warnings that the false worship of the last days will " 'deceive, if possible even the elect.' "[13] They also fail to connect the dots between this warning and Christ's observation in the same discourse that " 'many will come in My name . . . and will deceive many.' "[14] The prefix *anti* used in the term *antichrist* may be rendered either "in place of" or "against." The plain teaching of Jesus is that the last day deception will be Christian in name but not in character.

The worship of the beast and its image described in Revelation 13 is enforced by the strongest sanctions, including economic penalties and, ultimately, death. All who don't conform to this worship are slated to be killed.[15] This is reminiscent of the account in Luke 9, in which some of Jesus' disciples wanted to call fire down from heaven to destroy a Samaritan village. There was considerable antipathy between Samaritans and Jews, and this particular Samaritan village didn't want anything to do with Jesus because He was on His way to Jerusalem. Jesus' disciples, James and John, were highly offended and wanted revenge. Jesus rebuked them, declaring, " 'You do not know what manner of spirit you are of. For the Son of Man did not come to destroy men's lives but to save them.' "[16]

A religion that seeks to destroy those who don't worship in the "right" way is a false religion. Its teachings run contrary to the character of a loving God. The false christ—or antichrist—demands worship on pain of death. The true Christ gave His life to win our love and compels no one to return that love.

The true gospel is powerful. Christ declared that if He is lifted up, He will draw all people unto Himself.[17] He doesn't need the help of the state or its laws. No one must be coerced to believe or to worship. The love and righteousness of God revealed in the true gospel can turn the world upside down. They can also turn a human life right side up. This is what the real battle is all about—the battle to recover the real gospel of Jesus Christ.

---

1. David Kuo, *Tempting Faith: An Inside Story of Political Seduction* (New York: Free Press, 2006), 67; but see pages 170–172, where Kuo discusses the co-opting of conservative religious leaders by the Bush administration.

2. See Kuo; see also Cal Thomas and Ed Dobson, *Blinded by Might* (Grand Rapids, Mich.: Zondervan, 2000).

3. Psalm 146:3, NKJV.

4. Psalm 118:9, NKJV.

5. Isaiah 36:6, NKJV.

6. See Revelation 17:1–5.

7. See, e.g., John Paul II, *The Splendor of Truth: Encyclical Letter of John Paul II* (Boston: Pauline Books & Media, 1993).

8. This is the main theme of Revelation chapters 13, 14, 17, and 18.

9. Christian pollster George Barna has surveyed the church community extensively. Some of his findings are available at his Web site, www.barna.org. See, e.g., "Born Again Christians Just As Likely to Divorce As Are Non-Christians," September 8, 2004, http://www.barna.org/FlexPage.aspx?Page=BarnaUpdate&Barna UpdateID=170. See also "Faith Has a Limited Effect On Most People's Behavior," May 24, 2004, http://www.barna.org/FlexPage.aspx?Page=BarnaUpdate&BarnaUp dateID=164.

10. John 14:15, NKJV.

11. 1 John 5:2, 3, NKJV.

12. Romans 1:16, 17, NKJV.

13. Matthew 24:24, NKJV.

14. Matthew 24:5, NKJV.

15. Revelation 13:15, "cause all who refused to worship the image [of the beast] to be killed," NKJV.

16. Luke 9:55, 56, NKJV.

17. See John 12:32.

Part I

Foundations of Freedom

John Graz

CHAPTER 1

Liberty and the Gospel

For many years I have encountered the attitude that the idea of religious freedom came from philosophers who were reacting against religious intolerance and fanaticism. Many people believe that religion has been a root cause of intolerance, segregation, and persecution rather than a source of human rights and freedom. Sadly, there is some truth to this belief. Not withstanding the failings of religion, the Bible remains the primary source for the value of religious freedom. Those who have claimed that it justifies persecution have misunderstood and misrepresented its teachings. Historically, it wasn't the Enlightenment alone that contributed to the rise of religious freedom; religious faith played an indispensable role. Believers saw an expression of their faith in human rights.

The most widely accepted definition of religious freedom today, and probably the most elaborate one, is given in Article 18 of the Universal Declaration of Human Rights. It states, "Everyone has the right to freedom of thought, conscience and religion; this right includes freedom to change his religion or belief, and freedom, either alone or in community with others and in public or private, to manifest his religion or belief in teaching, practice, worship and observance."[1] This definition lays down the principle of the freedom of choice, both for the individual and for the religious community.

Freedom to choose one's religion may seem basic to those who live in democratic countries, but it is far from universal. Indeed, in the international arena, there is considerable resistance to recognizing even this most basic aspect of religious freedom. Many nations are identified with a particular religious tradition, and citizens are expected to remain members of the national religion. The problem is most acute in Islamic nations where Shari'a law is implemented. Citizens of these nations have no right to change their religion. The laws give the state the legal right to put to death those who have converted to another faith.[2]

The American tradition of religious freedom has its origins, not in the Enlightenment, but in the separatist Puritan minister Roger Williams (1603–1683). Before the Enlightenment made its contribution to developing ideas of individual rights, he constructed a mature theology of religious freedom on a strong biblical foundation. Roger Williams, not Thomas Jefferson, was the first to urge that, in his words, a "hedge or wall of protection" be erected to protect "the garden of the church" from "the wilderness" of the state. He may have derived some of his ideas from the Anabaptists, who may have been the first to advocate the complete separation of church and state. They were such a universally despised and persecuted religious minority in Europe that they came to their appreciation of religious freedom with good cause.

The Enlightenment's political ideas made a substantial contribution to the ferment that resulted in the American Revolution, but the seeds of liberty sown in the churches were just as responsible. A powerful spiritual revival, the First Great Awakening, blew through the American colonies in the 1740s and 1750s. The colonists were equally suspicious of religious and political tyranny, and their preachers fanned the fires of revolution in sermons throughout the churches. After the Revolution, it was the multiplicity of churches born of the Great Awakening that practically necessitated the adoption of the First Amendment and its guarantees of religious freedom.

However, the Christian tradition of religious freedom is much more ancient than the American experience. Tertullian[3] (A.D. 160–220), one of the early church fathers, was the first author to use the words *religious liberty* (*libertas religionis*). He wrote that every man has the right to freedom (*ius libertatis*). He also observed that "religion demands, by itself, the refusing of all kind of constraint in matters of religion,"[4] and he argued that religious freedom ought to be the natural outgrowth of religion.

Tertullian wrote at a time when Christians were still subject to intermittent persecution. About a century later, an intense decade of persecution ended with the Edict of Milan (A.D. 313), which was confirmed by Emperor Constantine and published by his brother-in-law, Licinius. Constantine's conversion to Christianity set the stage for Christianity to become the state religion. Within a century of that change, Christian theologians and church authorities sanctioned the persecution of so-called heretics. The persecuted became persecutors.

In Jesus' time, the government of the Roman Empire—which extended across many lands and peoples with many different religions—offered a good deal of religious toleration. The prevailing peace allowed for an expansion of trade and travel. As people moved about, they would change their religions or bring their own religions into new regions.[5] Religious pluralism was a fact around the Mediterranean Sea. Even Judaism was given legal recognition in spite of being an exclusive religion.

Christianity, however, was denied legal status, though at times Roman authorities protected Christians in disputes with Jewish authorities. Later, Rome persecuted Christians because they refused to be part of the emperor's cult. Christianity was perceived as a rejection of Rome and its gods.[6] Christians became scapegoats, though they weren't the only people whom the emperors persecuted for their religious beliefs.

Religious freedom in the New Testament

The life of Jesus, as well as His teaching, attests to the centrality of free will to the act of worship. At the beginning of His ministry, Jesus was led out into the wilderness, where the devil plied three temptations upon Him (see Matthew 4:1–11). He proposed a way for Jesus to gain control of the world and yet avoid the humiliation and torture of crucifixion. Jesus declined these temptations, choosing the harder path of obedience and faithfulness. Again, a few hours before His crucifixion, Jesus was sorely tempted to choose an easier path. He chose instead submission to God's will no matter the cost (see Mark 14:32–41). The Son of God Himself was free to follow His Father or to choose some other path. Freedom of choice is at the heart of a relationship with God. He didn't force His Son to obey Him, nor will He force any of His children to worship Him. God desires a relationship based on love, and without free choice, love cannot exist.

That the principle of love functions as the basis of the relationship between humanity and God is evident from the earliest biblical revelation. God granted Adam and Eve permission to eat of any tree save one. There was no coercion involved. Adam and Eve were restricted but weren't prevented from eating the forbidden fruit. Later, when God established His covenant with Israel as they were about to enter into the Promised Land, Moses expressed God's purpose for them. He said, " 'I have set before you life and death, blessings and curses. Now choose life, so that you and your children may live' " (Deuteronomy 30:19). Again, even though issues of life and death hinged on right choices and actions, these decisions weren't coerced. Israel was given the freedom to choose whether or not they would worship God. After Moses, Joshua led by example rather than by force when he declared to the nation, " 'Choose for yourselves this day whom you will serve, whether the gods your forefathers served beyond the River, or the gods of the Amorites in whose land you are living. But as for me and my household, we will serve the LORD' " (Joshua 24:15).

Following the temptations in the wilderness, Jesus began to gather disciples. He didn't compel anyone to follow Him. The decision to follow Jesus couldn't have been an easy one to make. Many of those whom Jesus called had businesses and families to care for (see Matthew 4:18–22). All of the disciples had good reasons to say no.[7] However difficult the decision to follow Jesus, though, it was a decision freely made.

In His teaching Jesus emphasized freedom as a profoundly spiritual principle rather than as a political right. He conveyed the idea of freedom from the penalty and power of sin, the freedom to do right.

Jesus' teachings were difficult, and at one point, many followers began to leave. This was a crisis point in His ministry. An opportunist might have manipulated the faithful, declaring, "We're going to win. Stick with me, and you will make history." Jesus could have resorted to working miracles to impress or terrorize the hesitant. Instead, He simply asked the Twelve, " 'You do not want to leave too, do you?' " (John 6:67).

Perhaps the ultimate expression of free choice in Jesus' life came in His dealings with Judas. Jesus knew that Judas would betray Him. At the Last Supper, He indicated to Judas that He knew what Judas was about to do, giving Judas further evidence of His Messianic authority. Yet Jesus did so discretely, giving Judas the opportunity to reconsider his intended betrayal without accusing him publicly or restraining him in any way. Instead, Jesus told Judas, " 'What you are about to do, do quickly' " (John 13:27). By quietly revealing to Judas that He knew his plans, Jesus actually gave Judas the opportunity to make a better choice.

Religious freedom means no coercion

Jesus met people from other faiths. He shared the good news with them, but He never forced people to change. He didn't preach with a sword in one hand and a cross in the other. He didn't order His disciples to destroy pagan temples. When a Roman centurion asked Jesus to heal his servant, Jesus answered the prayer without imposing any conditions (see Matthew 8:5–13). And when Jesus was traveling in the area of Tyre, a Greek woman asked Him to heal her little daughter. Jesus didn't heal the daughter under the condition that the mother would become His follower. He saw someone suffering who believed in His capacity to heal. That was enough (see Mark 7:24–30).

Consider the way Jesus talked with the Samaritan woman. She opened the debate and challenged Him. But though He could have argued with her about who had the right religion, He brought her the good news without coercion or harassment. He respected her opinion and simply shared His message with her (see John 4:7–42).

A few days before Jesus' arrest in Jerusalem, He decided to travel through the territory of the Samaritans. He sent His disciples to a village to find a place where they could rest for the night, but the citizens there refused to extend hospitality to Him. That is exactly what religious fanaticism has done for centuries and still does today. It refuses to welcome those who are different and destroys them instead.

Two of Jesus' disciples, John and James, became so furious that they wanted to pray that God would destroy the village (see Luke 9:51–56). "[Jesus] turned and rebuked [His disciples] and said, 'You do not know what kind of Spirit you are of' " (Luke 9:55, NASB). Religious intolerance and violence are not part of His teaching. He told His followers what to do if people don't accept the good news about Him that they preach: " 'If anyone will not welcome you or listen to your words, shake the dust off your feet when you leave that home or town' " (Matthew 10:14).

Luke concluded his story with the words, "They went to another village" (Luke 9:56). That is all. Jesus felt no need to curse or threaten the Samaritans. They had made their choice, and Jesus respected it. He and His disciples went to another village where people would be happy to welcome them.[8] That should have made it clear enough to all Christians that they should reject the use of force and violence in their mission. Unfortunately, it didn't.

Article 18 of the Universal Declaration of Human Rights defines religious freedom as an individual right. In actuality, the right is also a community right. The body of believers, the church, must also have the freedom to worship God as a group. In other words, the church as an institution may choose whether or not to serve Him. This seems to contradict its very *raison d'être*—the church is supposed to have made the right choice once and for all. Through the message to Laodicea in the book of Revelation, the risen Christ says to His church, " 'I stand at the door and knock. If anyone hears my voice and opens the door, I will come in and eat with him, and he with me' " (Revelation 3:20). The One who received the kingdom, the power, and the glory doesn't force Himself on the church.

The church is free to choose, but people are equally free not to join it. This principle was underlined when John came to Jesus after having encountered a man who was using Jesus' name without being part of Jesus' group. " 'Teacher,' said John, 'we saw a man driving out demons in your name and we told him to stop, because he was not one of us.' 'Do not stop him,' Jesus said. 'No one who does a miracle in my name can in the next moment say anything bad about me, for whoever is not against us is for us' " (Mark 9:38–40).

Like the rest of the Bible, the teachings of Jesus are crystal clear about the consequences of our choices. For Him, and for Moses and Joshua, the choice is between life and death. Those who choose to obey God will be saved (see Deuteronomy 30:19). There is no salvation outside Christ: " 'God so loved the world that he gave his one and only Son, that whoever believes in him shall not perish but have eternal life' " (John 3:16).

We are free to choose, but our choice has eternal consequences: " 'Whoever believes and is baptized will be saved, but whoever does not believe will be condemned' " (Mark 16:16).[9] The freedom we ask for ourselves and for everyone else doesn't compel us to be silent about our beliefs. Believers have the right to say, "I have the truth. I bring you the truth. We are the only true church. Our religion is the only true religion." That is their right, and other people have an equal right to disagree with them and to express such disagreement.

Because free choice brings responsibilities and leads to eternal consequences, Jesus was never a neutral observer of the choices people made. He did His best to lead people to make the right choice. He called the rich man to follow Him (see Mark 10:17–22). He prayed for His disciples to stay faithful (see John 17:6–26). He was sad when Jerusalem rejected Him (see Luke 13:34, 35). He commanded His disciples to go and preach the good news to everyone everywhere (see Matthew 28:19, 20). In spite of His willingness to guide people to the right choice, Jesus never substituted His choice for their own decision.

"Compel them to come in"

One of the biggest tragedies in the history of the Christian church is the justification of religious persecution and holy wars. At the beginning of the fifth century, St. Augustine (A.D. 354–430), one of the greatest theologians, used Jesus' words to justify persecution of heretics.[10] According to James Carroll, "it was the late Augustine who, no longer depending on the force of reason, justified the use of coercion in defending, and spreading, the orthodox faith: 'in being first compelled by fear or pain, so that they might afterwards be influenced by teaching.' "[11]

St. Augustine was locked in theological combat with the Donatists, a sect regarded as heretical that had grown increasingly influential and powerful in the East. In this conflict, Augustine made an unfortunate interpretation of Jesus' parable of the great banquet. A wealthy man organized a great supper and invited his friends. They declined the invitation. The man found this very humiliating—the dinner was ready and nobody was there to enjoy it. So, the man decided to send his servants out to the streets; they were to bring back with them all the people they could find. His order was, " 'make them come in' " (Luke 14:23). *Anagkazo,* the Greek verb Luke used in this verse, can be translated "to constrain" or "to compel," whether by force or by persuasion.[12]

Augustine believed the Donatists were refusing to accept the truth and that it was acceptable for church authorities to use civil law to force them to accept the truth (orthodoxy). Their will, according to the great theologian, was in a state of ignorance and trouble. Their will and habits needed to be broken.[13] Augustine opposed torture and the death penalty, but he considered it appropriate to force people in other ways. He believed that physical persecution could help them to make the right choice. He wrote, "Let the heretics be drawn from the hedges, be extracted from the thorns. Stuck in the hedges, they do not want to. But that is not the Lord's command. He said, 'Compel them to come in.' Use compulsion outside, so freedom can arise once they are inside."[14] To the Donatists, he said, " 'We love you, please accept the truth. We love you, but we want to correct you.' "[15] He believed that correction in this world would save heretics from eternal punishment in the next.

Augustine's view formed the basis of the doctrine and practice of the Middle Ages. It opened the way for the Inquisition.[16] A few centuries later the great theologian Thomas Aquinas (1224–1274) went even further. He justified the death penalty for heretics.

Christian theologians no longer support that interpretation of the parable. They agree that Jesus never forced people to believe in Him. He never instructed His disciples or the apostolic church to use force. Jesus repeatedly counseled His disciples to avoid controversy and retaliation for grievances. (See, for instance, Matthew 5:43–47; 6:14, 15; 7:1–5; 10:14.) He has always been on the side of the persecuted and not on the side of persecutors.

The examples of Augustine and Thomas Aquinas show how Jesus' teachings may be misinterpreted to justify the use of civil power to defend orthodoxy. Unfortunately, Jesus wasn't personally present to rebuke Augustine and Aquinas—to say to them, "You don't know what kind of spirit you are of."

Religious freedom and persecution

Persecution is omnipresent in the New Testament. It began with the slaughter of the children two years of age and under in Bethlehem. It continued with the beheading of John the Baptist, the crucifixion of Jesus, and the persecution of the apostles. It is interesting to notice that Jesus and the disciples didn't react against persecution brought on by a denial of human rights as we do today. In His time, authorities used persecution, torture, and violence to maintain their power and the public order—and those who challenged the authorities also used these methods. Of course, the law brought some humane treatment, but most of the time the last word belonged to the one who most effectively used violent force.

The prince of this world is the devil, and Jesus' disciples shouldn't expect an easy time from him as they fulfill their mission of preaching the good news to everyone everywhere (see Mark 16:15; John 12:31). The world offers them not honor but persecution. Jesus often warned that those who follow Him would suffer persecution throughout their journey home. (See, for instance, John 15:20.)

Persecution is part of the package that comes with choosing to be a Christian. Jesus didn't hide that cruel reality: " 'Then you will be handed over to be persecuted and put to death, and you will be hated by all nations because of me' " (Matthew 24:9; see also John 15:20). Disciples of Jesus will be persecuted by believers too: " 'A time is coming when anyone who kills you will think he is offering a service to God' " (John 16:2). This has happened for centuries, and it will happen again.

How should Christians react when they are persecuted? Activists may be disappointed by the answer Jesus gave to this question. He said, " 'Blessed are those who are persecuted because of righteousness, / for theirs is the kingdom of heaven. Blessed are you when people insult you, persecute you and falsely say all kinds of evil against you because of me. Rejoice and be glad, because great is your reward in heaven, for in the same way they persecuted the prophets who were before you' " (Matthew 5:10–12).

How are we to react when we are persecuted? By loving our persecutors! " 'I tell you: Love your enemies and pray for those who persecute you, that you may be sons of your Father in heaven' " (verse 44). This doesn't mean that Christians should provoke persecution. It isn't good in itself; in fact, it's the mark of the devil. Some people believe you need to be persecuted to be a good Christian. That isn't true. Persecution was never a goal for Jesus. Often, He did what He could to avoid it, and He told His disciples, " 'When you are persecuted in one place, flee to another' " (Matthew 10:23).

If Jesus didn't recommend to His disciples that they react with violence when they are persecuted, how could He have justified using violence to persecute those who don't want to follow His teachings? Though "Caesar makes himself God and persecutes God's people who don't want to worship him, Christians must resist. For Jesus' disciples during the three first centuries 'took the form of martyr.' "[17] Inspired by the teaching and the example of his Master, the apostle Paul told the Romans not to avenge themselves. (See Romans 12:19–21.) And he added, "Overcome evil with good" (verse 21).

However, the apostle Paul knew his rights, and when his rights weren't respected, he reacted. Once, in the Roman colony of Philippi, he was arrested, beaten, and put in jail. Paul took advantage of his Roman citizenship. "Paul said to the officers: 'They beat us publicly without a trial, even though we are Roman citizens, and threw us into prison. And now do they want to get rid of us quietly? No! Let them come themselves and escort us out' " (Acts 16:37). Paul's demand worked. "They came to appease them and escorted them from the prison, requesting them to leave the city" (verse 39).

On another occasion, when he faced an imminent beating in Jerusalem, he asked the centurion, " 'Is it legal for you to flog a Roman citizen who hasn't even been found guilty?' " (Acts 22:25). His objection worked again. "Those who were about to question him withdrew immediately. The commander himself was alarmed when he realized that he had put Paul, a Roman citizen, in chains" (verse 29).

The Universal Declaration of Human Rights didn't exist in Jesus' time.

The constitutions of most countries now recognize religious freedom. The number one superpower, the United States, has an Office for International Religious Freedom, an ambassador at large, and a commission that publishes an annual report on international religious freedom.[18] Countries that persecute believers are given the designation CPC—Country of Particular Concern.

Europeans also have the Human Rights Convention, and Article 9 is dedicated to religious freedom. Countries that have signed the convention have to protect this freedom. People who are persecuted in these countries can appeal to the European Court of Human Rights, and, if the country is found guilty, it will be sanctioned. Several countries have been sanctioned in this way.

Jesus' disciples should know their rights and responsibilities. Being a good citizen means respecting the law as long as it doesn't contradict God's commandments. It is always healthy to remind the authorities about the laws they're supposed to observe. In asking that these laws be implemented, we protect not only ourselves but others too, including the authorities—we help them to act in a way that is consistent with their own legislation.

A sign of a better world

The beautiful and universal principle known as the golden rule provides evidence that Jesus expected His followers to respect people's decisions. He said, " 'In everything, do to others what you would have them do to you, for this sums up the Law and the Prophets' " (Matthew 7:12). The golden rule teaches us to respect the freedom of others to worship God in the way that makes sense to them just as we desire the freedom to make our own religious choices. Unless everyone is free to teach their children their own religion and to share their faith with others, no one is free. If the authorities can restrict your religious freedom, then there is no security for anyone's religious freedom, even your own. The golden rule forms the basis for human rights and religious freedom.

When a teacher asked Jesus about the greatest commandment, He answered, " ' "Love the Lord your God with all your heart and with all your soul and with all your mind and with all your strength" ' " (Mark 12:30). And He added, " 'The second is this: "Love your neighbor as yourself." There is no commandment greater than these' " (verse 31). Jesus explained that our "neighbor" is any other human being. He told the story of the good Samaritan to illustrate this point (see Luke 10:30–37). When someone is suffering or is a victim of injustice, there is a human and a Christian obligation to help. Religion isn't a criterion when people are in need. All human beings are children of God and should have their freedom of religion protected.

Why should Christians defend religious freedom for all people everywhere knowing that persecution will happen anyway?[19] One might just as well ask why we build hospitals when we know that people will eventually die anyway, and why we help the poor when Jesus said, " 'You will always have the poor with you' " (Matthew 26:11).

Why do we defend religious freedom when we know that persecution will come again? Because persecution bears the signature of the devil.[20]

In Revelation 13, the apostle John describes the vision he had about persecution against Jesus' disciples in the last days. They will be persecuted by a power called the "beast," which comes out of the earth (see verse 11). What are the characteristics of this evil beast? Satan's intention is that "all who refused to worship the image to be killed" (verse 15). That would imply a systematic persecution. "He also forced everyone, small and great, rich and poor, free and slave, to receive a mark on his right hand or on his forehead, so that no one could buy or sell unless he had the mark, which is the name of the beast or the number of his name" (verses 16, 17). In that vision of what happens just before the end of the world, the antichrist coalition uses force to impose its worship on the people of the world. That demonstrates the fundamental difference between the kingdom of God and the kingdom of the devil.[21]

Jesus' disciples are called to be the "light of the world" (Matthew 5:14). They are to "shine before men" (verse 16). The apostle Paul used another image: "We are therefore Christ's ambassadors" (2 Corinthians 5:20). Being a "light" or an "ambassador" represents something else. These roles are signs of another world.

Intolerance denies human dignity, and persecution is the product of intolerance—which, in turn, is the product of sin. Coercion is the opposite of Christ's message, which respects freedom of choice. Those who would adhere to the teachings of Jesus will reject the idea that people should be forced to keep or give up a religion against their will. They won't accept discrimination—including discrimination based on religion or belief. Nor will they allow an organization or a government to take the role of God, asking for their worship and setting the parameters of their consciences.

Followers of Christ will reject the use of violence against believers because of their faith. They will respond to the cries of the voiceless, homeless, persecuted, and poor. Those who do this walk in the footsteps of Christ. Moreover, persecution isn't a sign of God's kingdom; people who love their enemies in spite of persecution comprise that sign.

Jesus consistently taught the value of human dignity. At Creation, God provided humanity with freedom of choice, and the atoning sacrifice of Christ enhanced this freedom. In the plan of salvation, the death of Jesus provides a means whereby all may choose to be saved. But God doesn't compel anyone to believe.

When as Christians we defend religious freedom, we do more than uphold a basic human right recognized by the international community. In defending religious freedom, we express our understanding of the character of God as our Creator and Savior.[22] Religious freedom is a fundamental gift of a God who loves His creatures and respects their right to choose. Love and freedom are inseparable because love cannot be commanded or coerced. God hasn't given the gift of freedom merely to entice human beings to worship Him. Rather, He created humanity free, and then, when human beings lost their freedom, He restored it because it is in His nature and character to do so—because God is love, and love must be free. " 'God so loved the world that he gave his one and only Son, that whoever believes in him shall not perish but have eternal life' " (John 3:16).

---

1. UN General Assembly, Third Session, *Universal Declaration of Human Rights,* adopted and proclaimed by UN General Assembly Resolution 217 A (III), December 10, 1948.

2. About eleven countries have the death penalty for those who convert from Islam to another religion. See Tad Stahnke and Robert C. Blitt, "The Religion-State Relationship and the Right to Freedom of Religion or Belief: A Comparative Textual Analysis of the Constitutions of Predominantly Muslim Countries," United States Commission on International Religious Freedom, http://www.uscirf.gov, March 2005.

3. See Roland Minnerath, "Tertullien précurseur du droit a la liberté de religion," *Méditerranées,* Moyen Âge chrétien et Antiquité, L'Harmattan, no. 18, 19 (1999), 33–43.

4. Ibid., 38 ("nec religionis est cogere religionem." *Ad Scapulam* 2:2).

5. Ibid., 34. "L'Empire était tolérant pour tous les cultes a condition qu'ils admettent par dessus tout le culte du pouvoir romain, sous la forme de la vénération de la déesse Rome et d'Auguste."

6. The first empire-wide persecution was in the middle of the third century. The Jehovah's Witnesses have had a similar experience to that of these early Christians be-

cause of their refusal on religious grounds to salute national flags or to participate in various patriotic events.

7. " 'If anyone would come after me, he must deny himself and take up his cross daily and follow me' " (Luke 9:23). " 'If' " means we have a choice. See also Mark 10:17–22: Jesus called the young man, but the young man declined to follow Him.

8. The story of the ten lepers is a good example. Jesus healed all ten, but only one came back and glorified God. Jesus didn't use His healing to force them to follow Him (see Luke 17:12).

9. See also the parable of the Sheep and the Goats in Matthew 25.

10. Tertullien, Origen, St. Cyprien, and Lactance were opposed to using force against heretics. See Michele-Marie Fayard, "Suz l'usage de la force pour la conversion des hérétiques," *Conscience et liberté* 13 (1977), 34–36.

11. James Carroll, *Constantine's Sword, The Church and the Jews* (Boston: Houghton Mifflin, 2001), 211.

12. See Frank E. Gaebelein, ed., *The Expositor's Bible Commentary* (Grand Rapids, Mich.: Zondervan, 1984), 8:978.

13. *Lib. arb.* 3.18, 51, 52.

14. Garry Wills, "*Sermones* 112.8," *Saint Augustine* (New York: Viking, 1999), 103.

15. Ibid., 109.

16. *De Civit Dei*, XXIII, 51.

17. Minnerath, 42.

18. *Annual Report on International Religious Freedom 2004,* November 2004, Washington, D.C.: U.S. Government Printing Office, 2005.

19. It is a little easier for Baptists or Adventists than for others because both these communions have had a strong tradition in favor of religious freedom. Adventists have a prophetic mission to defend and promote religious freedom for all. Ellen G. White stated, "The banner of the truth and religious liberty held aloft by the founders of the gospel church and by God's witnesses during the centuries that have passed since then, has, in this last conflict, been committed to our hands." *The Acts of the Apostles* (Nampa, Idaho: Pacific Press® Publishing Association, 1911), 68, 69.

20. "Any use of force or persecution in matters of religion is a policy inspired by the devil not by Christ." Francis D. Nichol, ed., *The Seventh-day Adventist Bible Commentary,* (Hagerstown, Md.: Review and Herald® Publishing Association, 1980), 5:810.

21. See the retribution the persecutors experience in Revelation 12:20.

22. "According to Jesus, religious liberty doesn't have the same nature as human rights. It is a right that comes from a duty to act according to conscience—duty for which we are responsible to God, the abandonment of which will have eternal consequences." Pierre Lanarès, "Jésus et la liberté de conscience et de religion," *Conscience et liberté,* no. 40 (1990), 81, 82.

Nicholas P. Miller

CHAPTER 2

"Render Unto God": How Should the State Relate to God?

I had just completed a week's worth of religious liberty meetings at Redwood Area Camp, a religious retreat in northern California. Escaping the dust and the heat, I headed for the pine trees and green waves of the coastal haven known as Shelter Cove. Paddling out on my surfboard, I soon found myself trading waves with the owner of an outdoor-sports store from Bend, Oregon. After exchanging observations on the beauty of the surroundings and the joy of connecting with nature through wave-riding, our conversation turned to current events and religion. I introduced myself as a lawyer who was interested in religion and the Constitution, and I expressed my concern that religion and politics were becoming too closely entwined. He said he wasn't religious and that he shared my concerns about the current influence of religion on politics and the erosion of the Constitution.

I agreed that the line between church and state had become blurry, but I also cautioned him that removing religion completely from public thought and concern could be dangerous to freedom. "Belief in God can provide a limitation, or check, on the power of the state," I said. "Do you want to know what a government looks like that denies belief in God?"

"What's that?" he asked, sitting up on his board.

"Communist Russia," I responded. "It had no restraint on its power. The government was everything and had no limits. Communists believe there is nothing greater than the state—nothing to which the state is accountable."

I wheeled around and scanned the horizon to avoid being surprised by an unexpected set of waves in the middle of our discussion. "In socialistic Communism, the state is the final and only authority," I continued. "The idea of God can create a space in society where the individual has some freedom and autonomy."

"Ah, I see," he responded. "A belief in a Higher Power can create a sense of humility or limitation in the state."

"That's exactly right," I called over my shoulder as I paddled into the next wave.

The conversation with my fellow surfer was relatively brief, and I was surprised to see how quickly and readily a nonbeliever could grasp the importance of God to freedom, human rights, and limited government. Perhaps this acquaintance's connection with nature and the humility inspired by interaction with the powerful forces of the ocean made him see that a "Higher Power" can instill respect.

Today, too often we see spiritual arrogance rather than humility and respect in politics. Inspired by their belief in Allah, fundamentalist Islamic terrorists are driven by a sense of self-righteousness to carry out the most horrible atrocities. Those living in the West are not immune from the same temptation. A fervent belief in God can inspire an overconfident arrogance that America is a chosen nation with a mandate to bring freedom, democracy, and equality to the world—even if it must be at the point of a gun. Rather than act as a check on power, the idea of God has justified the accumulation of power at home and abroad.

In light of the misappropriation of God's name, one can begin to understand why some secularists desire to strike God from our money and from the Pledge of Allegiance. But, as my discussion with the surfer shows, removing God from the equation could lead to even more oppression.

So, what is the right balance? How can the state acknowledge the limits placed on it by the idea of God without turning itself into a special tool to enforce the will of God? This question has kept political scientists, theologians, and philosophers thinking and writing for centuries. Rather than turning to them, let's turn to the book that has provided the foundation for their thinking—the Bible. What principles does the Bible establish in relation to how the state should—in Christ's words—"render to God," and how might those principles guide our thinking today?

Creation—the foundation of civil and religious freedoms

The idea of the creation of humanity by a Supreme Being has played a powerful and central role in the development of human rights and freedoms. Indeed, the U.S. Declaration of Independence explicitly draws this connection: "We hold these truths to be self-evident, that all men are created equal, that they are endowed by their Creator with certain inalienable Rights." To seek the earliest foundations of freedom in the Bible, we must return to Creation.

The Bible records that God said, " 'Let Us make man in Our image, according to Our likeness' " (Genesis 1:26, NKJV).[1] Many books have been written regarding what it means to be created in the image of God, but for our purposes this passage contains two important points. First, the image of God contains within it the inherent idea of freedom and autonomy to act, as God Himself showed in His choice of creation. The three great monotheistic religions agree that God was truly free in entering upon His creation. He did not have to create but freely chose to create. In making human beings, He passed this same freedom on to them. Theologian David Burrell has noted that the three traditions—Islam, Judaism, and Christianity—each avow God's free creation of the universe. He wrote that these three traditions "have developed a view of free human actors in relation to their initial affirmations that the universe is freely created by God."[2]

Part of the reason that God can freely create relates to the second point we take from the text—the multiplicity of God. He didn't say He created humanity in "My" image but in "Our" image. Isolated humans are lonely. But God wasn't "lonely" in some existential sense before the creation of humanity or the angels. Rather, He is multiple and hence relational even apart from His creation. That is why God can be, is, and always will be, love. If God were single at some deep dark distant point of time—if we can speak of time before Creation—His love would have been self-love. But God is not that way. His love has always been a giving, sharing, serving, overflowing love. God chose to make humanity in this relational, multiple, "Ourness" image of the Godhead.

We take from this simple passage humankind's inherent moral and social autonomy—not just individually but also in seeking relationships with others. Indeed, if creation was going to mean something, if God was going to create something other—something that was more than a mere extension of Himself—these elements were necessary. People with no real free choice would be computers or robots, mere appendages of their Maker. "To deprive man of the freedom of choice would be to rob him of his prerogative as an intelligent being, and make him a mere *automaton*. It is not God's purpose to coerce the will. Man was created a free moral agent."[3]

Political philosophers are fond of talking about a "state of nature" in which individuals existed as separate and unconnected units in a wilderness prior to coming together to seek protection and safety in communities. Such a state is mythical, of course. The closest we come to it is the description of God making a man and a woman in a garden. However, the story of Eden is not of disconnected, isolated beings but of people who were purposely created to enjoy a relationship with God and with one another. This biblical picture of Creation reveals the moral and social nature of humanity, the social nature of humanity, and the relationship of humanity to God.

Government is theend result not the begining, of pre-existing relationships. The state is obligated, then, to respect the fundamental capacity of people as moral and social beings who are in relationship with God.[4] This is a good core of principles, but, admittedly, they are somewhat vague. Society must be regulated, and laws often deal with both moral and social issues. So how do we achieve the proper balance between respect for core rights and order in society? Fortunately, the Creation account also provides a foundational example of the difference between inappropriate spiritual legislation and the proper regulation of morals. That example is the account of the forbidden fruit.

Freedom and the Fall

God placed a tree in the Garden of Eden and told Adam and Eve not to eat from it. How much simpler the whole matter would have been if the tree had been surrounded by a moat, barbed wire, or angels with swords of fire. God certainly had appropriately armed angels at His disposal, as He placed them at the entrances to Eden *after* the Fall. Surely, if God had positioned angels around the tree prior to the Fall, He could have avoided a lot of trouble.

Here lies the fundamental difference between invasive spiritual legislation and appropriate moral legislation. God knew that huge issues were at stake in the eating of the fruit of the forbidden tree, yet the consequences were primarily spiritual. The Bible records that the forbidden fruit was beautiful to look at and good for food. In other words, it was not poisonous or physically harmful. So, the test was spiritual, designed to determine whether Adam and Eve would trust God. Even God could not legislate or coerce their trust.

After Adam and Eve had fallen, however, their continued access to the forbidden tree would have imperiled others, including their offspring. The fruit would have prolonged their sinful lives in perpetuity, bringing misery and suffering to the world they lived in. This became more than a question of their trust in God because it involved direct harm to others. God, therefore, placed the forbidden tree forever off-limits to sinful, fallen humanity, and He used force to do so.

Since God Himself did not coerce trust and obedience, neither should the state compel people to engage in spiritual conduct or behavior that relates to worship. Prayers, days of worship, church attendance, financial support of religious institutions, veneration of images, and sacred or profane speech all relate to the spiritual pilgrimage of human beings and shouldn't be imposed or hindered by human laws. However, the state can and should regulate civil moral matters that relate to humanity's conduct towards each other—such as killing, theft, murder, adultery, prostitution, and other moral issues that directly impact others—even though these acts also have spiritual consequences.

In addition, when regulating and enforcing matters of civil morality, the state should take care to go no further than its legitimate civil goals. It should avoid becoming the crafter of the souls of its citizens and avoid seeking to inculcate virtues. The state has at its disposal only the crude tools of law, coercion, and physical punishment. These are sufficient to create a level of civic restraint but unsuitable for the delicate, nuanced job of character development. God Himself recognized this truth in His dealings with Adam and Eve.

> It is true that all liberty comes through keeping God's law, but God himself, who wrote that law in the hearts of men in the beginning, who spoke it amidst the thunders of Sinai, that all might hear and obey, who waits through the new covenant to rewrite it in every trusting soul,—God himself, who did all this, still made man as free to disobey these precepts as to obey them. Why did God allow all this fearful iniquity that man might be made free? To this there can be but one answer. It was because He knew the worthlessness of all forced obedience and that, therefore, the freedom to sin was absolutely necessary to the possibility of righteousness.[5]

If God recognized this truth and respected humanity's freedom, how much more should the state—with its almost infinitely weaker tools and exponentially poorer grasp of the standards of spiritual truth—do so?

The patriarchs

God has not left humanity without authorities, both civil and spiritual, to help guide them in their earthly sojourn. Although civil and spiritual authority are fundamentally different in nature, they have been combined at times.

The first form of earthly government as described in the Bible was patriarchal. Extended families were cared for and overseen by fathers, who were expected to provide their relatives with both spiritual and civil direction and oversight. A prime example is the biblical patriarch Abraham. God chose Abraham for His special plan of bringing redemption to humanity because He knew Abraham would " 'command his children and his household after him, that they keep the way of the LORD, to do righteousness and justice' " (Genesis 18:19). Abraham acted as both a civil and spiritual leader and authority in his household. Yet, while firm in his leadership as Scripture attests, he demonstrated the kind of flexible, servant leadership that should be a model for both civil and spiritual leaders.

We find a primary example of his style of leadership in his interactions with his nephew, Lot. Abraham refrained from asserting his prerogative as the senior male. Instead, he invited his nephew to choose first the part of the land where he wanted to dwell, and then he took the remainder. Abraham could have asserted both his civil authority ("I'm the senior and have the right to choose the better fields") and his spiritual authority ("You cannot live near Sodom because it will provide a risky moral surrounding for your family"). Instead, he graciously gave the younger man the first choice. No doubt Abraham told Lot about his spiritual concerns and prayed for his physical and spiritual well-being, knowing the moral challenges posed by living in proximity to Sodom. But he didn't compel him to make a sound spiritual decision.

In rescuing Lot and his family from the kings who sacked Sodom, Abraham probably went beyond his basic civil responsibilities, as Lot had left Abraham's household and was out on his own. Abraham had the courage, ability, and faith in God to rescue his nephew. He undertook the military venture on the grounds that are among the very limited circumstances that justify the use of force—the defense or rescue of weaker, innocent parties who are facing actual or immediate risk of death or destruction.

An event that occurred after the successful rescue tells us something even more profound about the exercise of spiritual authority. Abraham paid tithe to the priest of God, Melchizedek, on the booty he had recovered but then refused to keep the rest for himself (see Genesis 14:20–24). This simple act carried with it deeply profound implications that the apostle Paul described more than a thousand years later in chapter 7 of his Epistle to the Hebrews. Abraham was the father of the faithful, the friend of God, and the first and greatest of the patriarchs. Yet even he was not the ultimate earthly spiritual authority. He did not keep the tithe for himself but paid it to one who is a symbol or type of the heavenly Priest who was to come.

Paul cited this story of Abraham returning tithes to Melchizedek to demonstrate both the superiority of a heavenly priesthood and that there are limits to the spiritual authority of any earthly leader. There is no earthly priestly class that provides actual access to God in heaven. The Old Testament priests, like the patriarchs, were symbols of a heavenly Mediator, whom every person must access directly.

The implications are deeply profound for government and its relation to spiritual leaders. If there is no ultimate earthly spiritual authority, how can civil legislatures and tribunals enforce religious standards? Indeed, most Western governments recognize that they have no competence to legislate on spiritual matters. In the past, some of these same governments implemented the spiritual mandates of those perceived to be duly constituted religious authorities. Yet, as Paul explained, Abraham's simple act of paying tithe shows that no earthly spiritual authority has the right to act as conscience for the individual, and no government has the authority to enforce the spiritual mandates of religious leaders. If there was ever an exception to this rule, it was when the nation of Israel functioned as a theocracy. However, this isn't a true exception, as God Himself spoke to Jewish leaders through the Urim and Thummim stones (see Exodus 28:30; Numbers 27:21).[6] The civil state enforced the mandates of a heavenly authority, not an earthly one. Even in the Jewish theocratic state, power was divided between the civil and spiritual authorities. As we shall see, serious consequences arose whenever the nation violated this division.

Separation of civil and spiritual authority

As we've discussed above, Abraham recognized in Melchizedek a superior spiritual authority. And while Moses was both the civil ruler and leader of Israel and a great prophet "whom the Lord knew face to face" (Deuteronomy 34:10), yet God chose his brother Aaron to head Israel's priestly functions. During the period of Jewish theocracy that followed, God maintained a separation between civil and religious authorities—priests and judges played separate roles. Samuel, for instance, served as a prophet and didn't wield civil authority as would a king.

However, the children of Israel demanded a king. God eventually yielded to the nation's desire, yet He retained a firm commitment to the separation of civil and religious authority. This commitment was demonstrated very early in the period of monarchy. The first king, Saul, had scarcely been anointed when he usurped the priestly function by offering a sacrifice. Facing imminent war with the Philistines and eager to obtain God's blessing on the military campaign, Saul failed to wait for Samuel, as he had been instructed to do. Because of this act, God rejected Saul as king (see 1 Samuel 13:8–14). What may have appeared to be a simple act of impatient devotion was instead a profound violation of the separation between the kingly and priestly roles, incurring God's extreme displeasure.

Similar results occurred when other kings exceeded their authority and invaded the priestly role. King Uzziah, a ruler with a reputation for godliness, was stricken with leprosy when he entered the temple to burn incense over the objection of the priests (see 2 Chronicles 26:16–20). When King Jeroboam burned incense before the altar, a prophet of God cursed him, the altar split, and the king's hand withered (see 1 Kings 13:1–5).

King David is notable for accepting the limitation on his authority. He was eager to erect a temple in Jerusalem as a permanent center of worship, but before he began, he conferred with Nathan the prophet. Nathan told David that he was not to build the temple; his son would do that. David accepted Nathan's spiritual authority and obeyed (see 2 Samuel 7:4–13). This didn't dim David's enthusiasm for the project. Knowing that his son would be permitted to build the temple, David assembled materials and supplies for the project. Yet he was deprived of a form of glory sought by many ancient kings—having his name associated with the most elaborate architectural achievement in the nation. The edifice erected forever became known as "Solomon's Temple," not David's.

David showed a similar respect for the separation between his personal political fortunes and the spiritual status of Israel when he fled Jerusalem during Absalom's rebellion. Zadok the priest followed David out of the city, and he brought the ark of the covenant with him. Rather than associating his cause with the most sacred object in Israel, David sent Zadok and the ark back to Jerusalem. He recognized that his personal political success must be separated from the religious devotion of his nation—an extremely rare case of a national leader resisting the temptation to invoke God as an ally and supporter during a time of crisis (see 2 Samuel 15:23–26). In modern times, Abraham Lincoln's second inaugural address evidences the same humility. Lincoln acknowledged that it was likely that God was punishing both sides fighting in the American Civil War because of their sins and failings.

These examples from the lives of King David and President Lincoln illustrate that, regardless of the form of government, civil leaders needn't deny or ignore God. The Bible says "the fear of the Lord is the beginning of knowledge" (Proverbs 1:7) and that a ruler's throne is "established by righteousness" (Proverbs 16:12). That's true even in our age of secular democracies. "God would have the rulers of the nations know that He is the Supreme Ruler. Those who preside over the affairs of nations should realize that there is a King of kings. . . . He who has been placed where he has authority over others should seek the Lord for wisdom, that he may govern wisely."[7]

Both King David and Abraham Lincoln publicly acknowledged God's role in the life of the nation. In both cases, the leader's relationship to God resulted in humility and restraint rather than in attempting to justify national pride or political ambition.[8] This is a profound distinction that is all too often overlooked. Politicians shouldn't use belief in God as a justification to wield arbitrary power or legislate on spiritual matters. Rather, genuine faith will act as a restraint on the use of power. Religious belief ought to serve as a reminder to rulers that the power they exercise doesn't belong to them and that they are merely stewards who will be held accountable for how they use or abuse that power. This was Christ's message when He came face to face with an agent of the greatest civil state of His day—the proud, ambitious Roman Empire.

Christ and Caesar

It was Jesus, of course, who described the duties owed to God and Caesar in the succinct and memorable lines: " 'Render therefore to Caesar the things that are Caesar's, and to God the things that are God's' " (Matthew 22:21). Volumes have been written on what this means. At its most basic level, Jesus clearly identified a separation of the two spheres—the civil and the spiritual. Caesar is owed certain things, but Caesar should *not* require those things that are due to God.

What should Caesar render to God?

Jesus acted as a good citizen all His life and avoided encounters with Roman authorities until He was slandered and betrayed to the authorities at the end of His life. When He appeared before Pilate, Jesus demonstrated His understanding of the distinct roles of Caesar and God. Pilate asked Jesus whether He had claimed to be "king of the Jews" as He was accused of doing. Jesus assured Pilate that He had no designs on Caesar's realm, that His "kingdom is not of this world," and for this reason, His followers didn't wield the sword (see John 18:36). Pilate knew he had no basis to assert jurisdiction over Jesus as His dispute with the Jews was a matter of religion. Nevertheless, Pilate had Jesus flogged and questioned Him further because of his concern for crowd sentiment and the threat it posed to his own position. At this point, Jesus refused to answer any further questions.

Having established Jesus' innocence, Pilate had no business toying with Him further merely to placate a hostile crowd. He stepped beyond any legitimate inquiry as a state official, and undoubtedly he knew it. Yet he was affronted by Jesus' silence and resorted to arbitrary threats: " 'Are You not speaking to me? Do You not know that I have power to crucify You, and power to release You?' " (John 19:10). Christ's memorable response is the correct Christian response to all states and rulers that overstep their powers and invade the prerogatives of God: " 'You could have no power at all against Me unless it had been given you from above' " (John 19:11). Jesus reminded Pilate that his power was not his own to wield as he saw fit. He had been given power from above—from the emperor, certainly, but ultimately from God—and he was merely a steward of that power. Pilate was obligated to exercise power with justice and equity, not arbitrarily. This meant that he should release Jesus.

Pilate's response to Jesus demonstrates that he not only understood but agreed. "From then on Pilate sought to release Him" (verse 12). In the end, though, Pilate caved in to popular demand and didn't release Jesus. Pilate has become an enduring symbol of the weak, spineless authority that knows the right but chooses the wrong for safety, expediency, and popularity. Ever since that time, civil rulers have needed the prophetic voice of the church to remind them that they serve as stewards of power, not as masters.

If the words "under God" in the Pledge of Allegiance or "In God We Trust" on our money remind the state and its citizens of the duty to exercise power justly, fairly, and within the limits God has established, then these words do not advance religion. Rather, they limit government. If instead, people take these words as constituting evidence that America is God's chosen nation with authority to act in the world in a unilateral and heavy-handed manner and to legislate religious matters, then they should be struck down as violations of the Constitution. Further, Christians should be first to reject them as a blasphemous attempt by the state to usurp the role of God in spiritual matters.

Which meaning does America give to these words? Americans must decide for themselves. Today's generation needs to hear Christ's admonitions against using the power of the sword or the state for the advancement of His kingdom. The humility engendered by a genuine sense of a Higher Power—of the Divine—seems to be escaping our society.

Jesus escaped the temptation of using civil force in His spiritual ministry by taking refuge in God's Word. But He sought solace also in God's other book, that of nature. John records that when Jesus saw that the Jews were "about to come and take Him by force to make Him king," He went to two places where human beings are reminded of their weakness and smallness (see John 6:15–17). First, He climbed up a mountain alone, and then He walked out onto the sea. This takes us back to where this chapter began, with two men out on the sea, sensing the greatness of nature and their own insignificance. "Be still, and know that I am God" (Psalm 46:10).

Mountain climbing and surfing may not be the solution to our church-state dilemmas, but gaining a sense of wonder and awe in nature can only help us see—with our minds and souls—the true relation between God and humankind as well as between church and state. It can remind us that the state is under an obligation to God to exercise its civil authority with humility and restraint, as a steward of power, not as its master.

---

1. All other Scripture quotations in this chapter are from the New King James Version.

2. David Burrell, *Freedom and Creation in the Three Traditions* (Notre Dame, Ind.: University of Notre Dame Press, 1993), 5, 6, back cover.

3. Ellen G. White, *Patriarchs and Prophets* (Nampa, Idaho: Pacific Press®, 1958), 331, 332; emphasis added.

4. James Madison expressed this principle in his famous "Memorial and Remonstrauce."

5. White, *Spirit of Prophecy Counsels Relating to Church-State Relationships* (Silver Spring, Md.: Ellen G. White Estate, 1964), 27, http://maranathamedia.com/start/index .php?option=com_docman&task=doc_view&gid=1078.

6. The Urim and Thummim were still in use in the time of Ezra and Nehemiah, after the Babylonian exile, see Ezra 2:63; Nehemiah 7:65.

7. White, Letter 187, 1903, 5, reprinted in *Spirit of Prophecy Counsels Relating to Church-State Relationships*, 7.

8. Justice Roy Moore, the Alabama Ten Commandments judge, has publicly advocated the duty of the state to acknowledge God. While it is doubtful that the state has such a duty, leaders have every right to acknowledge God.

Alan J. Reinach

CHAPTER 3

"Render Unto Caesar": How Should the Church Relate to the State?

I watched as several thousand people stood reverently and pledged allegiance to the Christian flag. As they concluded this revised pledge, they recited together "with life and liberty for all who believe." They were gathered for a Reclaiming America rally, at which they attended seminars, workshops, and plenary sessions to train them for political action. They were taught that America is succumbing to Satan, secular humanism, and homosexuality and that it's the duty of the elect to take back America for God. Looking on, I wondered about the intended fate of those who don't believe. It was a chilling moment.

This Reclaiming America rally can be understood only in a theological context, for it is the product of Dominion theology, or Christian Reconstructionism. While few Christian leaders publicly profess this theology, many advocate Dominionist ideas. Christian Reconstructionism is faultily crafted from a biblical foundation, Genesis 1:28, where Adam was given dominion over the plants and animals. From this, Dominionists assert the right and authority of the elect to rule over the rest of humankind as well as the earth. The grandfather of the movement was a Reformed theologian, R. J. Rushdoony, whose work *The Institutes of Biblical Law* is a detailed discussion of how Old Testament law applies to modern society. It is essentially a blueprint for a theocracy in which the elect are empowered to rule in God's name.[1]

Christian Reconstructionism is an extension of the Calvinist doctrine of limited atonement. This doctrine holds that God didn't really love the whole world and give His Son Jesus Christ to die for the sins of everyone. Instead, He chooses to save a favored few and consigns the rest to the fires of hell.

These few fortunate ones are considered "the elect," and Christ died to save only them. Because of their unique status with the Almighty, they are presumed to know God's will and to possess authority to rule in His name.

As the Religious Right has grown in power and influence and given the Republican Party virtual control of all three branches of the federal government,[2] more and more journalists and scholars are examining the theological and philosophical basis for this unprecedented rise to power. Evangelical Christians, as well as those of other faiths or of little faith, have written critiques. While these commentators do a good job of examining the presuppositions and aims of the movement as well as the diversity of beliefs, they all make one glaring omission. None have placed this movement in a prophetic context.[3]

Prophetic Scripture warns against the reunion of church and state in the United States. (See especially Revelation 13:11–17, and compare Revelation 14:8 and chapter 17.) It warns that America will substitute a form of "national righteousness" in place of the power of godliness. The three angels of Revelation 14 give God's final warning to humanity. These messages, especially the first two, need to be given the prominence they deserve.[4]

Although these messages are expressed in symbolic language, their meaning is clear and direct. The second angel declares that the reunion of church and state will lead to oppression and persecution in God's name (Revelation 14:8). It will constitute a form of national apostasy that will incur the wrath and judgments of God and result in national ruin.[5]

The message of the first angel is equally urgent. In contrast with current efforts to produce moral and cultural reform and spiritual revival through political means, the first angel reminds us that we must recover authentic worship of the Creator God. This message is said to be the everlasting gospel. The message is more than a call to personal spiritual renewal; it has profound social and political implications as well. It is the antidote to the political gospel the second angel warns against. The second angel warns the church to flee from the state as the source of its power and to return to the arms of Christ. The first angel's proclamation of the everlasting gospel is the necessary corollary, as it reminds us to trust our Creator.

The "no win" question

The title of this chapter is taken from a simple and powerful saying of Jesus. Religious leaders who felt threatened by Jesus' growing popularity were seeking to discredit Him. Their agents dogged Jesus' steps, looking for opportunities to trap Him. One day, they crafted what they thought would be a surefire plan. They asked Jesus whether it was lawful to pay taxes to Caesar. They intended this to be a "no win" question. They expected that Jesus would alienate people if He supported the legitimacy of paying taxes. If, on the other hand, He opposed paying taxes, He would be vulnerable to charges of treason.

Jesus was neither fooled nor amused. He asked His foes to show Him a coin and then asked them whose picture appeared on the coin. "Caesar's," came the reply. Then Jesus issued a simple declaration that has echoed through the centuries: " 'Render to Caesar the things that are Caesar's; and to God the things that are God's' " (Matthew 22:21).[6] His answer silenced His foes. The principle Jesus stated is simple but profound. It contains the critical distinction between the respective roles of Caesar and God, though it doesn't define those roles.

The lines between those roles have often been blurred. After the fall of imperial Rome, the Roman bishops became the *de facto* heirs of the empire, and they blended civil and religious authority for more than a millennium. Early in the Protestant Reformation, the "chaos" of individual freedom was restrained by the principle that the inhabitants of a region must follow whatever religion the prince of that region chose for himself. The Pilgrims and Puritans who settled New England also failed to distinguish between church and state. People were fined and whipped and placed in stocks for violating what the authorities considered their religious duties. Laws were enacted to require attendance at worship services and to forbid travel and other work on the "Lord's Day." Free speech and press were circumscribed by blasphemy laws.[7] The profound principle that Jesus set forth has rarely been understood, much less practiced.

Jesus promised the church unlimited spiritual resources as well as profound spiritual authority. " 'Everything you ask in prayer, believing, you shall receive,' " (Matthew 21:22). Indeed, believers who are in agreement were given authority to bind both heaven and earth (see Matthew 18:18–20). In the Great Commission, Jesus asserted that all authority in heaven and earth belonged to Him and on that basis commanded His followers to make disciples, to baptize, and to teach (see Matthew 28:18–20). In effect, Jesus offered this unlimited authority to His followers. However, in light of the American church's emphasis on social and political activism, the absence of any "cultural mandate" is a glaring omission in Jesus' great commission.[8] He didn't command the disciples to transform Roman culture, to infiltrate the structures of power, or to battle against prevailing practices of abortion and homosexuality. When Jesus taught His followers to be "salt" and "light," He wasn't calling them to exercise power but to practice loving service. The greatest among men would be a servant (Matthew 20:25,26).

Before Jesus ascended to heaven, He had one final encounter with His disciples. They still expected Jesus to assume the throne and rule as an earthly monarch, so they asked Him, " 'Lord, is it at this time You are restoring the kingdom to Israel?' " (Acts 1:6). They remained eager to sit on His right and left hand and to exercise political power. Jesus had already told them to wait for the promise of the Father, referring to the Holy Spirit. Now He had to remind them again. " 'It is not for you to know times or epochs which the Father has fixed by His own authority; but you shall receive power when the Holy Spirit has come upon you; and you shall be My witnesses both in Jerusalem, and in all Judea and Samaria, and even to the remotest part of the earth' " (verses 7, 8).

Jesus' answer was tactful but firm. One can hear in it echoes of His answer to Pilate in the judgment hall, when He declared, " 'My kingdom is not of this world. If My kingdom were of this world, then My servants would be fighting' " (John 18:36). Jesus insisted that the establishment of the kingdom of God is in the Father's hands and was not His disciples' concern. It is not given to them to pursue power in this world. The kingdom isn't about power or use of force or political action. No, the kingdom of God is about restoring lost humanity to an intimate relationship with their Creator, based on love and trust.

The disciples sought to exercise power as the world defines power. Jesus offered a superior source of strength. The Spirit of God is not weakness. The Greek word Jesus used to describe the Spirit is *dynamis*. This word is the root of *dynamite, dynamo,* and *dynamic.* The Spirit is the power that re-creates the human heart and gives strength to the one who is weak and weary (see, e.g., Isaiah 40:28–31). The promised Spirit of God has never been a substitute for power—it is the real Source of the believer's power.

Jesus sought to correct the Pharisees' Messianic expectations of political triumph over the Romans by defining the kingdom in spiritual terms: " 'The kingdom of God is not coming with signs to be observed; nor will they say, "Look, here it is!" or, "There it is!" For behold, the kingdom of God is in your midst' " (Luke 17:20, 21). The kingdom of God is a matter of the heart. Jesus said that eternal life is to know God (see John 17:3). In the biblical sense, knowing is intimacy, not intellectual knowledge. The kingdom of God is founded in love. It was for love that Christ died on the cross (see, e.g., John 3:16).

Contrast this vision of the kingdom with a recent scene on the steps of the California State Capitol, where hundreds of Christian protesters were gathered in opposition to several gay-rights bills enacted by the legislature. They gathered to urge Governor Arnold Schwarzenegger to veto the bills. "Terminate these bills," they chanted, "or we'll terminate you!" With this and other slogans, the Christian activists brought a powerful spirit to the capitol, but it wasn't the spirit of love. It was pure hatred. These were the elect, the righteously indignant. They knew that homosexuality was evil. It was a matter of black or white. They were the chosen ones battling the forces of darkness.[9]

To those who don't share the hostility or the certainty that their politics and religion are flawless, such scenes seem to be discordant exceptions to the American spirit of tolerance. How quickly many forget that racial and religious intolerance have been constant themes in our national experience. The Puritans persecuted Quakers. The Anglicans jailed Baptist preachers. The Native Americans were driven from their lands. The economy of Southern states was dependent on the labor of imported African slaves. Following the American Civil War, the freed slaves faced social and legal obstacles to economic opportunity and equality in both the North and the South. Women finally obtained the right to vote in the early twentieth century, but to this day, they are often paid substantially less than men for the same work. Despite the civil rights movement of the 1960s and 1970s, race conflicts still exist in American cities. Jews have long been excluded from jobs and country clubs because of their religion. Since the 1980s, the biggest divide is no longer racial but religious. The culture war is definitely being fought on religious lines.

The main focus of prophecy

The misguided effort to establish the kingdom of God as an earthly dominion through political means is the main focus of prophecy. This effort is essentially about rendering to Caesar the things of God by asking Caesar to engage in the work of the church. Revelation 13 identifies the United States as the final dominant world power.[10] In the Bible, horns are a symbol of power. In chapters 7 and 8 of the book of Daniel, the blending of the powers of church and state during the medieval period is symbolized by a single horn. By contrast, the United States is pictured as having "two horns like a lamb." The lamb is a symbol of Christ (see, e.g., John 1:29). The two horns denote a separation of powers. In the American political system, power is divided in order to preserve civil and religious freedom. However, although this nation was founded on "lamblike" principles of power, it will speak as a dragon when it enforces worship. The worship to be enforced is said to be that of the first beast, a symbol of the union of church and state during the Middle Ages.

America was established on a uniquely Protestant principle. The primacy of individual conscience, to be respected by the state, derives from Reformation doctrines regarding personal religious conversion. Because the soul can and must respond directly to Christ to grasp salvation by faith, neither the church nor the state has any authority to interfere between the soul and Christ. Out of this simple discovery flowed the major Reformation doctrines: justification by faith, the Bible as the only rule of faith and practice, and the priesthood of all believers. Thomas Jefferson expressed a fundamentally Protestant idea in the Declaration of Independence when he wrote, "All men . . . are endowed by their Creator with certain inalienable rights." The American Constitution became the political expression of Protestant and republican principles—limited self-government designed to respect the rights of the individual.[11]

This good beginning is why the American effort to enforce worship described in Revelation 13 is said to be so deceptive, so confusing. The pursuit of national righteousness through legislating religious worship will appear to be good and godly. Yet, the effort to bring America back to God through political means is actually a repudiation of God's character and kingdom, which are based on love instead of force. It will also result in religious tyranny and persecution in opposition to our constitutional principles.

The picture in Revelation 17 is equally striking. There the church is symbolized as a harlot who is riding on a beast. This beast represents the political powers, the kings of the earth. The woman is on top—she's holding the reins, calling the shots. The name on her forehead, "Babylon," means "confusion." The church is confused. She has forsaken intimacy with Christ for intimacy with the state. The Bible doesn't mince words: it repeatedly calls this illicit connection between church and state fornication or adultery (see, e.g., Revelation 17:1, 2, 4; 18:3).

Revelation 14 pictures three angels with messages to give to the entire world. The first angel issues a call to worship the Creator in the hour of

God's judgment. It is a call to recover the genuine experience of righteousness by faith. This is a gospel that delivers us from both the penalty and power of sin. Those who are justified don't experience cheap grace—a feel good, do as you please, anything goes gospel. The fact that they have been saved by expressing their belief in Christ hasn't given them license to sin. Instead, the *just* shall live by faith; Paul insists that the truly converted are controlled by the love of Christ and "they who live should no longer live for themselves, but for Him who died and rose again on their behalf" (2 Corinthians 5:15).

The second angel warns that the fall of Babylon is caused by the reunion of church and state (Revelation 14:8). "Babylon" is the name written on the forehead of the harlot that symbolizes the church. She is in for a sudden and calamitous collapse, described in considerable detail in Revelation 18. The collapse is global and universal. The national and international political, economic, and social structures will descend into anarchy and chaos. It is sudden and complete. But it won't happen without warning. God intends that His servants faithfully warn the world about what will bring this to pass. Jonah didn't fulfill his prophetic task until God got his attention in a dramatic way. One can only wonder what sort of divine attention-getting intervention might be required for God's people to fulfill their prophetic function faithfully this time around, when the stakes are so much higher.

" 'Fallen, fallen is Babylon,' " the second angel declares emphatically. The cause of her fall is announced in symbolic language: " 'She who has made all the nations drink of the wine of the passion of her immorality' " (Revelation 14:8). The problem is defined as an immoral intimacy between church and state, described as fornication. Babylon, a comprehensive symbol of fallen churches working together, makes the nations drink her wine.[12] The church deems religious instruction and indoctrination inadequate to build up the kingdom of God—she believes she must employ the wrath of the state to enforce her doctrine. Righteousness has not been achieved through the power of the Spirit alone, she concludes, so civil means must supplement the power of God. The nations don't drink Babylon's wine voluntarily. They are forced to drink. Babylon grasps the reins of power and imposes her will through the exercise of civil authority. She has seized the power of Caesar to render forced obedience to God. The name *Babylon,* meaning "confusion," is an apt description of fallen churches that blend spiritual and civil authority in a misguided effort to build up God's kingdom, punishing religious dissent in the process.

Bloody Christian history

Jesus warned His followers, " 'An hour is coming for everyone who kills you to think he is offering service to God. And these things they will do, because they have not known the Father, or Me' " (John 16:2, 3). Christian history is bloodied with the corpses of dissenters. It should surprise no one that prophecy suggests a repetition of this sordid history.

Contrast this use of coercion with the picture of Christ in Revelation 3:20: " 'Behold, I stand at the door and knock; if any one hears My voice and opens the door, I will come in to him, and will dine with him, and he with me.' " Christ is the consummate gentleman. He doesn't force His way into the human heart. He knocks politely. His instruction to Peter to put away his sword stands for the church for all time (John 18:11). The warning—that the church that lives by the sword will die by the sword—is repeated in Revelation 13:10.

Revelation 13 declares three times that the United States will form an "image of the beast." An image is like the thing, but it is not the thing itself. In this case, the image is a likeness of the medieval union of church and state. It is an image of the first beast, whose deadly wound was healed. To understand where we are headed, we need to look back. We need to study our history. The medieval union of church and state gave the world the Inquisition. This was an institution founded on the moral premise that the end justify the means. It was permissible to destroy the body in the hopes of saving the soul. Torture was justified to achieve a positive religious goal and therefore seen as moral.

The United States forms an image of the sponsors of the Inquisition by repudiating both Protestant and republican principles respecting the primacy of individual civil and religious freedoms.[13] It is no wonder, then, that during a war on terror there is a national debate over the role of civil liberty. It isn't surprising that extraordinary and unconstitutional means are being employed for the common good of preventing terrorist attacks. Our most fundamental constitutional commitments are being called into question by the present conflict. At the same time, religious theology has come to dominate American policy.[14]

Michelle Goldberg relates a chilling picture of a politicized church. In Ohio, in the weeks leading up to the 2004 presidential election, John Kerry supporters appeared to dominate the streets. Everywhere, the Democrats seemed to be out in force, while Republican banners and campaigners were apparently absent. The upset in Ohio on election day was a stunning surprise. The Republican activists hadn't abandoned that state—they had concentrated their efforts in the churches.[15] While the church has been manipulated for partisan political purposes, it has also adopted a decisive political agenda itself. It seeks to reform and revitalize the nation by seizing the reins of power. The reunion of church and state has become a mutual courtship that has progressed well beyond the flirtation stage.

When Jesus invoked the famous distinction, to render to Caesar the things that are Caesar's and to God the things that are God's, He defined a critical boundary that every nation would do well to observe. The role of the state is essentially civil, not religious. Jesus told Pilate " 'You would have no authority over Me, unless it had been given you from above' " (John 19:11), pointing to God as the source of his civil authority. In Romans 13, Paul also taught that civil authority derives from God. When, after the Crucifixion, the rulers commanded the apostles not to teach and preach in the name of Jesus, the apostles refused to comply, insisting that they " 'must obey God rather than men' " (Acts 5:29). The lines are drawn quite clearly. The state exercises authority under God, but it is restricted to civil matters. The state has no right to meddle in religious affairs. It has no expertise for interpreting doctrine and no authority to enforce "truth."

In the Middle Ages, a single, universal church asserted the authority to define what is truth. Civil authorities acknowledged the spiritual authority of the church and accepted their role to uphold and enforce truth. The church defined heresy, and the state assumed the obligation to carry out the needed punishment. Today, there is vigorous dispute about the nature and content of religious truth. The genius of the American republican system is its institutional humility. In this system, the state lacks either the authority or expertise to determine which religion is correct and what doctrine should be taught or enforced by civil authority.

Revelation 13 depicts the United States as able to form an image of the medieval church-state union through the use of powerful deception. The blurring of the lines between church and state is inherently confusing because the goal of political power is the pursuit of a form of national righteousness. Tragically, such formal righteousness will become a counterfeit of the genuine experience of personal righteousness by faith, which is the central teaching of the Reformation.

The boundary between church and state

In the American experiment, the boundary between church and state has often been symbolized as a distinction between the first and second tables of the law. This metaphor is credited to Roger Williams, the founder of Rhode Island and the first Baptist church in New England. The first table is said to define the human obligation to worship and obey God, while the second table of the law contains social duties, some of which are suitable for state enforcement.[16] In this conception, the state crosses the line when intruding on matters of faith, belief, and worship. God and Caesar each receive their proper respect.

The consequences of failing to heed the warning of the first two angels—the warning to the church to turn from pursuing political power and to recover the power of the gospel—results in a third and final warning. The final message warns against receiving the infamous "mark of the beast." Legislative efforts to enforce worship misrepresent the character of God. Such efforts mark the end of a long path, not the beginning. In place of official humility in matters of faith, the Religious Right insists on manipulating the powers of state to promote Christian prayer, Bible reading, and Ten Commandments displays. Too often, there is little respect for the rights of conscience.

Some wonder whether speaking out will delay the coming of Christ since prophecy must be fulfilled. In fact, the opposite is true. Prior to the coming of Christ, the earth will suffer the judgments of God for its universal apostasy. These judgments are described in the seven last plagues (see Revelation 15; 16). God doesn't judge the nations without warning. He doesn't want any to perish (see 2 Peter 3:9). This is why the warnings of the three angels are to be given universally and with a loud voice (see Revelation 14:6–12). The giving of the warning doesn't delay the coming of Christ. In fact, Christ will not come until the warning has been faithfully given.

There is a truth critical for our time—the truth that a loving God doesn't coerce the conscience but extends freedom to all. If fundamentalists of all religions would adopt this principle, violence and war in the name of God would cease and the world would be a far safer place. This truth is central to the gospel. If God could have forced us into the kingdom, Jesus wouldn't have had to die. Jesus' sacrifice satisfied the legal claims of the broken law, but it did more than that. It restored a relationship between God and human beings based on love and freedom. The truth is that, contrary to the increasingly popular Calvinist conception that God alone chooses, humans must respond to the love of Christ by the exercise of free will. If we love and serve Christ, it is because we choose to, not because God compels us. God has chosen everyone for salvation, but some choose not to accept the eternal life freely given. It is in the nature of things that the human heart cannot be compelled to love God.

In the end, everyone will have to choose to worship the God of freedom or the god of force. No one will be left sitting on the fence. The powers of church and state will unite to compel belief and worship in Christ's name. Those who resist will be marginalized, demonized, economically sanctioned, and even killed (see Revelation 13:11–17). God is misrepresented as a tyrant who will kill those who disobey.

The blending of faith and patriotism, God and country, Jesus and guns, has powerful and nearly universal appeal. Those who object to this patriotic appeal may be derided as unpatriotic, irreligious, and even heretical. Yet, these are the true patriots. Though opposed by the combined powers of church and state, they will remain faithful to God. Empowered by the Spirit of God, they will know the truth and defy church and state. In so doing, they will render faithful service to God and Caesar, reminding both church and state that Caesar's authority can never be allowed to usurp the authority of the Creator.

---

1. Current critical discussions of impending theocracy overlook the obvious: that in the genuine theocracy of Israel, the supposed model, God destroyed the people who asserted their power and authority to interpret His will. See Numbers 16.

2. This was written prior to the midterm elections of 2006. At that time, the Republicans controlled Congress and the White House and had made two new Supreme Court appointments, effectively shifting the balance on the Court to the Right.

3. Time would be well spent with the following volumes: (1) Randall Balmer, *Thy Kingdom Come: How the Religious Right Distorts the Faith and Threatens America: An Evangelical's Lament* (New York: Basic Books, 2006), a critique of evangelicals. (2) Michelle Goldberg, *Kingdom Coming* (New York: W. W. Norton & Co., 2006). (3) Kevin Phillips, *American Theocracy: The Peril and Politics of Radical Religion, Oil, and Borrowed Money in the 21st Century* (New York: Viking, 2006). In this book, a conservative political analyst documents how thoroughly conservative Christian theology has influenced both foreign and domestic policy in the United States. (4) Rabbi James Rudin, *The Baptizing of America: The Religious Right's Plans for the Rest of Us* (New York: Thunder's Mouth Press, 2006). Rabbi Rudin has been a leader in the interfaith community as a leader of the American Jewish Committee. He writes from firsthand experience. (5) Cal Thomas and Ed Dobson, *Blinded by Might:Why the Religious Right Can't Save America* (Grand Rapids, Mich.: Zondervan, 2000), the groundbreaking critique of the Religious Right written by two former Moral Majority board members.

4. The third of the three angels' messages pertains to the time when the mark of the beast is being enforced, which is yet to come. The first two messages are both relevant and timely today.

5. Consider the following observation: "A time is coming when the law of God is, in a special sense, to be made void in our land. The rulers of our nation will, by legislative enactments, enforce the Sunday law, and thus God's people be brought into great peril. When our nation, in its legislative councils, shall enact laws to bind the consciences of men in regard to their religious privileges, enforcing Sunday observance, and bringing oppressive power to bear against those who keep the seventh-day Sabbath, the law of God will, to all intents and purposes, be made void in our land; and national apostasy will be followed by national ruin." Ellen G. White, *Review and Herald,* December 18, 1888. Quoted in Francis D. Nichol, ed., *The Seventh-day Adventist Bible Commentary* (Hagerstown, Md.: Review and Herald®, 1957), 7:977.

6. Unless otherwise noted, all Scripture quotations in this chapter are from the New American Standard Bible.

7. See William Addison Blakely, ed., *American State Papers* (Hagerstown, Md.: Review and Herald®, 1943), 31, 79.

8. The "cultural mandate" is what evangelicals refer to as the command to be "salt" and "light" and transform the culture and politics to reflect the values and morals of the kingdom of God.

9. This event was observed by Michael D. Peabody, Esq., a contributor to this volume.

10. This interpretation is explained in some detail by C. Mervyn Maxwell in *God Cares, Volume 2: The Message of Revelation* (Boise, Idaho: Pacific Press®, 1985), 309ff.

11. See, e.g., White, *Maranatha* (Hagerstown, Md.: Review and Herald®, 1976), 185; also White, *Spirit of Prophecy* (Nampa, Idaho: Pacific Press®, 1884), 4:277.

12. See Nichol, 7:831.

13. "When Protestantism shall stretch her hand across the gulf to grasp the hand of the Roman power, when she shall reach over the abyss to clasp hands with Spiritualism, when, under the influence of this threefold union, our country shall repudiate every principle of its Constitution as a Protestant and Republican government, and shall make provision for the propagation of papal falsehoods and delusions, then we may know that the time has come for the marvelous working of Satan, and that the end is near." White, *Testimonies for the Church* (Nampa, Idaho: Pacific Press®, 1948), 5:451.

14. The most thorough discussion of this is found in Phillips, *American Theocracy.* See also Walter Russell Mead, "God's Country," *Foreign Affairs,* vol. 85, no. 5 (Sept./Oct. 2006).

15. Goldberg, 52, 53.

16. Covetousness is not only unsuitable to state prohibition, it has become the foundation of the global economy.

Douglas Morgan

CHAPTER 4

Marching to the Call of History

On January 28, 2003, the leader of the wealthiest and most powerful empire[1] in history spoke with solemn resolve about the likelihood that its power would soon be used in a dramatic, new manner. President George W. Bush put the world on notice in his State of the Union address that he was prepared to attack a foreign government that, while unquestionably reprehensible and antagonistic to the United States, had not directly attacked the United States, its interests, or its treaty commitments. Such action, said the president, would be necessary for the United States to fulfill its unique role in history—its destiny in spreading to the world the divine gift of liberty. "If war is forced upon us, we will fight with the full force and might of the United States military—and we will prevail," he declared. "And we go forward with confidence, because this call of history has come to the right country."[2]

These stirring sentiments, reinforced on numerous occasions by the president and his associates, point us to the fact that something more basic than wiping out terrorist networks has been driving the global war on terrorism since 2001. Something deeper than the threat of weapons of mass destruction or the brutality of a tyrant. Something deeper even than the thirst for oil—namely, "the call of history," the role and destiny of the American republic in the human drama as a whole.

Just over nineteen hundred years earlier, a ringleader of a suspicious dissident movement, exiled by the empire of that time to the Mediterranean island of Patmos, wrote feverishly about a different but also sweeping and dramatic vision of history. The apostle named John, writing at a time when the Roman Empire had reached its zenith, dissented from the seemingly obvious fact that history had reached its fulfillment with the *Pax Romana*—arguably the most powerful, efficient, just, and peace-enhancing empire in history to that point. In John's view of history, a Ruler other than Caesar had already won sovereignty over the earth (see Revelation 1:5, 6), though the relatively few who recognized His reign held no territory and had no army or law-enforcement systems.

Questions about history's meaning—about their location in the unfolding drama of the ages and what that meant for their lives—also preoccupied the early Seventh-day Adventists. In the midst of an America already taking on aspects of an empire, they scrutinized John's book of Revelation for answers. In 1851, for example, John N. Andrews opened his pioneering exposition of Revelation 13 and 14 with the question, "What position do we now occupy? No question of greater importance can now engage our attention."[3]

Andrews and the others came to see in Revelation 13 the point at which John's book of apocalyptic prophecy brings the American empire most directly into its scope. After describing a thoroughly vicious, multiheaded beast that came up out of the sea blaspheming, demanding worship from people all over the world, and persecuting the faithful worshipers of God, this chapter describes the emergence of a second beast from the land—one that looks benign with its two "lamblike" horns but that speaks like a dragon.

If this second beast lacks the ferocity of the first one, it has finesse that it uses to deceive, delude, and seduce people into its control. It appears to be something other than it really is. We discover that it isn't at all hesitant to use coercion ruthlessly to consolidate and maintain the power it gains through persuasive deception. It is, after all, in the business of making an image to the sea beast, whose very nature was to "make war" (verse 7) and "kill with the sword" (verse 10, NRSV).

In verse 18, the reader is bidden to use "wisdom" in assessing this scene. To protect ourselves against the "organized deceit" characteristic of Revelation 13's land beast, writes Eugene H. Peterson, the author of Revelation wants us to use our heads: "Figure out what is going on. Most of the conspicuous religion that is in vogue at any one time in the country derives from the land beast. Expose these religious pretensions."[4]

In President Bush's 2003 State of the Union message, "the call of history" beckons the United States to fight for freedom—the liberty that "is not America's gift to the world, it is God's gift to humanity." Though not the source of liberty, the armed forces of the United States are regarded as designated by "history"—and thus God—as the chosen instrument for the destruction of whomever or whatever stands in the way of the realization of that liberty throughout the world.

The president's characterization of U.S. military power as a primary agency of world redemption reflects the ascendance—and convergence—of two ideological movements that have been gathering strength since the 1970s: neoconservatism and the New Christian Right. These movements draw their power from deeper sources than the public policy agendas they advocate. Both are theologies of history—ways of envisioning the past and the future that give meaning to the present. Both bear surface similarities to the biblical worldview. Our project is to examine their claims, taking the gospel highlighted by the book of Revelation as the measure of authenticity.

Power to transform the world

The neoconservative movement took shape as a reaction against the moral relativism of the 1960s counterculture. If the goal of plain old conservatism was to *conserve* traditional values and the standing order of society, the neoconservatives believed that the democratic ideals of America could *transform* the world. The essence of their aspirations, writes international relations scholar Andrew J. Bacevich, was "to fuse American power to American principles, ensuring the survival of those principles and subsequently their propagation to the benefit of all humankind."[5] Forward-thinking, unflinching confrontation with dictatorship and repression would bring victory for democracy and human rights around the globe.

With the collapse of Communism in 1989, it seemed that the neoconservative moment had arrived. President Reagan's forthright condemnations of Soviet totalitarianism and the major buildup of American military strength appeared to have vindicated the neoconservatives. The Communist evil had not merely been contained but defeated.

For the neoconservatives, this triumph most emphatically did *not* mean that the United States should stand down from military dominance now that its great superpower rival, the Soviet Union, had disintegrated. It wasn't the time to look for a "peace dividend" now that the threat of Communism no longer existed to justify massive military expenditures. Rather, this was the moment for the United States to press its advantage by further expanding and renovating its military power. By this policy it could ensure total and unassailable military dominance in the world. In turn, that would empower democracy's continuing drive to world triumph and the defeat of its linger-ing foes.

After the terrorist attacks of September 11, 2001, President Bush turned to the neoconservative plan of ensuring the defense of democracy with an aggressive "offense": strong, bold confrontation of the enemies of liberty, making use, without hesitance or hand-wringing, of whatever military re-sources might be required.

Though the decisiveness of the president's turn would only gradually become fully apparent, he signaled it just days after the 9/11 attacks in the memorial service held at the National Cathedral: "Our responsibility to his-tory is already clear: to answer these attacks and *rid the world of evil*"[6] (em-phasis added). Then, in his January 2002 State of the Union address, the president specified Iraq, Iran, and North Korea as the "axis" of world evil that had to be confronted.

Thus, the direction taken by the United States in the "war on terror" entails more than foreign policy doctrine and strategy. It is a utopian escha-tology that envisions the worldwide defeat of opposition to America's global program for liberal democracy. The title alone of a book published in 2003 establishes this point. David Frum, the presidential speechwriter who took credit for the "axis of evil" phrase, teamed up with Richard Perle, "the intel-lectual guru of the hard-line conservative movement in foreign policy," to author *An End to Evil: How to Win the War on Terror*.[7] So, in our effort to discern through "prophetic perspective" what is going on, it is of paramount importance for us to grasp that in all this we face a *theology of history* that stands in marked contrast to that presented in the book of Revelation.

President Bush is by no means the originator of this theology of history. In the best-selling tract *Common Sense,* which did much to persuade Amer-ican colonists to take the final, radical step of violent revolution against the British crown, Thomas Paine wrote, "We have it in our power to begin the world over again. A situation, similar to the present, hath not appeared since the days of Noah until now. The birthday of a new world is at hand."[8] Re-garding the overmatched patriots' military struggle, Virginian John Page wrote to Thomas Jefferson, "We know the race is not to the swift nor the battle to the strong. Do you not think an angel rides in the whirlwind and directs the storm?"[9] Belief that violence, when exercised on behalf of Amer-ican values, is "redemptive violence" that in some sense advances a new ep-och of freedom and justice that is the historic destiny of humanity under God, has pervaded the national consciousness ever since.[10]

Thus, though not unique in declaring this faith, our forty-third president gives it sharply defined expression in a new context, thereby raising it to a significance far above the commonplace. Religion scholar Bruce Lincoln identifies five propositions that form the basis of the theology of history preached from the pulpit of the Bush presidency: "1) God desires freedom for all humanity; 2) this desire manifests itself in history; 3) America is called by history (and thus, implicitly by God) to take action on behalf of this cause; 4) insofar as America responds with courage and determination, God's purpose is served and freedom's advance is inevitable; 5) with the triumph of freedom, God's will is accomplished and history comes to an end."[11]

Another gospel

This theology of history has important features similar in appearance to those of the gospel. It presents a God invested in history and directing it to a glorious culmination that upholds human freedom and makes it forever secure. And while God is finally sovereign, the free response of human agents is indispensable for moving history to its goal. Thus, it is a form of *millennialism*.[12]

The word *civil* points to the fact that a civil government, the United States of America, is presented as the principal agent through which the redemption of history—the defeat of evil and the triumph of liberty—is accomplished. The "call of history has come to *the right country*," Or, as President Bush stated it in his second inaugural address in January 2005, history "has a visible direction, set by liberty and the Author of Liberty," and the corresponding policy of the United States is to support democratic liberty everywhere "with the ultimate goal of ending tyranny in our world."[13]

Is it really such a problem, though, that the United States, rather than Jesus, is depicted as the means through which history reaches its goal? The outcome of triumph for liberty and defeat for tyranny seems to harmonize with the future God has promised. Could it not be that the United States is a leading instrument for the fulfillment of God's plan for history?

The *content* of the "freedom" offered by civil millennialism speaks to those questions. In his commencement address at the U.S. Coast Guard Academy on May 21, 2003, President Bush encapsulated what he means by the "freedom" for which the nation fights: "America's national ambition is the spread of free markets, free trade, and free societies."

I confess to being easily moved by the patriotic rhetoric of liberty, which my mind associates mainly with freedoms of worship, speech, and political representation enjoyed equally by all without regard to distinctions of race, gender, and wealth. So, I have found it a useful exercise in clarification to remember, when I hear our leaders speak of liberty, the part of the package usually left unmentioned: "free markets and free trade." In other words, capitalism American-style, and in one word, *globalization*.

The eloquent apostle of globalization, Thomas Friedman, makes it plain: "For globalization to work, America can't be afraid to act like the almighty superpower that it is. . . . The hidden hand of the market will never work without a hidden fist. McDonald's cannot flourish without McDonnell Douglas, the designer of the F-15, and the hidden fist that keeps the world safe for Silicon Valley's technology is called the United States Army, Air Force, Navy and Marine Corps."[14]

Clearly, then, the "civil" millennialism we are examining is also "militaristic." It places a large measure of faith in the "almighty" military power of the United States to accomplish the redemption of history. In the president's victory speech aboard the USS *Lincoln* on May 1, 2003, he congratulated American troops for having "taken up the highest calling of history." They carried a "message of hope" that is "ancient and ever new" expressed by the prophet Isaiah in the words, " 'To the captives, "Come out,"—and to those in darkness, "be free." ' " The passage quoted, Isaiah 49:9, is part of the cycle of "servant songs" that Christians have traditionally seen fulfilled in the redemptive work of Jesus Christ.

Indeed the president had already appropriated to America what the Gospel of John has to say about Jesus as the redeeming "light of the world." The previous fall, on the anniversary of the 9/11 attacks, with a spectacularly lit Statue of Liberty in the background, he declared the ideal of America to be the "hope of all mankind"—the light that "still shines in the darkness" and which the darkness will not overcome (see John 1:1–5). In thus describing the United States with "the same language that the New Testament reserves for Christ alone," President Bush takes the language of civil religion a crucial step further than the commonplace usage made by all presidents, according to Duke University biblical scholar Stephen B. Chapman.[15] Despite his care to avoid references to the war on terrorism as a Christian crusade, President Bush clearly casts American military power in the Messianic role of effecting the global elimination of tyranny and the triumph of liberty, just as in the neoconservative vision.

Religion influences foreign policy

The rise and unprecedented political clout of the Christian Right, the second ideological force we must examine, does not need rehearsal here. The challenge is to convey its significance. What seemed an ominous *possibility* in the 1970s and 1980s has become a stunning *reality* in the first decade of the twenty-first century: dispensationalist prophecy belief exerting substantive influence on American foreign policy.

Dispensationalism, popularly known as the "secret rapture" teaching, is also known as Christian Zionism because it sees the modern Zionist movement and the Israeli state as the centerpiece of biblical prophecy. The establishment of the state of Israel in 1948 provided apparent vindication for this entire system of prophecy interpretation. Then, the amazing, sweeping victories in the Six Days' War of 1967 brought the territory controlled by the Israeli government much closer to the biblical specifications of the land promised to the ancient Israelites and dramatically heightened still further the interest of American evangelicals in biblical prophecy. Hal Lindsey's *The Late Great Planet Earth* became the best-selling Christian book in America ever, and it held that honor until the recent, mega-best-selling Left Behind™* books came along.[16]

Dispensationalism appears to be quite Christian. It makes copious use of the Bible, which its advocates loudly proclaim to be inerrant. It teaches that the second coming of Christ, the millennium, and the final judgment will be real events and that history is moving toward the demise of all sinful human institutions and an eternity in which God reigns and believers will enjoy everlasting life. Successful TV preachers, best-selling Christian writers, and hot contemporary Christian musicians espouse it. Might this be a means for pointing millions to the Lamb of God?

While envisioning the ultimate demise of American democracy along with all human governments, popular dispensationalist belief sees a special role for the United States in prophecy that dovetails nicely with the militaristic, utopian nationalism that drives the neoconservative movement. In this theology of history, America's specific task is to be Israel's military protector, providing unconditional support for policies to defend and strengthen Israel's control over all of Palestine. All other considerations—the rights of the Palestinians, international law, the criteria for "just war," the give-and-take of diplomacy—are at best secondary to cooperation with God's prophecy-

---

* Trademark owned by Tyndale House Publishers, Wheaton, Illinois.

revealed plan for the survival and strength of the state of Israel. Put another way, in the words of Jerry Falwell, "To stand against Israel is to stand against God."[17]

Bible prophecy is thus construed to confer on the armies of Israel and of the United States an exceptional status that sets them above all other nations of the earth. The buildup of U.S. military power to ensure unchallenged world supremacy thus became a central tenet of the Christian Right in its rise to political power.[18]

The drama unfolding since 2001 has made clearer than ever that right-wing Christian voices "have fostered among the legions of believing Americans a predisposition to see U.S. military power as inherently good, perhaps even a necessary adjunct to the accomplishment of Christ's saving mission. In so doing, they have nurtured the pre-conditions that have enabled the American infatuation with military power to flourish."[19]

Prophecy-based militarism displayed new heights of political power in the renewed antagonism between the United States and Iran in 2006, for which fighting between Israel and the Iranian-backed Hezbollah movement in Lebanon became an arena. A new organization dedicated to lobbying Congress on behalf of Israel, Christians United for Israel (CUFI), was formed in 2006 under the leadership of John Hagee, pastor of the eighteen-thousand-member Cornerstone Church in San Antonio, Texas. Coinciding with the launch of CUFI, Hagee published and extensively marketed a new book, *Jerusalem Countdown,* in which he urges that the United States, in order to fulfill the role designated for it in end-time prophecy, must join Israel in a preemptive military strike against Iran.[20]

More than thirty-four hundred delegates representing all fifty states attended CUFI's kickoff banquet held in July 2006 at the Washington Hilton, while numerous leaders among the nation's power elite flocked in for their turn at the podium. While much of the world reacted with stunned horror at Israel's massive bombing of civilian-populated areas in Lebanon, Hagee declared that CUFI's aim was to urge the U.S. government "not to restrain Israel in any way in the pursuit of Hamas and Hezbollah." Hagee promised that CUFI would cause a "political earthquake" and that its influence could surpass that of the famously powerful American Israel Public Affairs Committee (AIPAC): "When a congressman sees someone from AIPAC coming through the door, he knows he represents six million people. We represent 40 million people."[21] With a mass appeal far surpassing that of neoconservativism as such, Christian Zionism not only sanctifies but makes it a positive religious duty for millions of voters to support the same militant foreign policy.

In a time of fear and insecurity, American civil millennialism beckons us to trust its power to save us from our terrors and free us for pursuit of our comforts. Come, worship the image we have set up, it says. See its newness, its amazing feats of technological and military wizardry, and its capacity to generate prosperity. See how religion thrives, and see the wonder-working power produced when faith communities and government support each other.

Viewed in the light shed by the book of Revelation, one thing, at least, about this offer is unmistakably clear: The system that beckons, may be more benevolent and free than other political systems.We may render it respect and acquiescence as an instrument for the restraint of evil and chaos. However, as an agency for ending tyranny and evil in the world, it is a counterfeit, a dangerous fraud.

Opposing the American empire

Seeing this when few others did was one of the most remarkable features of the Seventh-day Adventist movement that coalesced in the 1850s. John N. Andrews was barely out of his teens when, in 1851, the *Second Advent Review and Sabbath Herald* published his seminal interpretation of the "two-horned" beast of Revelation 13:11–18 as symbolizing the role of the United States in apocalyptic prophecy's "grand drama" of empires. Within the five years previous to his writing, a war of aggression with Mexico[22] and negotiations with Great Britain over the Oregon Country had capped the still-young nation's expansion across the continent. Now, Andrews wrote, "the great circuit of empire will be accomplished, for the boundary of the vast Pacific has been reached."[23]

The stunning rapidity of this expansion, along with the "great wonders" of steam power captured to send "chariots with the speed of lightning coursing their way through the land" and ships to "traverse the mighty deep" at similar speed, functioned, in Andrews's view, as tools of deception because they popularized confidence in the Enlightenment myth of progress.

The "wonder" of America's shining new system of government itself joined these "remarkable elements of deception" because it held before the world the "delusive dream" of an era in which peace and freedom would triumph everywhere in human affairs. Indeed, just a year before Andrews's article appeared, one of America's greatest writers, Herman Melville, wrote in *White Jacket,* "We Americans are the peculiar, chosen people—the Israel of our time; we bear the ark of the liberties of the world. . . . Long enough have we been skeptics with regard to ourselves, and doubted whether, indeed, the political Messiah had come. But he has come in *us,* if we would but give utterance to his promptings."[24]

John Andrews dissented from all this. The presence of "three millions of slaves . . . bought and sold like brute beasts" as well as the intolerance of the dominant religious bodies that expelled believers "for no other crime than that of looking for the coming of Jesus Christ"[25] demonstrated that America, the lamb of Revelation 13 is such only in pretension. "His ostensible appearance is that of a lamb; but the power by which he speaks is that of a dragon. The true kingdom of the Lamb—the King of kings is not set up on earth until the destruction of all the wicked powers that now bear rule. Then the Jubilee will end the bondage of the saints. 'God speed the right.' " The "coming of the Just One" would check the republic's "astonishing career."[26]

With America at the zenith of its appeal as trailblazer of liberty for the world, the fledgling Adventist movement was defined by a covenant to "keep the commandments of God and the faith of Jesus Christ"[27] and thus not deviate from following the Lamb of God for the sake of any lesser loyalty. Even in the Civil War that soon followed, a war that, in the end at least, was about ending the slavery they abhorred, Adventists couldn't in good conscience depart from the Lamb's way of nonviolent, self-sacrificing love in order to follow their government's bidding to take up arms. To the military authorities in charge of the Union army draft, they declared themselves "a people unanimously loyal and anti-slavery, who because of their views of the ten commandments and of the teaching of the New Testament cannot engage in bloodshed."[28]

During subsequent decades, Ellen White was among those encouraging Adventists to keep a lively and clear distinction between "earthly kingdoms" that "are established and upheld by physical force" and the "Messiah's kingdom" in which "no carnal weapons were to be used, no coercion practised; no attempt would be made to force the consciences of men." Additionally, "prophecy has plainly stated the nature of Christ's kingdom. He planned a government which would use no force; his subjects would know no oppression. The symbols of earthly governments are wild beasts, but in the kingdom of Christ, men are called upon to behold, not a ferocious beast, but the Lamb of God."[29]

Ellen White understood Christ's kingdom to be a "spiritual" one in the present age. But "spiritual" did not mean intangible in its impact in the real world of strife, sin, and suffering. This peaceable kingdom of active benevolence demanded the total allegiance of those who would be Christ's. We may "cooperate with Christ in the upbuilding of His kingdom," she wrote; one way of doing this being to give "aid and protection to the oppressed."[30]

Seeing through the pretense

At the next critical juncture in America's imperial career—the Spanish-American War—the prophetic perspective empowered Adventists to see through the pretenses of preachers who wrapped the cross in the flag and politicians who hijacked Christian idealism for a militaristic agenda. With the declaration of war in 1898 against Spain over its abusive rule of Cuba, the continental empire that John Andrews had written about in the 1850s entered a new phase. It now joined the imperial powers of Europe in projecting military power overseas to establish colonies or spheres of influence among subjugated peoples. The swift decision to extend the war to the Far East by ousting the Spanish from rule over the Philippines most clearly demonstrated the new drive for an overseas empire.

Historian Sydney Ahlstrom points out that during the period of the Spanish-American War and the subsequent Filipino-American conflict, "patriotism, imperialism, and the religion of American Protestantism" stood in more "fervent coalescence than ever before."[31] Several Adventist leaders, however, viewing America from the critical perspective of Revelation 13, spoke out against the "spirit of militarism" abroad in the land and fostered "right within the bosom of the church." They warned against allowing this spirit to turn the followers of the Lamb away from the path marked out by the Sermon on the Mount.[32]

Alonzo T. Jones, at this point editor both of the *Review and Herald* and the *American Sentinel* (predecessor to *Liberty*), characterized the imperialist venture in the Philippines as "national apostasy" from the principle of "republicanism" that the "two-horned" beast appeared to offer but in reality would finally betray. While leading American Protestants, including President William McKinley, "proceeded in the limited time available to convert the war into a crusade to rationalize imperialism as a missionary obligation,"[33] Adventist educator Percy T. Magan pointed to Jesus' repeated refusal of the temptation to use force to aid His mission. If the "doctrine of the Bible in one hand and the shotgun in the other is a good one for the Philippine Islands, how long," asked Magan, "will it be ere it is considered a good one for every State in the Union?"[34]

Magan's critique of American imperialism took the form of a book, *The Peril of the Republic,* published in 1899 by the evangelical publishing house Fleming H. Revell. This volume shows an Adventist peace witness, informed by apocalyptic prophecy, at work not just as denunciation and announcement of judgment to come, but also as a call to peacemaking in the interim before Christ returns. According to Magan, "ambassadors of Jesus Christ" should make their voices heard "in the courts and congresses of human powers, of earthly governments." And he called upon all citizens of the coming kingdom of God to be true to principle "in things national as well as personal" and to "work for right principles while it is day."

In a time of a virulent new coalescence between patriotism, imperialism, and religion, how do we hear the call of history? Whose marching orders will we heed? Will the inducements of empire so seduce us and the popular American spirituality concocted of individualism, consumerism, and militarism so stupefy us that our hearts, minds, and hands will come to bear the marks of the counterfeit system of coercion? Or will we hear the call of history in the book of Revelation and follow the Lamb wherever He leads? The Lamb stands on Mount Zion, to which, the prophet Isaiah tells us, people of all nations will stream in the latter days to receive from the Lord the instruction and authoritative rulings that will put an end to the futile spiral of violence between nations (see Isaiah 2:1–4). Following the Lamb, taking our marching orders from Him, commits us to being people of peace on our earthly journey to the Holy City.

The burden of engineering "world peace" is not placed on our shoulders. Yet if we are in fact marching to Zion, we will be peacemakers. "We are not marching to Zion because we think that by our own momentum we can get there," writes John H. Yoder. "But that is still where we are going. We are marching to Zion because, when God lets down from heaven the new Jerusalem prepared for us, we want to be the kind of persons and the kind of community that will not feel strange there."[35]

Following the Lamb's marching orders puts us out of step with a world dominated by powers that promise peace through military dominance and that demand our full allegiance in the struggle. We, however, find boldness to take the Lamb's unpopular and seemingly unpragmatic marching orders because we have been clued into the meaning and direction of history and know that He holds the keys (see Revelation 1:17, 18). The gracious call of history's Redeemer, the Lamb who was slain and is worthy " 'to receive power and wealth and wisdom and might and honor and glory and blessing' " (Revelation 5:12, NRSV) comes to *us,* unworthy though we be. The Lamb who takes away the sin of the world grants us, even now, the privilege of participating in the peacemaking program of His kingdom.

"O house of Jacob, come, let us walk in the light of the Lord!" (Isaiah 2:5, NRSV).

1. The application of the term *empire* to the United States has been disputed during the past five years but appears to be increasingly accepted. Some neoconservative scholars, charged with advocating expansion of the American empire, insist on differences between America and the great empires of history and propose other terms for their policies, such as "benevolent global hegemony"; see the exchange between Jay Bookman and Donald Kagan in the *Atlanta Journal-Constitution*: Jay Bookman, "The President's Real Goal in Iraq," September 29, 2002; Donald Kagan, "Comparing America to Ancient Empires Is 'Ludicrous,' " October 6, 2002. However, another neoconservative spokesman, Max Boot, sees no value in fighting the term; see "American Imperialism? No Need to Run Away From the Label," *USA Today,* May 6, 2003. Charles S. Maier gives a detailed and nuanced historical perspective on the issue in his book *Among Empires: American Ascendancy and Its Predecessors* (Cambridge, Mass.: Harvard University Press, 2006).

2. "President Delivers 'State of the Union,' " January 28, 2003, quoted in the White House Web site, http://www.whitehouse.gov/news/releases/2003/01/20030128-19.html.

3. J. N. Andrews, "Thoughts on Revelation XIII and XIV," *Second Advent Review and Sabbath Herald* (May 19, 1851): 81.

4. Eugene H. Peterson, *Reversed Thunder: The Revelation of John and the Praying Imagination* (New York: HarperCollins, 1991), 125, 126.

5. Andrew J. Bacevich, *The New American Militarism: How Americans Are Seduced by War* (New York: Oxford University, 2005), 71; see also 69–96. Among the growing list of studies on neoconservativism, one of the most helpful in analyzing it from a theological standpoint is Gary J. Dorrien, *Imperial Designs: Neoconservatism and the New Pax Americana* (New York: Routledge, 2004).

6. Cited in Tony Carnes, "The Bush Doctrine," *Christianity Today* (May 2003): 38–40.

7. New York: Random House, 2003.

8. Quoted in Michael Northcott, *An Angel Directs the Storm: Apocalyptic Religion and American Empire* (New York: Palgrave Macmillan, 2004), 6. See also Nathan Hatch, *The Sacred Cause of Liberty: Republican Thought and the Millennium in Revolutionary New England* (New Haven: Yale University Press, 1977).

9. Quoted in Northcott, 9.

10. James C. Juhnke and Carol M. Hunter, *The Missing Peace: The Search for Nonviolent*

Alternatives in United States History (Scottdale, Pa.: Herald Press, 2001), 9–14; Walter Wink, "The Myth of Redemptive Violence: Exposing the Roots of 'Might Makes Right,'" *Sojourners Magazine* (April 1992): 8–12, 35.

11. Bruce Lincoln, "Bush's God Talk: To a Born-again Theology of Individual Salvation, Bush Has Added a Providential View of America's Role in World History," *Christian Century* (October 5, 2004): 27.

12. For the purposes of this discussion, I am setting aside questions of the exact nature of the millennium of Revelation 20 and its place in the sequence of final events and am using the term *millennialism* here simply as code for the general belief that God is guiding history toward an ideal future.

13. "President Sworn-In to Second Term," January 20, 2005; quoted in the White House Web site, http://www.whitehouse.gov/news/releases/2005/01/20050120-1.html.

14. Eugene McCarraher, "'The Most Intolerable of Insults:' Remarks to Christian Infidels in the American Empire," quoted in Wes Avram, ed. *Anxious About Empire: Theological Essays on the New Global Realities* (Grand Rapids: Brazos Press, 2004), 111.

15. Stephen B. Chapman, "Imperial Exegesis: When Caesar Interprets Scripture," in Avram, 91–102.

16. Timothy P. Weber, *On the Road to Armageddon: How Evangelicals Became Israel's Best Friend* (Grand Rapids: Baker Academic, 2004), 191–196.

17. Anatol Lieven, *America Right or Wrong: An Anatomy of American Nationalism* (New York: Oxford University Press, 2004), 173–186; Falwell quoted on p. 182.

18. In his book *The 1980s: Countdown to Armageddon* (n.c.: Westgate Press Inc., 1983), Lindsey wrote, "The Bible supports building a powerful military force. And the Bible is telling the United States to become strong again" and "use our vast and superior technology to create the world's strongest military power." Quoted in Bacevich, 135.

19. Bacevich, 146.

20. Sarah Posner, "Holy War," posted on *The American Prospect* Web site, July 19, 2006; http://www.prospect.org/cs/articles?articleId=11742.

21. Posner, "Lobbying for Armageddon," posted on the AlterNet Web site, August 3, 2006; http://www.alternet.org/story/39748/; Richard Allen Greene, "Evangelical Christians Plead for Israel," posted on the BBC News Web site, July 19, 2006; http://news.bbc.co.uk/2/hi/americas/5193092.stm.

22. Joseph Bates issued a blistering critique of "Christian" America's hypocrisy in the war with Mexico in his tract "Opening Heavens, Seventh-Day Sabbath, and Waymarks," excerpt reproduced in Douglas Morgan, ed., *The Peacemaking Remnant: Essays and Historical Documents* (Silver Spring, Md.: Adventist Peace Fellowship, 2005), 93, 94.

23. Andrews, 81–86.

24. Quoted in Richard T. Hughes, *Myths America Lives By* (Urbana and Chicago: University of Illinois Press, 2003), 35, 36.

25. Early in the nineteenth century, Baptist layman William Miller's interpretation that Bible prophecies indicated that Jesus' second coming would take place in 1843 or 1844 stirred much excitement in the northeastern United States. Many of the people who accepted Miller's ideas were disfellowshipped—dropped from membership in the churches to which they had belonged.

26. Andrews, 83.

27. "Doings of the Battle Creek Conference, Oct. 5 & 6, 1861," *Review and Herald* (October 8, 1861): 148.

28. *The Views of Seventh-day Adventists Relative to Bearing Arms, as Brought Before the Governors of Several States, and the Provost Marshal General, with a Portion of The Enrollment Law* (Battle Creek, Mich.: Steam Press of the Seventh-day Adventist Publishing Association, 1865), 16; tract in Document File 320, Ellen G. White Estate, Silver Spring, Md.

29. Ellen G. White, "The Kingdom of Christ," *Review and Herald* (August 18, 1896): 1.

30. Ibid.

31. Sydney Ahlstrom, *A Religious History of the American People* (New Haven: Yale University Press, 1972), 879, 880.

32. See Morgan, "Apocalyptic Anti-Imperialists," *Spectrum* 22, no. 5 (January 1993): 21, 22.

33. Ahlstrom, 879, 880.

34. Quotations from Magan in this paragraph and the next quoted in Morgan, *Adventism and the American Republic* (Knoxville: University of Tennessee Press, 2001), 68–70.

35. John H. Yoder, *The Original Revolution: Essays on Christian Pacifism* (Scottdale, Pa.: Herald Press, 1977), 159.

James D. Standish

CHAPTER 5

The Rise and Fall of Religious Free Exercise

Elton John said that if he had the power, he "would ban religion completely."[1] The popular singer's view is apparently a minority one—at least in the United States. In a recent poll, 96 percent of Americans agreed that one of the greatest things about this nation is the religious liberty we enjoy.[2] This is all well and good, but what does our concept of "religious liberty" mean, and how far are we willing to extend it?

Let me illustrate. When I was a boy, I grew up on a small island off the coast of Malaysia that was a microcosm of world religions. Christians, Muslims, Sikhs, Hindus, and Buddhists had roughly equal claims on the culture of the island. It seemed like a major holiday celebration occurred every week—from the end of Ramadan to Christmas, from Chinese New Year to the Hindu festival of Diwali. It made for a marvelously interesting childhood. However, one of those religious holidays still haunts me—a holiday called Thaipusam.

The premise of Thaipusam is fairly simple. A believer makes a deal with the gods. If the gods fulfill their part—for example, heal the believer's child, bring success in business—then the believer will do his or her part by participating in an annual parade. This event is not your average parade with floats and balloons. Rather, the participants begin by going into a trance at a temple. Then large skewers are forced through their cheeks, gruesome hooks are placed through the skin of their backs, and large contraptions ride on their shoulders, held on by hundreds of small spears that penetrate their flesh.

Every year, the parade route went almost directly past our home. Music blared night and day in advance of the event. When I was a child, that music aroused in me simultaneously a fascination with the macabre and a dread of the gruesome scenes that would soon pass in front of my home.

Perhaps you belong to the 96 percent of Americans who support religious freedom. Do you support the right of people to put huge hooks through their backs and parade through your streets? You may well say yes, but my guess is that most Americans wouldn't be so sure. We believe in religious liberty, but intuitively we believe there must be limits. Even those of us who believe religious liberty should extend to Thaipusam would likely agree that it cannot extend to even more horrible religious practices such as female genital mutilation, human sacrifice, or the suicide bomber's "martyrdom." We instinctively know that religious liberty cannot mean a license to harm others, but where and how do we draw the line? How can we simultaneously support both religious liberty and restrictions on religiously motivated behavior?

This isn't a novel question—it is one this nation has struggled with for more than two hundred years and has yet to resolve. It certainly isn't clear in the U.S. Constitution. The religion clauses of the First Amendment consist of only sixteen words: "Congress shall make no law respecting an establishment of religion, or prohibiting the free exercise thereof."

The First Amendment doesn't impose any limit on the free exercise of religion or even hint at what that limit should be. The Founding Fathers left it to succeeding generations to determine. Not surprisingly, legal theorists, scholars, legislators, and courts have had vastly different ideas.

Early decisions

The Church of Jesus Christ of Latter-day Saints (the Mormon Church) was established in the mid-nineteenth century. Its founding generation suffered merciless persecution—so much so that they decided to leave "civilization" for the great untamed West. Settling in Utah had many advantages, not the least being that they were far from the mobs that murdered Joseph Smith and harassed Mormon believers. However, they soon discovered that Utah also had one distinct disadvantage: It was a federal territory, and, as such, the federal government could pass laws regulating every facet of society, and those laws would be interpreted by federal courts under the federal Constitution.[3]

In an effort to target Mormons living in the territory of Utah, Congress passed a law banning bigamy in U.S. territories. One of the individuals prosecuted under the new law was George Reynolds, the personal secretary of Brigham Young, who was the Mormon Church president. After being tried, Mr. Reynolds was found guilty and fined five hundred dollars—a large sum of money at the time—and sentenced to two years of hard labor.

The Mormons decided to appeal the trial court's ruling. They argued that polygamy was a religious practice and should be free from federal interference. Indeed, Mr. Reynolds's marriages had been performed by Mormon Church leaders and sanctified under the teachings of the church.

The appeal went up to the U.S. Supreme Court. Chief Justice Morrison Waite delivered the opinion of the Court, and it was not good news for Mr. Reynolds:

> Laws are made for the government of actions, and while they cannot interfere with mere religious belief and opinions, they may with practices. Suppose one believed that human sacrifices were a necessary part of religious worship, would it be seriously contended that the civil government under which he lived could not interfere to prevent a sacrifice? . . . So here, as a law of the organization of society under the exclusive dominion of the United States, it is provided that plural marriages shall not be allowed. Can a man excuse his practices to the contrary because of his religious belief? To permit this would be to make the professed doctrines of religious belief superior to the law of the land, and in effect to permit every citizen to become a law unto himself. Government could exist only in name under such circumstances.[4]

According to that Supreme Court decision, American citizens had the right to believe anything they wished, but when their religious practices conflicted with the law of the land, the law of the land prevailed. That decision, while sounding reasonable, was very troubling in practice. Certainly, the freedom to believe is a significant freedom. But religion is more than abstract ideas—as the book of James states: "Faith by itself, if it is not accompanied by action, is dead" (James 2:17). Put another way, if religion is reduced to abstract ideas with no practical application, it is reduced to nothing at all.

Virtually every faith has action associated with it. These actions may include helping the poor, the sick, the imprisoned, and the least fortunate in society; specific worship requirements; the wearing of particular clothing, and in some cases, personal grooming requirements. In addition, each tradition has actions followers are forbidden from engaging in. These forbidden actions include consuming alcohol, carrying weapons, engaging in secular work on holy days, assisting with the killing of human fetuses, taking oaths, and many other actions, depending on the faith tradition. All of these require people to act in a particular manner no matter what the general laws of society may require. A freedom to believe without freedom to act in accordance with those beliefs is no freedom at all.

The *Reynolds* Court questioned whether a government can endure if it permits its citizens to practice their faith freely even when that faith conflicts with the law of the land. The United States was soon going to find out.

Religious freedom matures

Originally, the First Amendment applied only to federal laws and action. It wasn't until 1940 that the Supreme Court decided a case in which it applied the free exercise clause to protect religious freedom from state interference.[5] The case involved Newton Cantwell and his sons, Jesse and Russell. Newton, Jesse, and Russell were Jehovah's Witnesses. As part of their effort to spread their message, they went to a Catholic neighborhood in New Haven, Connecticut, set up a gramophone and began to play a record promoting a book titled *Enemies*. The book was a frontal attack on the Roman Catholic Church. Not surprisingly, the locals didn't take kindly to the content, and a couple of Catholic men vigorously confronted Mr. Cantwell. Subsequently, the Cantwells were prosecuted under a state statute that banned solicitation of funds for religious activities without prior state approval and a statute that banned inciting others to breach the peace.

The case raised a number of intriguing questions. First, did the federal Constitution apply at all since the laws in question were state, not federal, statutes? Second, if the federal Constitution did apply, did it protect action as well as belief, and if so, which actions did it protect?

In answer to the first question, the Supreme Court declared, "The fundamental concept of liberty embodied in [the Fourteenth] Amendment embraces the liberties guaranteed by the First Amendment."[6] The Fourteenth Amendment was adopted after the American Civil War to guarantee the rights of African Americans. It declares, in part, that no state shall "deprive any person of life, liberty, or property, without due process of law." It was this clause that the *Cantwell* Court interpreted as requiring states to honor people's First Amendment rights. Today, this may seem like a modest proposition, but *Cantwell* was a remarkable development as one of the first of many cases to apply First Amendment freedoms to state and local government laws and actions.

Not only did the *Cantwell* Court find that the federal religious liberty guarantees protection against all government action, but it also abandoned, at least in part, the *Reynolds* belief/action dichotomy. The Court stated, "The Amendment embraces two concepts,—freedom to believe and freedom to act. The first is absolute but, in the nature of things, the second cannot be. Conduct remains subject to regulation for the protection of society. The freedom to act must have appropriate definition to preserve the enforcement of that protection. In every case the power to regulate must be so exercised as not, in attaining a permissible end, unduly to infringe the protected freedom."[7]

In *Reynolds,* the Court had given carte blanche to the state to regulate religious actions. In *Cantwell,* the Court made it clear that there were limits on state regulation of religious practices. The Cantwells' convictions were overturned. After *Cantwell,* the state was forced to prove that state regulation of religious action didn't "unduly infringe" on religious freedom. Although this was a somewhat vague legal standard, it protected religious action for the first time, which was a major step forward.

At about the same time that the Court was deciding *Cantwell,* it heard another key religious liberty case involving Jehovah's Witnesses. The case involved an emotional issue: Could the state expel two public school students ages ten and twelve, who, for religious reasons, refused to salute the American flag? The Court answered that it could.[8] After all, the Court reasoned, to decide any other way would undermine both national unity and security.[9] The decision seems preposterous. How could two school children refusing to salute the flag undermine national security? It helps to keep in mind that the world was descending into the chaos of World War II when the case was decided. Some observers believe this explains the willingness of the Court to assign to the state the power to coerce sincerely held religious beliefs, even to the point of expelling little children from school.

In explaining the Court's decision, Justice Frankfurter wrote for the majority that "conscientious scruples have not, in the course of the long struggle for religious toleration, relieved the individual from obedience to a general law not aimed at the promotion or restriction of religious beliefs." Remember these words, because you will read very similar sentiments expressed by a current member of the Supreme Court later in this chapter.

In 1943, only three years after the first flag salute case, the Supreme Court reconsidered its decision.[10] In one of the most dramatic moves in its history, the Court reversed itself. In explaining why the Court decided that the First Amendment protects the right of students to refuse to salute the flag for religious reasons, Justice Jackson memorably wrote:

> The very purpose of a Bill of Rights was to withdraw certain subjects from the vicissitudes of political controversy, to place them beyond the reach of majorities and officials and to establish them as legal principles to be applied by the courts. One's right to life, liberty, and property, to free speech, a free press, freedom of worship and assembly, and other fundamental rights may not be submitted to vote; they depend on the outcome of no elections. . . . If there is any fixed star in our constitutional constellation, it is that no official, high or petty, can prescribe what shall be orthodox in politics, nationalism, religion, or other matters of opinion or force citizens to confess by word or act their faith therein.[11]

Shortly thereafter, the Supreme Court further held that in order to justify restricting religious freedom, the state must not only be attempting to prevent a "grave and immediate danger" to lawful interests but also that those state interests themselves must be sufficiently urgent and compelling. This later case arguably brought religious liberty protections in America to their legal pinnacle—and it involved a Seventh-day Adventist standing for her religious beliefs in her place of work.

The peak of religious liberty

We often look to the superstars of our world to act with courage and conviction to advance the cause of freedom—to presidents, academics, pastors, and social activists. No doubt each of them plays a part. Yet often it is regular people just going about their lives who are the ones with the character and commitment to be champions of freedom—people like Rosa Parks and Adelle Sherbert. This nation reached the next milestone in the constitutional development of religious liberty in Ms. Sherbert's case.

You've never heard of Adelle Sherbert? You aren't alone. However, almost every lawyer and judge in America has heard of her, for it was this simple factory worker from South Carolina who changed the way America views religious liberty.

Adelle Sherbert was a Seventh-day Adventist Christian who believed in keeping all ten of God's commandments. This included the fourth commandment, which calls on us to rest from secular work on the seventh day of the week—Saturday. When her boss at the textile factory where she worked demanded that she work on Saturday, her Sabbath, Ms. Sherbert said that she couldn't. Rather than respect the fidelity of this faithful woman, her employer fired her.

Ms. Sherbert searched for a new job. But she couldn't find an employer willing to accommodate her religious practice of resting on the Sabbath. So, like other citizens of South Carolina unable to find employment, she applied for unemployment benefits.

It wasn't to be that simple. South Carolina ruled that Ms. Sherbert had made herself unavailable for work on Saturdays without "good cause" and so didn't qualify for unemployment benefits.[12] There were two problems with the state's reasoning. First, South Carolina had a rule that said if employees were fired because they wouldn't work on Sunday, the state would give them unemployment benefits.[13] Second, Ms. Sherbert's position wasn't a whimsical personal preference; it was a sincerely held religious belief, a belief expressed through action in a nation that guarantees the right of the "free exercise of religion."

Ms. Sherbert wasn't a belligerent person, but like Rosa Parks, neither was she a wilting flower. She believed that America should practice what it preaches about "liberty and justice for all," so she appealed the state's decision.

The Supreme Court surprised many by deciding in favor of Ms. Sherbert. In its ruling, the Court announced a new legal standard in religious liberty cases. The Court held that a state cannot regulate religious behavior unless it can show that it has a "compelling interest" to do so. The Court then quoted from a flag salute case, *Barnette*: "In this highly sensitive constitutional area, '[o]nly the gravest abuses, endangering paramount interests, give occasion for permissible limitation.' "[14] This new test was consistent with the approach taken by President George Washington in a letter he wrote to a group of Quakers: "The liberty enjoyed by the people of these States, of worshipping Almighty God agreeably to their consciences, is not only among the choicest of their blessings, but also of their rights. . . .

"And it is my wish and desire, that the laws may always be as extensively accommodated to them, as a due regard to the protection and essential interests of the nation may justify and permit."[15]

Finally, 172 years after the adoption of the religious liberty protections in the First Amendment, America had a legal standard that protected religious liberty unless, as President Washington put it, "essential interests" of the nation were at risk. After the *Sherbert* decision, a state could still prevent religious actions that were dangerous to others, that damaged people's property, or that involved other similarly compelling state interests. Yet such restrictions were to be the exception, invoked only to prevent real harm. Otherwise, the state was required to respect individual conscience in all its beauty and variance.

The Court had established a rule in which every individual conscience superseded the laws of the land—the very anarchy the Justices had warned against in the *Reynolds* case. Or was it? The *Sherbert* compelling-interest standard was in place in this nation for almost three decades. During that time the nation didn't collapse into anarchy, the economy didn't stop functioning, the state didn't refrain from making and enforcing laws, and no one became a law unto him or herself. Instead, in a very few cases, people of deep faith successfully asserted their right to believe and to practice their faith free from state interference. This is hardly an immodest outcome in a nation founded on liberty and pledged to support individual freedom.

One of the most important cases decided during this high point of religious liberty was *Wisconsin v. Yoder*.[16] The state of Wisconsin argued that it had the right to force Amish children into a conventional high school setting until they turned sixteen years old. The Amish responded that a core part of their faith was to live a simple agrarian life and that this required that young people obtain a vocational education after completing the first eight grades of school.

Citing *Sherbert*, Chief Justice Warren Burger, writing for the majority, stated, "A regulation neutral on its face may, in its application, nonetheless offend the constitutional requirement for governmental neutrality if it unduly burdens the free exercise of religion."[17] In considering whether the state's interest in the case was sufficiently compelling, Chief Justice Burger noted there was no evidence that the Amish practice would harm the mental or physical health of the children or that it would result in the children becoming a burden to the state.[18] The Court therefore ruled in favor of the Amish and reaffirmed that religious freedom is to be respected except in rare cases. "The essence of all that has been said and written on the subject is that only those interests of the highest order and those not otherwise served can overbalance legitimate claims to the free exercise of religion."[19]

The decline of religious liberty

As the saying goes, all good things must come to an end. In 1990, the Supreme Court heard a case involving two Native Americans who worked as drug rehabilitation counselors. Their employer discovered that they had ingested peyote, a hallucinogenic drug, during a Native American religious ritual. Fired from their jobs, and, like Adelle Sherbert, denied unemployment benefits, they appealed all the way to the Supreme Court.

Most observers thought the case would turn on whether the state had a compelling interest in discouraging illegal drug use. Instead, Justice Scalia, writing for the majority, redefined the standard under which free exercise of religion cases are decided. He wrote, "The right of free exercise does not relieve an individual of the obligation to comply with a 'valid and neutral law of general applicability.' "[20] This meant that when a law doesn't specifically target religious practice and when it applies to everyone no matter their faith, the state can enforce it regardless of any burden imposed on religious practice, and even if the government interest in applying the law is relatively trivial. It was a return to Justice Frankfurter's opinion that gave the green light for public schools to expel little children whose religious beliefs prevented them from saluting the flag.

Some people didn't see a problem with Justice Scalia's opinion. They asked, shouldn't everyone have to obey all the laws of the land—especially our narcotics laws? Justice Sandra Day O'Connor, a Reagan appointee to the Supreme Court, explained the heart of the concern: "Laws neutral toward religion can coerce a person to violate his religious conscience . . . just as effectively as laws aimed at religion."[21] If you don't believe her, consider Justice Scalia's justification for his new standard. As an example of the kind of "neutral laws" that could be applied to people even if it burdens their religious practices, Justice Scalia pointed to Sunday-closing laws, saying, "We upheld Sunday-closing laws against the claim that they burdened the religious practices of persons whose religions compelled them to refrain from work on other days."[22] He was right. Back in 1961, before the *Sherbert* case, the Supreme Court had found that Sunday laws were constitutional even when applied to Sabbath keepers.[23] The 1990 *Smith* decision shut the door on overturning the Sunday law ruling.

Justice Scalia insisted that those seeking to protect their religious liberty must appeal to the legislatures rather than the courts. Scalia was not troubled by the claim that religious minorities lack the political clout to obtain such protection. He wrote, "It may fairly be said that leaving accommodation [of religious practices] to the political process will place at a relative disadvantage those religious practices that are not widely engaged in; but that [is an] unavoidable consequence of democratic government."[24]

In response, Justice O'Connor wrote, "The Court today suggests that the disfavoring of minority religions is an 'unavoidable consequence' under our system of government. . . . However, the First Amendment was enacted precisely to protect the rights of those whose religious practices are not shared by the majority."[25] In other words, the majority doesn't need the Bill of Rights because its rights are protected by the legislature, which is elected by majority vote. The Bill of Rights is needed to ensure that the rights of individuals and minority groups cannot be violated regardless of what the majority as represented by the legislature desires to do.

Justice O'Connor may have won the rhetorical battle, but it is Justice Scalia's opinion that became law.

The Court's ruling caused an enormous outcry among religious groups and legal scholars alike. With the support of a broad coalition of religious liberty advocates, Congress passed the Religious Freedom Restoration Act (RFRA) in 1993. The vote was nearly unanimous. The Act eloquently states:

> The Congress finds that—
> (1) the framers of the Constitution, recognizing free exercise of re-ligion as an unalienable right, secured its protection in the First Amendment to the Constitution;
> (2) laws "neutral" toward religion may burden religious exercise as surely as laws intended to interfere with religious exercise;
> (3) governments should not substantially burden religious exercise without compelling justification;
> (4) in Employment Division v. Smith, 494 U.S. 872 (1990) the Supreme Court virtually eliminated the requirement that the gov-ernment justify burdens on religious exercise imposed by laws neu-tral toward religion; and
> (5) the compelling interest test as set forth in prior Federal court rulings is a workable test for striking sensible balances between reli-gious liberty and competing prior governmental interests.

The heart of the Act was the requirement that the state must prove it has a compelling interest when it limits religious practice—a return to the

Sherbert standard. Thus, the Religious Freedom Restoration Act was an attempt by Congress to reverse the Supreme Court's decision in *Smith,* and reinstate the religious liberty protections that Americans enjoyed previously under the First Amendment. But there is an inherent problem with statutes—they are subordinate to the Constitution, and courts can strike them down. Not surprisingly, the Religious Freedom Restoration Act was quickly challenged.

In 1997, the U.S. Supreme Court heard *City of Boerne v. Flores,* a constitutional challenge to the Religious Freedom Restoration Act. A Texas town had invoked historic preservation laws to restrict a Catholic Church from renovating and expanding an old church building. The church argued that under RFRA, the town was obligated to permit the church to carry out the desired renovation. The city argued, on the other hand, that Congress lacked the authority to enforce RFRA on local and state governments.

In deciding this case, the Supreme Court found that Congress had indeed overstepped its authority[26]—though the Court didn't strike down RFRA entirely, as it confirmed in 2006 when it held that RFRA remains valid when applied to the federal government.[27]

After the *Boerne* decision, what power did state and local governments have to restrict religious practices? Some state constitutions had religious liberty protections that already protected religious freedom with the *Sherbert* compelling-interest standard. However, many states were left with a dangerously low level of protection. A national effort to pass state versions of the Religious Freedom Restoration Act was successful in twelve states.[28] Adding together the states with constitutions that provide RFRA-like protection and those with state RFRAs, roughly half of all states now provide a high level of religious liberty protection against state and local government action.[29] What about the remaining states? In them, citizens' religious freedom can be taken away by "neutral laws" even if the state has a seemingly trivial interest in restricting religious practices by application of the neutral law in question.

After the federal RFRA was found unconstitutional as applied to the states, a second effort was made to pass a national religious liberty bill. However, bill supporters were divided over how broad it should be. The American Civil Liberties Union (ACLU) led the effort to limit the scope of the religious liberty protections because they feared that a broad bill might impact their gay-rights and abortion-rights agendas. The ACLU effort proved successful. The bill originally designed to replace RFRA was eventually enacted to protect only two categories—land use (zoning, building permits, etc.) and people who are in state-run institutions (prisoners, those in state mental hospitals, etc.). The resulting bill, which goes by the rather ungainly title of the "Religious Land Use and Institutionalized Persons Act," was signed into law in 2000.

Conclusion

We began by asking a rather simple question: What are the limits of religious freedom in the United States? How do we answer that question 225 years after the Bill of Rights was adopted?

In practice, religious liberty is alive and well. People of almost every faith live and worship in the United States without government interference. Americans enjoy vigorous protection for their religious freedom from the laws, regulations, and actions of the federal government and in about half of the states. In these states, the government has the burden to justify infringing a religious practice by demonstrating that the law doesn't target religious activity and that it has a compelling interest in enforcing the law against the religious activity in question. In the other half of the states, Americans enjoy this protection only in regard to federal law. When state law conflicts with a religious practice, the state need only demonstrate that the law isn't intended to target religion and that it applies to everyone. There are exceptions for cases involving the use of land for religious purposes and for cases involving those who are incarcerated.

It is important to understand the vulnerable nature of the religious liberty protections we currently enjoy. At the federal level and in many states, the promise of liberty for religious practice depends upon a statute and not a constitution. But statutes can be quickly superseded by new legislation, and court decisions can severely limit their applicability.

Where the Constitution is interpreted to provide strong protection for religious liberty, it is often only because courts view the issue through the prism of a separate constitutional freedom, ranging from the guarantee of free speech to equal protection under the law rather than because of the religious liberty protections in the Constitution itself. So, today, the constitutional promise of religious liberty is held together by a fragile string that can easily be severed. The religious liberty that 96 percent of Americans celebrate as one of the greatest features of our land has become an orphan right of the American Constitution, stripped of its inheritance and vulnerable.

The free exercise of religion enjoyed a remarkable rise as the Supreme Court developed and refined its respect for individual religious conscience and practice. Now, this right has suffered a stunning fall, left to the vagaries of the political process and subject to the whims of majority vote. And the story of this vitally important freedom is far from over. From predictions of religion-based anarchy to the patchwork of constitutional, statutory, and case law we have today, American ideas about religious liberty continue to develop, along with a plethora of challenges to this sacred freedom.

Thomas Paine forecasted correctly in 1776 that "those who expect to reap the blessings of freedom must . . . undergo the fatigue of supporting it." Today those words ring truer than ever as we look toward an uncertain future in which economic interests, security mandates, and the various social agendas of activists aim to supersede our first and most precious of freedoms, the right to worship God according to the dictates of our conscience.[30]

---

1. "Elton John 'Would Ban Religion,' " *United Press International*, http://www.upi.com/NewsTrack/Entertainment/20061111-115442-7664r/.

2. Charles Haynes, "Poll Shows Americans Value the Right of Religious Freedom," *Inside the First Amendment*, http://www.freedomforum.org/templates/document.asp?documentID=13297.

3. This may seem like a minor point since we are used to the First Amendment of the federal Constitution applying to all government action and laws at the local, state, and federal level. But back in the mid-1800s this wasn't the case; the First Amendment was applied only to federal action.

4. *Reynolds v. United States*, 98 U.S. 145 (1878).

5. *Cantwell v. Connecticut*, 310 U.S. 296 (1940). Six years earlier, the Supreme Court decided *Hamilton v. Regents of the University of California* (1934) and assumed that the liberty guarantees of the Free Exercise Clause would apply to the states through the Fourteenth Amendment. But ruling against the liberty interest, they didn't explore the meaning or interpretation of the Free Exercise Clause in that case.

6. *Id.*, 303.

7. *Id.*, 304.

8. *Minersville School District v. Gobitis*, 310 U.S. 586 (1940).

9. *Id.*, 595.

10. *West Virginia State Board of Education v. Barnette*, 319 U.S. 624 (1943).

11. *Id.*, 642.

12. *Sherbert v. Verner*, 374 U.S. 398, 401 (1963).

13. *Id.*, 406. "Significantly South Carolina expressly saves the Sunday worshipper from having to make the kind of choice which we here hold infringes the Sabbatarian's religious liberty."

14. *Id.*

15. "Reply to an Address Sent by the Religious Society Called Quakers from Their Yearly Meeting for Pennsylvania, New Jersey, Delaware, and the Western Parts of Maryland and Virginia, September 28, 1789" (undated); quoted in Edwin S. Gaustad, ed., *A Documentary History of Religion in America to the Civil War* (Grand Rapids, Mich.: Wm. B. Eerdman's, 1982), 277, 278.

16. *Wisconsin v. Yoder,* 406 U.S. 205 (1972).

17. *Id.,* 220.

18. *Id.,* 234.

19. *Id.,* 216.

20. *Employment Division, Department of Human Resources of Oregon v. Smith,* 494 U.S. 872, 879 (1990).

21. *Id.,* 901.

22. *Id.,* 880.

23. *Braunfeld v. Brown,* 366 U.S. 599 (1961).

24. *Employment Division,* 494 U.S. 872, 890.

25. *Id.,* 902.

26. *City of Boerne,* 521 U.S. 507 (1997).

27. *Gonzales v. O Centro Espírita Beneficente União do Vegetal,* 546 U.S. 418 (2006).

28. Douglas Laycock's, "Theology Scholarships, the Pledge of Allegiance, and Religious Liberty: Avoiding the Extremes but Missing the Liberty" *Harvard Law Review,* 118, no. 1 (November 2004): 155ff.

29. *Id.*

30. If you want to be active in the next stage of this sacred cause of liberty, visit http://www.religiousliberty.info.

Jonathan Gallagher

CHAPTER 6

An American Ayatollah?

Kill all the unbelievers just as they would kill you all!
—Ayatollah Khomeini[1]

Cotton Mather, the colonial Massachusetts spiritual and political leader, heard that a shipful of Quakers led by William Penn was on its way to the New World. He sent a brief letter to a friend outlining the plan of the colony's government, known as the General Court, for dealing with the heretics when they arrived. The plan of these God-fearing leaders was to intercept the Quaker ship, seize all those on board to prevent them from bringing "heathen worship" into the colony, and then sell them as slaves in Barbados. This brilliant scheme had, in the view of its creators, the threefold benefit of excluding heretics, punishing them by enslavement, and then making a profit for the Lord's "minister and people" by exchanging these slaves for rum and sugar. In this way, wrote Mather, they would "do the Lord great service" and ensure that "the Lord may be glorified"![2]

That Christians could even contemplate such a plan vividly illustrates the danger of a too-close proximity of religion and state. Like an atomic bomb when its two hemispheres of fissile material are brought together, the resulting critical mass of religious and civil power explodes with devastating effect.

The key question is this: Were the early examples of church-state combinations in America just a stage in the progression towards a pluralistic society that separates church and state or are they indicators of what may arise once more with particular regard to "Christian America"? What of the calls for a "return" to Christianity as the religion of the nation? Should we be concerned about those who demand "Christian" laws and morals and government? Where should we draw the line of separation between personal conviction and social mores, between individual belief and political power?

"Kill them all"

In the early thirteenth century, the French king responded to the pope's call for a crusade against the "heretic" Cathars of southern France. Military victory was not difficult against those whose leadership counseled nonviolence, though some Cathar followers did fight in self-defense. Besieging the city of Béziers in 1209, the French king's crusader-soldiers asked the church representative what to do with the city's inhabitants, a mixture of Cathars and Catholics. "Kill them all. God will know His own," was the response of the abbot of Cîteaux.[3] As a result, twenty thousand men, women, and children were slaughtered, many after gruesome torture and mutilation.

Such a horrific order exemplifies the self-assured confidence of those who are completely convinced that they have the truth and that God has given them the responsibility to impose it on others. Absolute power exercised on behalf of religious authority has rarely been tolerant of those with differing beliefs. In fact, it is hard to even think of any such cases. When the exclusive claims of faith that deny any other belief system are allied with civil power, intolerance inevitably follows. Such absolutism in religion combined with civil implementation means that concepts of tolerance and mutual respect are hard for the faithful to practice.

The theocrat's argument goes like this: if I have the truth and you don't and you won't accept my truth, then, in the name of my truth, I'm required to deny you freedom and to prevent you from propagating your views. Such faulty logic isn't the prerogative of any one religion, but it is common to those who claim certain knowledge of what is truth and the prerogative to impose that truth on others. The problem is not inherent in belief systems that profess to be exclusive or have absolute ways of understanding the world. Rather, the problem arises when religion is combined with state and an absolute system of truth seeks enforcement through state power. Once truth is defined according to an exclusive religious perspective and state power is obtained in support of that truth, those who differ in their theology or religious belief are at the state's mercy.

The rule of the religious has indeed been the historical norm, not the exception. The combination of religion and state continues to have broad appeal and affects hundreds of millions. In diverse regions of the globe and among different religious traditions, the majority religion claims to be the religion of the state. Americans are most familiar with Islamic rule in Middle Eastern countries such as Saudi Arabia and Iran, but we forget that the most populous Muslim nation is Indonesia, which has its own unique set of religious problems and conflicts. In Greece, the Orthodox Christian Church dominates, while in Buddhist Bhutan, intolerance is on the rise. India may be religiously diverse, but in several states, Hindu fundamentalism is the dominant force. In these and many other places, majority religious beliefs form the policy of the state to a greater or lesser extent, and religious minorities find themselves marginalized—victims of discrimination, persecution, and worse.

The interface—even the alliance—between religion and power in society is today's battle line. Napoleon said that religion was useful for keeping people quiet. Marx rejected religion on much the same grounds—that it was a useful opiate to paralyze the masses. Roman philosopher Seneca the Younger observed, "Religion is regarded by the common people as true, by the wise as false, and by rulers as useful." The philosopher John Stuart Mill concluded, "It is conceivable that religion may be morally useful without being intellectually sustainable."[4]

Some dream of a righteous kingdom of God on earth ushered in by His loyal lieutenants. It's been tried many times before. Modern-day theocrats should study the history of the second-century Montanists or the tenth-century Millennialists or the sixteenth-century Munsterites. Questions remain: Do we want a theocratic elite to enforce their views of God and social order in place of democracy? Is religious government the way of the future? Thomas Jefferson reflected critically on the history of "righteous rule": "History, I believe, furnishes no example of a priest-ridden people maintaining a free civil government."[5]

Those who came of age after the Iranian Revolution of 1979 may be unfamiliar with the term *ayatollah*. By definition, an *ayatollah* is a "holy man" in Islam—a Muslim leader roughly on par with a Catholic cardinal, or, in the case of Khomeini, with the pope himself. Ayatollah Khomeini was the leader of the Iranian Revolution that deposed the shah and installed an Islamic government in Iran. He is perhaps most famous for his anti-American rhetoric, such as calling the United States "the great Satan," and for holding hostage some fifty Americans who were captured after an assault on the American embassy in Tehran.

To most minds, an ayatollah has become synonymous with a radical—even an extremist—religious leader, whose religious ideology is backed up by civil force. The phrase "an American ayatollah" brings the ideas of freedom and force into conflict, a deliberate oxymoron that seems an impossibility.

Could there ever be an American ayatollah?

On the surface, the question seems ridiculous. How could there ever be such a merging of religious authority and civil might? Surely it is absurd to suggest that a representative of ecclesiastical authority could ever have such control in the land of the free and the home of the brave.

It could never happen here . . .

Americans tend to complacently assume such a church-state regime could never arise in our country. The problem is that it already did! Despite the experience of fleeing state-imposed religion in the countries of Europe, the early settlers in North America were quick to establish laws and practices as exclusive and discriminatory as those they left behind. They wanted to set up their own "kingdom of God" in this new land and were quite prepared to use the same kind of force that had been used against them. Church power and civil power were blended in what probably seemed to those colonial leaders to be part of their divinely ordained "manifest destiny." Though the colonists had seen the results of state-imposed belief, many were ready to do likewise and compel observance of "the one true religion" by force if necessary. This "enforced uniformity of religion"[6] mixed religion and state in a highly oppressive form. Baptists were exiled, Catholics persecuted, and Quakers hung. In New England, religion dominated every aspect of government and society, with nonchurch attendance punishable by whipping, and the stocks the penalty for kissing in public. Massachusetts made blasphemy and worship of any deity other than the Christian God capital offenses. One Puritan preacher stated the colonists were enemies of toleration.

The same spirit of intolerance was felt farther south as well. In 1632, the House of Burgesses in Virginia enacted legislation that required throughout the colony uniformity to the canons and constitution of the Church of England. Virginia passed laws that included the death penalty against Quakers, and Maryland imposed English penal laws against Catholics.

The American experience of religious intolerance surely ended with the Revolution, the ratification of the Constitution, and the adoption of the Bill of Rights. Or did it? Today, there are many who oppose the separation of church and state and who seek to establish America as a Christian nation.

Various proposals have been advocated—for example, that the Constitution should be amended to identify the United States as a Christian nation or to add the words "one nation under God" to the federal Constitution.[7] At the heart of suggestions such as these is the idea of claiming Christian sovereignty and excluding other belief systems. Combined with nationalism, the goal of making America Christian "once more" seems to resonate with many. Crying "God bless America!" these activists seek to define God their way. The clarion call leaves no room for doubt. Those who oppose it are declared unpatriotic at the least, and more likely, hostile enemies of both America and God.

We are witnessing a determined grasp for civil power to enforce religious convictions. These self-appointed agents of the Lord are motivated by an exclusive faith, and they claim a duty to impose that faith on others. The historian Thomas Macaulay explained it this way: "The doctrine which, from the very first origin of religious dissensions, has been held by bigots of all sects, when condensed into a few words and stripped of rhetorical disguise, is simply this: I am in the right, and you are in the wrong. When you are the stronger, you ought to tolerate me; for it is your duty to tolerate truth. But when I am the stronger I shall persecute you; for it is my duty to persecute error."[8] In other words, since their cause is God's cause, to permit dissent would be to tolerate falsehood. This logic is inherent in religious intolerance.

Do those who claim to speak for God really demand compliance with what they believe are divine requirements? Consider the rhetoric, for example, of George Grant, former director of Coral Ridge Ministries:

> Christians have an obligation, a mandate, a commission, a holy responsibility to reclaim the land for Jesus Christ—to have dominion in the civil structures, just as in every other aspect of life and godliness. . . . World conquest. That's what Christ has commissioned us to accomplish. We must win the world with the power of the Gospel. And we must never settle for anything less. . . . Thus, Christian politics has as its primary intent the conquest of the land—of men, families, institutions, bureaucracies, courts, and

governments for the Kingdom of Christ. It is to reinstitute the authority of God's Word as supreme over all judgments, over all legislation, over all declarations, constitutions, and confederations.[9]

Note the language—"dominion," "conquest," "win," "authority," "supreme." This is the language of a dictatorship based on supposed divinely ordained demands. Enforced compliance is the program. It's promoting a religion not by choice or personal conviction but by ramming down the throat, with the absolute demand that piety be professed as if it were from personal conviction. The declaration that "the authority of God's will" supersedes even constitutions is reminiscent of the requirement in Afghanistan under the Taliban that Islamic law take precedence over the national constitution.

Consider another source: "Our Lord demands universal submission to His rule; and that He has predestined His people to victorious conquest and dominion over all things in His name. We must make no compromise and give no quarter in the great battle of history. We are commanded to win."[10] The rationale for such conquest is explained: "This is God's world, not Satan's. Christians are the lawful heirs, not non-Christians."[11] Such convictions derive from a biblical interpretation that views the ancient theocratic kingdom of Israel as the model for modern society:

> Those who are obedient to His commands will rule the world, reconstructing it for His glory in terms of His laws. Psalm 2 shows God laughing and sneering at the pitiful attempts of the wicked to fight against and overthrow His Kingdom. He has already given His Son "all authority in heaven and earth," and the King is with His Church until the end of the age (Matt. 23:18-20)! Is it possible that the King will be defeated? He has, in fact, warned all earthly rulers to submit to His government, or perish (Ps. 2:10-12). And the same is true of His Church. The nation that will not serve us will perish (Isa. 60:12); all the peoples of the earth will be subdued under our feet (Ps. 47:1-3)—promises made originally to Israel, but now to be fulfilled in the New Israel, the Church.[12]

Those who advance this position aren't content to wait for the Lord to establish His kingdom. What is truly frightening is that they are willing to "help" the Lord and do it for Him. Here is justification for extreme action, including the imposition of harsh punishments and very rigorous behavioral laws that demand compliance with what they believe are God's requirements. "The significance of Jesus Christ as the 'faithful and true witness' is that He not only witnesses against those who are at war against God, but He also executes them."[13]

This is extreme rhetoric, foreign to modern ears. We are unaccustomed to recalling the violent excesses of a more religious age, when wars of religion were common and heretics were tortured or killed on account of their beliefs. Could this spirit arise again in a Christian context? Is the violent rhetoric above intended merely to serve as a rallying cry for the faithful, or does it portend something more ominous?

If taken seriously, there is little difference between such a Christian system of government and the religious totalitarianism of an Ayatollah Khomeini. At present, such believers claim to endorse religious freedom because they wish to use it for their own purposes. Once they achieve sufficient power, they no longer need to protect individual rights or religious freedom. The imperative is to enforce "the truth." Gary North, leading Christian Reconstructionist and son-in-law of theological-political innovator R. J. Rushdoony, doesn't mince words: "So let us be blunt about it: we must use the doctrine of religious liberty to gain independence for Christian schools until we train up a generation of people who know that there is no religious neutrality, no neutral law, no neutral education, and no neutral civil government. Then they will get busy in constructing a Bible-based social, political and religious order which finally denies the religious liberty of the enemies of God."[14]

Such reasoning is not only blunt but also chilling. Who are these "enemies of God" if not anyone who dares to dissent from the sectarian wisdom of those in power? The dangerous combination of exclusive "truth" claims and power is here unmasked.

R. J. Rushdoony was the leading theologian of Christian Reconstructionism. Reconstructionism advocates a "Bible-based" social and political order, invoking history for support and enthusiastically endorsing the time when Christianity became the state religion of the Roman Empire: "Because the saints were called to *manage* or govern the world, very quickly it became their purpose to move into positions of authority and power."[15]

The leaders of this movement condemn as heretics and idolaters those who won't accept and obey the religious order they intend for America. In very inflammatory language, they consign their opposition to the ranks of unbelievers, judging them guilty of idol worship as were the enemies of Israel of old. The implications are apparent: "All who are content with a humanistic law system and do not strive to replace it with Biblical law are guilty of idolatry. They have forsaken the covenant of their God, and they are asking us to serve other gods. They are thus idolaters, and are, in our generation, when our world is idolatrous and our states also, to be objects of missionary activity. They must be called out of their idolatry into the service of the living God."[16]

The heresy of democracy

Advocates of such a biblical order consider the current condition of the state as "bankrupt." The only alternative is to work to establish God's rule on this earth through imposition of "His will." There is no place for democracy in such a system: "The church today has fallen prey to the heresy of democracy."[17] Those devoted to democracy are condemned: "Democracy is the great love of the failures and cowards of life."[18]

Ayatollah Khomeini came to power in Iran in a revolution that surprised the West. Missing the religious component, intelligence analysts didn't anticipate the revolution until it was too late. In an orgy of revenge, followers of radical Muslim cleric Khomeini attempted to destroy all the influences of the apostate West, especially the "great Satan" America. The religion-inspired imposition of rules that regulated every aspect of life demonstrated just what happens when religion is used as a blunt political instrument. The long-running embassy hostage crisis, the abortive raid, and the final release hit the collective American psyche hard. But the words of Khomeini have a familiar ring: "Don't listen to those who speak of democracy. They all are against Islam. They want to take the nation away from its mission. We will break all the poison pens of those who speak of nationalism, democracy, and such things."[19]

There is a striking parallel between the attitudes expressed by Khomeini and those of the "Christians" quoted above. They say that those who oppose religious domination are against the will of God and are heretics to be destroyed. "Those who are against us are like cancer tumors that need to be removed surgically; otherwise they will corrupt everything. . . . These writings, these speeches, these wrong activities, these democratic programs are separations from Islam. All these voices are blasphemy and are atheistic."[20]

God's own authority is invoked in support of such violence and oppression. "Those who are trying to bring corruption and destruction to our country in the name of democracy will be oppressed. They are worse than Bani-Ghorizeh Jews, and they must be hanged. We will oppress them by God's order and God's call to prayer."[21]

If the rhetoric from both Islamic and Christian sources were rephrased, disguising which religion were being referred to in each case, it would be impossible to distinguish one from the other. The next quote sounds equally like the Ayatollah Khomeini and R. J. Rushdoony. It is in fact Rushdoony: "The purpose of regeneration is that man reconstruct all things in conformity to God's order, not in terms of man's desire for peace. This purpose and mission involves law and coercion."[22] Note that final word—*coercion*. This is no peaceful invitation, no free choice, no appeal to the heart. This is absolute compulsion. There is no chance for religious liberty here, no freedom of conscience, and no respect for the personal dignity of religious choice: "The goal is the developed Kingdom of God, the New Jerusalem, a world order under God's law."[23] "All law is religious in nature, and every non-Biblical law-order represents an anti-Christian religion."[24] "Every law-order is a state of war against the enemies of that order, and all law is a form of warfare."[25]

Are these the ravings of a fanatic? Are they merely extremist ideas like all the others that bounce around the margins of society? The polls say otherwise.[26] Although the names of R. J. Rushdoony, Gary North, and David Chilton are not well recognized, their ideas have gained an increasingly strong foothold in the Christian community, strongly influencing the conservative Christian approach to politics.

> The significance of the Reconstructionist movement is not its numbers, but the power of its ideas and their surprisingly rapid acceptance. Many on the Christian Right are unaware that they hold Reconstructionist ideas. Because as a theology it is controversial, even among evangelicals, many who are consciously influenced by it avoid the label. This furtiveness is not, however, as significant as the potency of the ideology itself. Generally, Reconstructionism seeks to replace democracy with a theocratic elite that would govern by imposing their interpretation of "Biblical Law." Reconstructionism would eliminate not only democracy but many of its manifestations, such as labor unions, civil rights laws, and public schools. Women would be generally relegated to hearth and home. Insufficiently Christian men would be denied citizenship, perhaps executed.

So severe is this theocracy that it would extend capital punishment beyond such crimes as kidnapping, rape, and murder to include, among other things, blasphemy, heresy, adultery, and homosexuality.[27]

The idea of a Christian America is dear to many churchgoers, and the desire to return to "happier" days leaves them open to the seductive voices of those who promise to make it happen. Yet the foundational principles are all wrong—righteousness cannot be legislated and enforced. The attempt leads only to hypocrisy and oppression as people are pressured to conform to ideas and behaviors they don't believe in. It is far easier to advocate the need for laws and behaviors to conform people to divine standards of righteousness than it is to preach genuine spiritual renewal and voluntary devotion to God. Thus, the language of religious revival is linked with that of political activism, as though politics can save America. Jerry Falwell said, "I am convinced that America can be turned around if we will all get serious about the Master's business. It may be late, but it is never too late to do what is right. We need an old-fashioned, God-honoring, Christ-exalting revival to turn America back to God. America can be saved!"[28] "The idea that religion and politics don't mix was invented by the Devil to keep Christians from running their own country."[29]

God and coercion

Jesus explicitly rejected the use of force to impose belief or to compel obedience. What He said was so profoundly opposed to the use of compulsion in any form that it is surprising that any could advocate the use of force to advance Christianity, as a methodology consistent with the Christian religion. Yet throughout the ages, such claims have been all too common in the church.

As Jesus was being betrayed, He rejected Peter's rash resort to violence: " 'Put your sword back in its place,' Jesus said to him, 'for all who draw the sword will die by the sword. Do you think I cannot call on my Father, and he will at once put at my disposal more than twelve legions of angels?' " (Matthew 26:52, 53). Jesus reminded Peter that if the issue could be resolved by force, the Father could deliver "shock and awe-level" legions. And Jesus later declared to Pilate, " 'My kingdom is not of this world. If it were, my servants would fight to prevent my arrest by the Jews' " (John 18:36).

Those who fight to establish the kingdom of God by that very act betray that they aren't part of that kingdom—at least if Jesus' own definition is to be taken seriously. His servants are those who do not fight, because fighting and force have no place in His kingdom. Jesus knows of no compulsion in belief—and accepts no such worship.

Jesus, who claimed to have shown us the Father, revealed a God of freedom. This truth would set us free, make us free indeed (see John 8:32, 36). This is freedom from sin and from the law of sin and death (see Romans 6:18; 8:2). In fact, reading from Isaiah in the synagogue, Jesus boldly announced the kingdom by proclaiming liberty to the captives and the opening of the prison to those who are bound (see Luke 4:18). He never compelled anyone to believe. Only if God is very different from the portrait given by Jesus can violence and persecution be legitimized.

One's concept of God is essential. As Thomas Paine so rightly observed, "Belief in a cruel God makes a cruel man."[30] A religious dictatorship gains its endorsement from a dictator God. There may be a logical consistency, but the results are horrendous—and contrary to the God revealed by Jesus.

James Madison expressed the best in the American tradition of religious freedom, a tradition consistent with the teachings of Jesus: "We hold it for a fundamental and undeniable truth, 'that religion or the duty which we owe to our Creator and the manner of discharging it, can be directed only by reason and conviction, not by force or violence.' The religion then of every man must be left to the conviction and conscience of every man; and it is the right of every man to exercise it as these may dictate."[31]

Building on this American tradition more than a century later, a Christian champion of religious freedom observed: "It is just as improper to enforce a true religion as a false religion. It is just as tyrannical to prohibit the propaganda and free exercise of a false religion as of the true religion. All religion should be left unmolested, free and independent to proclaim what it considers the truth, so long as it respects and observes the civil statutes of the state and the equal rights of all men. Force has no place in religion. Religion is a personal and voluntary matter between each individual and his God."[32]

The peculiar danger of oppression in the name of religion lies not in its inherent evil but in its appearance as a great good. The desire to make America truly Christian, to blend faith and patriotism, God and country, may increase in popularity until it reaches an overwhelmingly seductive crescendo. But the gravest threat comes from good intentions, not evil ones. As Henry Brooks Adam observed, "It is always good men who do the most harm in the world."[33] Blaise Pascal echoed the sentiment: "Men never do evil so completely and cheerfully as when they do it from religious conviction."[34] And U.S. Supreme Court Justice Louis D. Brandeis wrote, "Experience should teach us to be most on our guard to protect liberty when the government's purposes are beneficent. . . . The greatest dangers to liberty lurk in insidious encroachment by men of zeal, well meaning but without understanding."[35]

So, how much religion do you want in government?

"As much as I can get," says a fervent believer.

"None at all," says the avowed atheist.

"Enough in others to keep the peace," says the skeptic.

"Sufficient to provoke some change," says the activist.

"More—so we can control the deviant and dysfunctional in society," says the religious official.

"Less—so we can keep moralists and bigots out of modern society," says the secularist.

The American Founding Fathers would have answered this question rather differently. They insisted that the state should stay out of religious matters except to protect the religious freedom of its citizens. Absolute neutrality toward religion might be overstating it, as this could result in a state ignoring the abuse of religious minorities by a social majority. Some scholars have chosen the phrase "benevolent neutrality" to capture the neutral yet protective role the Founders envisioned the state taking towards religion, which they viewed as essential to providing the moral and social framework needed for self-government.[36]

The undesirable blend of church and state is a recurring theme in history. Calvin's Geneva, Cromwell's England, the Salem witch trials, and even the Holy Roman Empire—all are examples of righteous rule becoming oppressive. The dangerous mix of religion and political power is equally evident from a survey of the conditions of religious believers around the world today. It is true of all the major religious traditions of the world; somewhere, each of them is sufficiently dominant and arrogant as to oppress persons of other faiths.

When you consider the question of how much religion you want government to push, don't overlook the logical end such a path may produce—the logic of Ayatollah Khomeini: "The Great God has given His gifts to you, and if you are not thankful of your current conditions, I am afraid of Almighty God's wrath toward you, and then, God forbid, everyone will burn, both dry and wet [that is, both the innocent and the guilty], and there will [be] no path to escape for any of you."[37]

---

1. Robert Spencer, "Khomeini in Dearborn," *Human Events,* November 22, 2004; quoted in http://findarticles.com/p/articles/mi_qa3827/is_200411/ai_n9470612. This quote was taken from the paragraph that follows: "Khomeini accordingly delivered notorious rebuke to the Islam-is-a-religion-of-peace crowd: 'Those who know nothing of Islam pretend that Islam counsels against war. Those [who say this] are witless. Islam says: Kill all the unbelievers just as they would kill you all! Does this mean that Muslims should sit back until they are devoured by [the unbelievers]? Islam says: Kill them, put them to the sword and scatter [their armies]. . . . Islam says: Whatever good there is exists thanks to the sword and in the shadow of the sword! People cannot be made obedient except with the sword! The sword is the key to Paradise, which can be opened only for the Holy Warriors! . . . Does all this mean that Islam is a religion that prevents men from waging war? I spit upon those foolish souls who make such a claim.' "

2. Adapted from the *New York Times* of March 8, 1897 (see http://query.nytimes .com/gst/abstract.html?res=9E05E0D71339E433A2575BC0A9659C94669ED7CF):
Sept. 15, 1682
To the Aged and Beloved Mr. John Higginson:
There is now a ship at sea called the *Welcome,* which has on board a hundred or more of the heretics and malignants called Quakers, with W. Penn, who is the chief scamp, at the head of them.
The General Court has accordingly given secret orders to master Malachi Huscott, of the brig *Porpoise,* to waylay the said *Welcome,* slyly as near the Cape of Cod as may be, and make captive the said Penn and his ungodly crew, so the Lord may be glorified, and not mocked on the soil of this new country with the heathen worship of this people.
Much spoil can be made by selling the whole lot to Barbados, where slaves fetch good prices in rum and sugar, and we shall not only do the Lord great service by puniching [sic] the wicked, but we shall make great good for his minister and people. Master Huscott feels hopeful and I will set down the news when the ship comes back.
Cotton Mather
3. This is a well-known remark, see, e.g., E. L. Skip Knox "History of the Crusade," an online course from Boise State University, http://crusades.boisestate.edu/Albi/.
4. John Stuart Mill, quoted in "Familiar Quotations: Conceivable" *Webster's Online Dictionary* http://www.websters-online-dictionary.org/definition/conceivable.
5. Eyler Robert Coates Sr., "Thomas Jefferson on Politics & Government," The University of Virginia Alderman Library Electronic Text Center, http://etext.virginia .edu/jefferson/quotations/jeff1650.htm.
6. *The Founders' Constitution,* "Roger Williams, 'The Bloody Tenent, Of Persecution

for Cause of Conscience,' " vol. 5, amendment 1(religion), document 4, The University of Chicago, http://press-pubs.uchicago.edu/founders/documents/amendI_religions4.html.

7. See, e.g., http://www.acknowledgegodamerica.com; http://www.christianamerica.net; http://www.cc.org; http://www.achw.org.

8. Positive Atheism's Big List of Quotations, "Lord Macaulay, *Macintosh's History of the Revolution*," at http://www.positiveatheism.org/hist/quotes/quote-m.htm.

9. George Grant, *The Changing of the Guard* (Ft. Worth, Tex.: Dominion Press, 1987), 50, 51; quoted in http://www.serve.com/thibodep/cr/worldcnq.htm.

10. David Chilton, *The Days of Vengeance: An Exposition of the Book of Revelation* (Fort Worth, Tex.: Dominion Press, 1984), 44; quoted in http://www.serve.com/thibodep/cr/commandd.htm.

11. Gary North, quoted in James W. Lett, "The Evolution of Religious Freedom," http://faculty.ircc.edu/faculty/jlett/The%20Evolution%20of%20Religious%20Freedom.pdf.

12. Chilton, 117; quoted in http://www.serve.com/thibodep/cr/under.htm.

13. R. J. Rushdoony, *The Institutes of Biblical Law* (Nutley, N.J.: Craig Press, 1973), 574; quoted in http://www.serve.com/thibodep/cr/execute.htm.

14. Gary North, "The Intellectual Schizophrenia of the New Christian Right," *Christianity and Civilization: The Failure of the American Baptist Culture,* no. 1 (Spring 1982), 25; quoted in http://www.serve.com/thibodep/cr/liberty.htm.

15. Rushdoony, 742; quoted in http://www.serve.com/thibodep/cr/manage.htm.

16. Rushdoony, *Law and Society: Volume II of the Institutes of Biblical Law* (Nutley, N.J.: Craig Press, 1982), 468; quoted in http://www.americanfundamentalists.com/cast/rushdoony.html.

17. Rushdoony, *The Institutes of Bibilical Law,* 747.

18. Rushdoony, *Thy Kingdom Come: Studies in Daniel and Revelation* (Vallecito, Calif.: Ross House Books, 2001), 39; quoted in http://www.americanfundamentalists.com/cast/rushdoony.html.

19. Ayatollah Khomeini in a meeting with Iranian students and educators, Qom, March 13, 1979; quoted in http://www.iran-heritage.org/interestgroups/government-article2.htm.

20. Ayatollah Khomeini in a talk to the representatives from Tabriz, Qom, September 19, 1979; quoted in http://www.iran-heritage.org/interestgroups/government-article2.htm.

21. Ayatollah Khomeini in a talk at the Fayzieah School, Qom, August 30, 1979; quoted in http://www.iran-heritage.org/interestgroups/government-article2.htm.

Bani-Ghorizeh Jews were a tribe that constantly fought against Mohammed. An Islamic scholar discusses Khomeini's theocratic statements: Dr. Jalal Matini, "Democracy? I Meant Theocracy," introduction and translation by Farhad Mafie, http://www.oranian.com/Opinion/2003/August/Khomeini/.

22. Rushdoony, *The Institutes of Biblical Law,* 777; quoted in http://www.serve.com/thibodep/cr/regen.htm.

23. Ibid., 357; quoted in http://www.serve.com/thibodep/cr/rc.htm.

24. Ibid., 113; quoted in http://www.theocracywatch.org/dominionism.htm.

25. Ibid., 93.

26. Frederick Clarkson, "Theocratic Dominionism Gains Influence," *Christian Reconstructionism,* March/June 1994; quoted in http://www.ucpress.edu/books/pages/8830/8830.ch01.html; http://www.firstthings.com/ftissues/ft9610/reeves.html.

27. Frederick Clarkson, "Theocratic Dominionism Gains Influence" *The Public Eye* vol. 8, no.1; quoted in http://www.publiceye.org/magazine/v08n1/chrisre1.html.

28. Jerry Falwell, *Moral Majority Report,* September 1984; quoted in http://www .ethicalatheist.com/docs/separation_church_state.html.

29. Jerry Falwell, sermon, July 4, 1976; quoted in http://www.ethicalatheist.com/ docs/separation_church_state.html.

30. "Thomas Paine Quotes," ThinkExist.com Quotations, http://thinkexist.com/ quotation/belief_in_a_cruel_god_makes_a_cruel/193806.html.

31. James Madison, *Memorial and Remonstrance to the Assembly of Virginia*; quoted in "A Chronology of US Historical Documents," University of Okalahoma, College of Law, http://www.law.ou.edu/ushistory/remon.shtml.

32. C. S. Longacre, *Liberty* 34, no. 4 (1939), 29.

33. "Quotes by Henry B. Adams," What Quote, http://www.whatquote.com/ quotes/Henry-B--Adams/18530-It-is-always-good-me.htm.

34. "Blaise Pascal," Quote DB, http://www.quotedb.com/quotes/2148.

35. "Quotes on Liberty," Eric Raymond, http://www.catb.org/~esr/fortunes/liberty .html.

36. See Robert T. Miller and Ronald B. Flowers, *Toward Benevolent Neutrality: Church, State, and the Supreme Court,* 4th ed. (Waco, Tex.: The Markham Press Fund of Baylor University Press, 1992).

37. Ayatollah Khomeini, message on the fifth anniversary of the establishment of the Islamic Republic, April 1, 1983; quoted in http://www.iran-heritage.org/interestgroups/ government-article2.htm.

Part II

Current
Issues

James D. Standish

CHAPTER 7

Caught Between God and Mammon: Religion in the American Workplace

The name Eric Liddell may have faded into obscurity, but at the 1924 Paris Olympic Games, that name was on everyone's lips. Eric, a strapping Scotsman with enormous athletic prowess, had done what few others have. After years of training and with the Olympic expectations of his country riding on his shoulders, he chose to turn down the opportunity to run in his specialty event, the 100-meter sprint. Even more remarkably, he turned down the opportunity because of his religious faith.

Liddell was not only a serious athlete but also a man of serious faith. He believed that participating in athletics on Sunday was sinful. Because the qualifying heats for the 100 meters were held on Sunday, he declined to compete in that event. Liddell was vilified by some, who saw his choice as the action of a fool and a betrayal of his nation. Nevertheless, he was firm in his commitment. In an accommodation of Liddell's religious faith, he was permitted to enter the 400 meters, an event he had little expectation of winning.

Liddell ran well in the qualifying heats of the 400 meters, but hopes for his victory faded at the outset of the final. He came out of the blocks at a 100-meters pace, and it appeared clear to those watching that he couldn't sustain the pace over 400 meters. To everyone's surprise, however, he stayed well ahead of his more experienced competitors and flew over the finish line, not only taking the gold but also setting a new world record. Liddell's inspiring story of adversity and achievement was eventually told in the film *Chariots of Fire*. Although his name may have faded, his example continues to burn bright.

The race for respect

There are Eric Liddells in the American workplace today. They are men and women who desire to work hard to support their families, their communities, and their nation, and they aim for the very highest levels of performance. Before all of this, however, they value their commitment to their faith. Unfortunately, like those who met Liddell's decision with hostility and ridicule, some of today's employers treat these faithful men and women shamefully. Surprisingly, employers can often do this with legal impunity.

The case of Teresa George is a prime example.[1] Ms. George is a Roman Catholic who felt convicted that she shouldn't work on Sundays. She communicated this conviction to her employer, Home Depot. The company offered to permit Ms. George to have time off on Sundays to attend Mass but refused to accommodate her need to spend all of Sunday in rest and spiritual reflection. When Ms. George remained steadfast in her religious conviction, Home Depot refused to explore other options, and instead, promptly fired her.

Ms. George's case would seem to be open-and-shut. After all, civil rights law states that employers have a duty to accommodate an employee's religious practices as long as they can "reasonably accommodate" the practice and the accommodation doesn't cause "undue hardship" on the employer's business.[2] In this case, Home Depot hadn't explored whether Ms. George could swap shifts with other employees or ways in which her shifts could be arranged around her religious beliefs. Nor had it offered her an alternative position. Rather, the company had given her a take-it-or-leave-it offer, an offer that clearly didn't permit her the spiritual rest she believed God requires on Sundays.

Ms. George's case was heard by the Eastern District of Louisiana and was decided on December 6, 2001. Home Depot filed for summary judgment, claiming that in firing Ms. George, they had acted well within their legal rights. The court agreed, finding that Home Depot had satisfied its legal obligation to accommodate Ms. George and that she was in the wrong for refusing to accept the "accommodation" offered by the employer.

In coming to its conclusion, the court stated: "George refused to accept the accommodation offered, refused to consider any accommodation except on her terms and therefore did not make a good faith effort to cooperate in the search for a resolution. Home Depot was not obligated to search for other accommodations that were more favorable to plaintiff. By providing at least one reasonable accommodation [note: the accommodation offered was no accommodation at all, as George would still have had to violate her conscience by working on Sunday], the defendant discharged its obligation. . . . Because Home Depot offered George a reasonable accommodation, it need not prove that it could not offer such accommodation without undue hardship."[3]

It may come as a surprise to Americans, who are used to hearing about the wide range of civil rights enjoyed in the workplace, that religious beliefs remain so vulnerable. While civil rights law requires employers to attempt to accommodate their employees' faith,[4] the Supreme Court has interpreted this requirement to impose on employers only a minimal level of responsibility. The statutory language requires employers to provide a reasonable religious accommodation unless it would result in an "undue hardship." Surprisingly, the Supreme Court has interpreted this to mean "not much hardship at all." The Court ruled that even a minimal out-of-pocket cost is more than the law requires.[5] In addition, as in the *George* case, courts frequently find that as long as an employer offers an accommodation, even if such an accommodation doesn't resolve the conflict, the employer has met its legal responsibility.

Some employers have taken advantage of these decisions, refusing to make any real effort to accommodate the sincerely held religious beliefs of their workers even when doing so is well within their ability. Because of the minimal legal protection available, employers can engage in such arbitrary actions with impunity. Indeed, lawyers who represent people of faith in the workplace point to an increasing number of cases in which employers have refused to take even the most basic steps to accommodate the religious faith of their employees. The U.S. Equal Employment Opportunity Commission reports that claims involving religious discrimination in the workplace went up a staggering 82 percent between 1993 and 2003 and have remained high since. In contrast, racial discrimination claims held steady during the same decade. Thus, it isn't simply that American employees have become more prone to complain. Rather, there is growing hostility toward religion in the American workplace.

In part, this growing intolerance is a natural outgrowth of the increase in religious diversity in America—and our shift toward a twenty-four-hour-a-day, seven-days-a-week economy in which Americans are spending more of their lives in the workplace. However, these factors don't appear to explain the increasing caseload completely. After all, many employers have expended significant resources on building a sensitive workplace in which ethnic, gender, and sexual-preference diversity is respected and accommodated. In addition, in 1990, Congress passed the Americans with Disabilities Act to ensure that those with disabilities are accommodated in the workforce. The tendency of employers to demonstrate increased disregard for their employees' religious practices is inconsistent with the general trend toward inclusiveness and toleration in the workplace.

The human face

Who is being placed in the impossible position of choosing between their commitment to God and their ability to earn a living to support their families? Regular, run-of-the-mill Americans with sincerely held religious beliefs. Consider the following cases:[6]

Teri Strickland, personnel manager—Ms. Teri Strickland, a member of the Seventh-day Adventist Church, worked for a temporary-personnel-placement agency located in Oklahoma City. Her supervisor was aware that she, like all Seventh-day Adventists, kept the Sabbath by avoiding non-humanitarian work from sundown Friday until sundown Saturday each week. One Saturday, her supervisor called and requested that she come in to work on a project. Ms. Strickland replied that she would be happy to come into work after sundown but due to her religious convictions, she couldn't come in before that time. The supervisor became upset and informed Ms. Strickland that if she didn't come in, she would be fired. After being fired, Ms. Strickland struggled to find a new position. She did some part-time bookkeeping and eventually turned to cleaning homes and selling her plasma to make ends meet. During this time, she completely depleted her savings and lost her home. And a repossession team came to her church during services to repossess her car.

Amric Singh Rathour, traffic enforcement agent—Mr. Amric Singh Rathour, a practicing Sikh, was sworn in as a new officer in the New York Police Department on June 18, 2001. During the eight weeks of training that followed the swearing in, Mr. Rathour's supervisor requested that he shave his beard and remove his turban. When Mr. Rathour refused to compromise the tenets of his faith that require men to wear turbans and beards, he was fired. In contrast, the D.C. Metropolitan Police Department is not only willing to make the appropriate religious accommodation for Sikhs but has actively encouraged Sikh Americans to become officers. Similarly, police forces in the United Kingdom, Canada, and many other nations around the world accommodate Sikhs by permitting them to wear beards and turbans while serving as officers.

Zeinab Ali, receptionist—Ms. Zeinab Ali, a practicing Muslim, worked as a receptionist for Alamo Rent A Car. In accordance with her religious faith, Ms. Ali wore a headscarf. Her supervisor asked her to remove the headscarf. Rather than going bareheaded, Ms. Ali replaced the scarf with a smaller head covering. After a protracted period of negotiations over the issue, Ms. Ali was laid off. Her efforts to gain legal redress have failed.

Peter Howard, warehouse worker—Mr. Peter Howard worked in the warehouse of Haverty Furniture Companies. A number of years after he began his employment there, he was ordained as a Methodist minister. On two occasions, Mr. Howard was forced to miss work because of his ministerial duties. On the second occasion, one of Mr. Howard's parishioners died, and the funeral was set for a Saturday. Mr. Howard asked on Thursday to have the Saturday off so that he could perform the service and was told to wait until Friday for a response. On Friday at 5:00 P.M., the supervisor told Mr. Howard he couldn't take Saturday off to fulfill his religious duties. Mr. Howard went ahead and conducted the funeral, and when he returned to work, he was fired.

Richard Katz, repair technician—Mr. Richard Katz, an Orthodox Jew, applied to work as a repair technician for Sears. Mr. Katz received high marks on the employer's test but was told he wouldn't be hired because he wouldn't work on his Sabbath. Mr. Katz offered to work on Sunday nights instead of Saturdays, but this offer was rebuffed. Sears consistently told Mr. Katz that the reason for its refusal to hire him was that Saturday was the busiest day for repair technicians. Later investigation established that in fact Saturday was not the busiest day.

While 75 percent of religious accommodations historically involve weekly Sabbath days, periodic religious holidays, religious garb (e.g., turbans), and religious grooming (e.g., beards), there are many other types of cases. These include the following:[7]

- a Jehovah's Witness employee who requests to opt out of raising the flag and pledging allegiance at work;
- a Methodist attorney who requests accommodation not to work on tobacco litigation;
- a Quaker (Society of Friends) employee who requests to be transferred to a division that doesn't work on armaments;
- an Orthodox Jewish woman who requests permission not to shake the hands of male customers;
- a Hindu employee who requests permission not to greet guests with the phrase "Merry Christmas";
- a Christian employee who requests to be assigned to work that doesn't involve embryonic research;
- a Muslim hospital employee who requests to be exempted from duty in which she would be present when a member of the opposite sex is unclothed;
- a Christian Web page developer who asks to be reassigned from a pornographic Web site development project; and
- a Muslim truck driver who requests to be assigned to routes that don't involve hauling alcoholic beverages.

What can we do?

Freedom of belief is central to the American experience. It is the essence of what it means to be free. Religious freedom is at the heart of human dignity; and it is this freedom that defines America as a nation of liberty. That this freedom should be protected as much as possible in the workplace flows naturally from our core values. Indeed, there is a broad coalition dedicated to stopping the arbitrary mistreatment of people of faith.

A group of forty-five diverse organizations has formed to push for legislative change. The focus of this coalition is a piece of proposed legislation entitled the Workplace Religious Freedom Act (WRFA). This act is designed to rectify the current legal imbalance. It has two central provisions. The first requires employers to accommodate employees' religious practices unless such accommodation would require significant difficulty or expense.

The second provision declares that an accommodation of religious beliefs is not sufficient unless it removes the conflict between the religious practice and the work requirement.

The coalition recognizes that there must be a balance between the right to religious accommodation and the business interests of the employer. After all, the employees are hired to do a job, and the employer has a right to insist that the job be done. Nevertheless, limitations on religious freedom should only be imposed if they are really necessary. In most cases, there are reasonable steps that employers can take to provide religious accommodation without undermining their business interests.[8] WRFA doesn't mandate that employers always accommodate religious beliefs. Rather, it requires employers to provide accommodation if that can be accomplished without incurring significant difficulty or expense. This is similar to the balance struck by the Americans with Disabilities Act.

WRFA's second central requirement would appear obvious. It says that employers haven't accommodated their employees until the conflict between work and faith is resolved. The *George* case demonstrates, however, that such a clarification of the law is necessary.

When the issue of accommodation of people of faith in the workplace is raised, it is sometimes suggested that employees who experience problems in the workplace should simply find a new employer. While many employees do exactly that, sometimes the situations they face aren't that easily resolved. Frequently, low-paid and poorly educated workers find their employers unwilling to accommodate their religious beliefs. These workers often have skills suited only to industries in which virtually all employers maintain similar practices, so changing employers provides no relief. In addition, finding a new employer can be exceedingly difficult, particularly in times of recession. Some employees are tied to a specific location where employers are few and moving from one to another is very difficult. Moreover, sometimes employees cannot afford the disruption in health care and other benefits that frequently occurs in transition between employers.

Even if these exigent circumstances aren't present, losing employment isn't an insignificant event. It can be destructive to family relationships as well as devastating financially and emotionally. Recognizing the dire impact of losing employment, our laws have been carefully crafted to protect the disabled from dismissal, for example, requiring efforts to accommodate their needs. It isn't too much to ask from a nation founded on the principles of religious freedom that people of faith be given the same respect.

Because of the hardships posed by losing one's employment, an influential set of leading legislators have taken up the call to pass the Workplace Religious Freedom Act. In recent years, the list has included leading Republicans, like Senator Rick Santorum, Senator Orrin Hatch, Senator Sam Brownback, and Senator Elizabeth Dole. It has also included leading Democrats, such as Senator John Kerry, Senator Hillary Rodham Clinton, and Senator Charles Schumer. However, despite robust bipartisan leadership, the WRFA hasn't yet been enacted into law. Why not? There are two good reasons—opposition from business groups and opposition from the Far Left.

The ACLU attacks

Despite the claim that the American Civil Liberties Union (ACLU) supports religious freedom, in recent years, it has become an increasingly powerful barrier to passing legislation to protect it. This is not to imply that all the ACLU does is wrong. Its support of prisoner rights and opposition to torture is laudable. However, the ACLU agenda gives priority to abortion rights and gay rights, and this organization will support religious liberty only if doing so poses no conceivable conflict with its other agenda.

The ACLU has aggressively opposed the Workplace Religious Freedom Act, even sending out an e-mail accusing the bill of being a "sneak attack" on abortion rights and gay rights.[9] It claims the WRFA will protect those who harass gays at work and that it will bar access to abortion.

Here is the ACLU's first example: A gay employee works in the cubicle next to an evangelical Christian. The evangelical tells his gay colleague that his lifestyle is wrong and that he's going to go to hell as a result of following it. The evangelical continues this line of commentary from day to day, creating a very hostile work environment. The gay employee complains to his supervisor. The supervisor calls in the evangelical employee and instructs him to stop the harassment. However, the evangelical refuses to stop expressing his religious beliefs and claims that WRFA protects his right to express his religious beliefs no matter who might be offended.

If you don't know anything about the law and are willing to indulge your wildest fears no matter how unreasonable, this can present a compelling scenario. However, despite the ACLU's pejorative stereotypes, they have presented no evidence that evangelicals are any more likely to harass gay employees than gay employees are likely to harass evangelicals. Indeed, there is no evidence that religion-based harassment is a problem in the workplace. In fact, there are only a handful of reported cases in the entire country. Nevertheless, should such harassment occur, the law already permits the employer to discipline or discharge the harasser if necessary.

This is exactly what happened in a recent case involving an employee at Hewlett-Packard. The company instituted a campaign to promote diversity that included posting photos of gay couples around the workplace. In response, the employee displayed Bible texts in his cubicle condemning homosexuality. When the employee's managers asked him to remove the texts because they were offensive, he refused to take them down unless the company removed the posters advocating toleration of gays. Eventually, the employee was fired.

When the case was tried, the court rejected the employee's claim that he had a right to religious accommodation of his antihomosexual beliefs. Instead, the court found that an employer needn't tolerate harassment. While Hewlett-Packard must tolerate some degree of employee discomfort in the process of taking the steps required by Title VII of the Civil Rights Act of 1964 to correct the wrongs of discrimination, it needn't accept the burdens that would result from allowing actions that demean or degrade or are designed to demean or degrade members of its workforce.[10]

Whether or not one believes this is the correct outcome in this case, a broad range of experts in the area of religious accommodation law have been consulted and agree that WRFA wouldn't change this result. Harassment is illegal, and WRFA doesn't extend protection to otherwise illegal conduct. Nor does the bill require religious accommodation under all circumstances, but only when an accommodation can be provided absent a significant cost or inconvenience to the employer. The courts have always given substantial weight to the rights of third parties in evaluating whether a religious accommodation is required. Harassment in the name of religion is highly offensive and disruptive in a workplace. It is fanciful to imagine WRFA would be interpreted to privilege such actions.

If the ACLU were correct in thinking that WRFA permitted religious harassment, the bill would be opposed by many religious groups since it would pose as much of a problem for people of faith as for gays. Jews don't want to be harassed by Christians. Christians don't want to be harassed by atheists. Atheists don't want to be harassed by Muslims. And Muslims don't want to be harassed by Jews. In short, in a country as large and diverse as the United States, we are all minorities in some workplaces. If WRFA declared that people were free to harass people of other faiths, the most vocal supporters of this bill would become its most vigorous opponents.

It isn't necessary to speculate about the possible impact of the Workplace Religious Freedom Act because New York State has enacted identical provisions. Governor Elliot Spitzer, a pro-gay rights Democrat, publicly critiqued the ACLU's perspective when he was serving as attorney general. He wrote, "I have the utmost respect for the ACLU, but on this issue they are simply wrong. New York's law has not resulted in the infringement of the rights of others, or in the additional litigation that the ACLU predicts will occur if WRFA is enacted. Nor has it been burdensome on business. Rather, it strikes the correct balance between accommodating individual liberty and the needs of businesses and the delivery of services. So does WRFA."[11]

The ACLU's claims that WRFA would bar access to abortion are even more far-fetched than its gay-rights scenario. So, neither of the ACLU's objections has any merit. The WRFA coalition includes many groups who agree with the ACLU's position on gay rights and abortion, and these groups wouldn't support a bill that undermines rights they care about. Moreover, several employment-law experts have examined the ACLU's claim and have rejected it outright.

Despite the ACLU's claims to the contrary, it has become increasingly hostile to mainstream religions, especially those religions that maintain beliefs contrary to the ACLU's own ideology that gay rights and abortion rights take precedence over religious liberty. The ACLU's opposition to the Workplace Religious Freedom Act doesn't appear to be a sincere effort to protect the rights of homosexuals so much as an effort to marginalize and stigmatize those who hold religious beliefs that they disagree with. This opposition is also central to a broader ACLU effort to ensure that gay rights and abortion rights trump religious liberty.

The Chamber of Commerce resists

On the other end of the spectrum, the U.S. Chamber of Commerce has conjured up its own parade of abuses focusing on fanciful religious claims. Once again, their emotive scenarios have no basis in fact. New York's WRFA hasn't instigated any cases involving an employee with a religious obligation to drink a six-pack of beer on lunch break. No one has claimed the right to sacrifice animals on company property or to perform a Black Mass by the watercooler, or any other far-fetched scenario that furtive imaginations picture.

Even more importantly, in New York State the claims filed relating to religious discrimination actually *dropped* after the state Workplace Religious Freedom Act was passed. Why would the Chamber of Commerce oppose the Workplace Religious Freedom Act if it actually reduces litigation? The Chamber has opposed virtually every piece of pro-employee legislation that has ever been introduced in Congress, so it would be a surprise indeed if it were to break with tradition.

Whether it involves a parade of fanciful claims, emotive scenarios, or playing on people's worst prejudices, the campaign to discredit the Workplace Religious Freedom Act has had an impact. Some legislators who at first boldly endorsed the bill have since meekly decided to sit out the debate on the sidelines. As a staffer for a Democratic senator stated, "No matter the validity of their claims, as long as the ACLU opposes the bill, there are many Democrats who aren't able to support the Workplace Religious Freedom Act." Similarly, there are many Republicans who view opposition by the Chamber of Commerce a complete bar to doing what they must know in their hearts is the right thing. It seems as though everyone in politics wants to play the religion card, but few are willing to do anything of substance when there is something serious to be done.

However, there are men and women on both sides of the aisle who have had the courage to stand up and be counted. They focus not on the hypothetical and the fanciful but rather on the real and tangible. The most pertinent is the undeniable fact that faithful American believers are increasingly being arbitrarily forced out of their jobs, losing their health insurance, their financial security, and in some cases their homes and their cars for no crime other than being faithful to what they believe God requires of them. Nothing could offend American values more.

We began by examining Eric Liddell's experience. It is fitting to end with a lesson from his experience. All of Great Britain rejoiced when Liddell won the gold in the 400 meters. This rejoicing was compounded when a fellow Briton won the gold in the 100 meters. By accommodating Liddell, Great Britain got two gold medals instead of only one. Similarly, accommodating employees' religious faith in the workplace is not a zero-sum game. Rather, meeting the needs of people who take their faith seriously can and often does result in retaining star performers. It is fitting for society to protect what its citizens value so highly—the right to worship according to one's own conscience and belief free of unnecessarily coercive job requirements.

I have high hopes that the Workplace Religious Freedom Act will pass. When it does, it will restore the balance between faith and work. Then the Eric Liddells in the American workforce will be a step closer to enjoying the respect their fidelity deserves.

---

1. *George v. Home Depot, Inc.,* 2001 WL 1558315 (E.D.La.). The facts presented in this article are based on the court's opinion.

2. 42 US.C. § 2000e(j). (Employers have a duty to accommodate an employee's religious practices as long as they can "reasonably accommodate" the practices and the accommodation does not cause "undue hardship" on the employer's business.)

3. *George* 2001 WL 1558315.

4. See note 2.

5. *Trans World Airlines, Inc., v. Hardison,* 432 U.S. 63, 84 (1977). (Accommodation of religious beliefs requiring "more than a *de minimis* cost" to the employer normally results in "undue hardship" and therefore is not required by current law.)

6. Case summaries prepared by the Coalition for Religious Freedom in the Workplace.

7. List compiled by the Coalition for Freedom of Religion in the Workplace.

8. See Alan J. Reinach, "Religious Accommodation in a Post 9/11 World (Minorities and the Workplace)," *Employee Rights Quarterly,* March 22, 2002. "Willing employers can provide religious accommodation."

9. From an ACLU "Take Action" e-mail sent by Matt Howes, national Internet organizer for the ACLU, to ACLU Action Members. The author received the e-mail June 9, 2004.

10. See *Oncale v. Sundowner Offshore Servs., Inc.,* 523 U.S. 75, 140 L. Ed. 2d 201 (1998), and *Peterson v. Hewlett-Packard,* 2004 U.S. App. LEXIS 72 (9th Cir., January 6, 2004).

11. Eliot Spitzer, "Defend the Civil Right to Freedom of Religion for America's Workers," *The Forward,* June 25, 2004, 1, 7; quoted in http://www.forward.com/articles/5867/.

Alan J. Reinach

Chapter 8

Can Johnny Pray in Public School?

Jimmy was a bright and eager second-grader as he entered his homeroom on the first day of school. Before class began, the teacher asked the students to raise their hands if they were Catholic or Jewish. Three hands went up, including Jimmy's. The three students were told to leave the classroom for the morning Bible reading and prayer since they weren't Protestants. Jimmy didn't know what a Protestant was. He was Jewish. The other two kids were Catholic. They sat together in the hall for what seemed like an eternity as students from other classes hurried by, giving them funny looks.

This morning ritual was repeated for two weeks, until Jimmy broke down and cried in front of his parents. His father went with him to the principal's office and demanded that the principal put a stop to the teacher's practice. The principal was a Southern Baptist who respected the historic American tradition of the seperation of church and state. He knew that a state-run institution like the public school was no place for imposing sectarian religion. He called the teacher into his office and in front of Jimmy and his dad demanded that she stop the daily Bible reading and prayer. The year was 1953, ten years before the Supreme Court would rule on such practices.[1]

When confronted by an offended child and his father, this Baptist principal applied the historic Baptist principles of respect for the rights of individual conscience. He also understood that the freedom, dignity, and respect this student deserved were more important than the freedom of the Protestant majority to engage in an act of worship at the beginning of the school day. The Supreme Court came to the same conclusion a decade later in two of its most controversial decisions, which banned devotional Bible reading and prayer from the public-school classroom.[2]

These two decisions are probably the most misunderstood and intentionally distorted rulings in the Supreme Court's history. For the past forty years, the Supreme Court has been wrongly accused of kicking God, prayer, and the Bible out of public school. Not surprisingly, some teachers and school administrators who are either misguided or hostile to religion claim to believe that these rulings did just that, and they act accordingly. Consequently, anecdotes have circulated widely that accuse teachers of preventing kids from saying grace at lunch or including religious content in homework assignments. Such anecdotes fuel the fire of culture wars and fill the coffers of culture-war fund-raisers. Sadly, by manipulating prayer and the Bible as weapons in this culture war, both Left and Right have desecrated what is sacred.

The starting point for understanding the battle over school prayer must be with the facts of the Supreme Court case itself. What did the Court actually decide, and what really is the status of prayer in public school?

The Regents' prayer

In the case of *Engel v. Vitale,* the New York State Board of Regents, the governing body of the state's public schools, had drafted the following prayer and adopted a regulation that this prayer be recited in every public-school classroom throughout the state: "Almighty God, we acknowledge our dependence upon Thee, and we beg Thy blessings upon us, our parents, our teachers and our Country."[3]

As the Supreme Court noted, the prayers were to be led either by the teacher or by a student selected by the teacher. No official comment by any teacher was to be permitted; the students were simply to recite this prayer. Shortly after the Regents adopted this prayer, ten parents filed a lawsuit that challenged the practice as a violation of the First Amendment's prohibition against the "establishment of religion." The New York State courts upheld the prayer practice, and the case went to the U.S. Supreme Court.

Justice Hugo Black wrote the opinion for the Court. Only one judge dissented—Justice Potter Stewart. Black was known as a constitutional literalist—the sort who is popular today among conservatives. Long before conservatives made popular the doctrine of relying on "the original intent of the Framers," Justice Black carefully considered the lessons of history and the Framers' intent. He reviewed the history of England and colonial America to determine the scope of the First Amendment's prohibition on the "establishment of religion." He observed that the English settlers of the

American colonies fled religious persecution in England, where the Book of Common Prayer was enforced as the standard of worship. Those who deviated from the established worship were punished by law. He noted that once safe on the western side of the Atlantic, those who had been persecuted for their own forms of worship now established them as the legal norms, and they themselves punished dissenters. Eventually, however, the American colonies rejected the legal establishment of religion and its modes of worship in favor of the separation of church and state.

Justice Black concluded that formal prayer, as adopted by the New York State Board of Regents, offended the constitutional prohibition against the establishment of religion. He rejected the argument that the prayer's constitutionality was assured by its "nondenominational" character. Instead, he asserted that the "Establishment Clause" had several purposes. He said, "Its first and most immediate purpose rested on the belief that a union of government and religion tends to destroy government and to degrade religion."

He might have argued, as many did later, that the Regents' prayer was evidence that the political process had degraded religion. The prayer, if it can even be called prayer, hardly meets the standards set forth by Jesus in the Sermon on the Mount. Indeed, when Congress conducted hearings about school prayer in 1964, Edwin H. Tuller testified in this vein on behalf of the National Council of Churches: "I live in fear of identifying this [the Regents' prayer] with prayer. Because if the children are taught this prayer, then my teaching that prayer is a vital relationship between the individual and his Creator through Jesus Christ is contrary to that teaching."[4]

Justice Black invoked history in support of his premise that both government and religion suffer when the relationship is too close:

> The history of governmentally established religion, both in England and in this country, showed that whenever government had allied itself with one particular form of religion, the inevitable result had been that it had incurred the hatred, disrespect and even contempt of those who held contrary beliefs. That same history showed that many people had lost their respect for any religion that had relied upon the support of government to spread its faith. The Establishment Clause thus stands as an expression of principle on the part of the Founders of our Constitution that religion is too personal, too sacred, too holy, to permit its "unhallowed perversion" by a civil magistrate.[5]

Preserved from unholy perversion

Justice Black's observation that the separation of church and state preserves religion from unholy perversion contradicts the popular portrait that pictures a humanistic and liberal court banning prayer out of hostility to religion. Justice Black anticipated that the Supreme Court would be accused of such hostility to religion, so he reminded us of the real intent of the Founding Fathers:

> These men knew that the First Amendment, which tried to put an end to governmental control of religion and of prayer, was not written to destroy either. They knew rather that it was written to quiet well-justified fears which nearly all of them felt arising out of an awareness that governments of the past had shackled men's tongues to make them speak only the religious thoughts that government wanted them to speak and to pray only to the God that government wanted them to pray to. It is neither sacrilegious nor antireligious to say that each separate government in this country should stay out of the business of writing or sanctioning official prayers and leave that purely religious function to the people themselves and to those the people choose to look to for religious guidance.[6]

Justice Black insisted that the Establishment Clause is designed to *prevent religious persecution*:

> Another purpose of the Establishment Clause rested upon an awareness of the historical fact that governmentally established religions and religious persecutions go hand in hand. The Founders knew that only a few years after the Book of Common Prayer became the only accepted form of religious services in the established Church of England, an Act of Uniformity was passed to compel all Englishmen to attend those services and to make it a criminal offense to conduct or attend religious gatherings of any other kind—a law which was consistently flouted by dissenting religious groups in England and which contributed to widespread persecutions of people like John Bunyan who persisted in holding "unlawful [religious] meetings . . . to the great disturbance and distraction of the good subjects of this kingdom. . . ." And they knew that similar persecutions

had received the sanction of law in several of the colonies in this country soon after the establishment of official religions in those colonies. It was in large part to get completely away from this sort of systematic religious persecution that the Founders brought into being our Nation, our Constitution, and our Bill of Rights, with its prohibition against any governmental establishment of religion.[7]

To those who pushed for a constitutional amendment to overturn the Supreme Court, the fears of religious persecution arising on the foundation of religious establishments must have seemed unreasonable, especially when compared to the real problems they were trying to correct. Rep. Frank Becker (R-NY) introduced an amendment to the Constitution and repeatedly urged, "The welfare and the entire future of our beloved America depends upon how we handle the most dynamic tradition in our national life—dependence upon Almighty God." Becker's amendment received an endorsement from the Reverend Billy Graham: "We have reaped a whirlwind in delinquency. Young people do not know what is right or wrong any more. Our young people are not being taught moral values; they are at sea morally. . . . I back the Becker amendment."[8]

Billy Graham's logic has been repeated countless times, blaming the Supreme Court for the nation's declining morals. On a monthly basis, widely circulated e-mails repeat the twisted logic that America's moral decline is the result of God being ejected from public schools by the Supreme Court. Few realize how much more absurd the argument has become with the passing of time. If the students were morally depraved at a time when prayer was being offered in the public schools of many states, as Billy Graham contended, then the problem must have been something else. It appears that the Supreme Court has now taken the place that Elvis Presley and rock 'n' roll occupied in a previous generation. It has become the scapegoat for the declining morals of American youth. In light of the social and political upheavals of the 1960s, it is doubtful that any single event or action has shaped American culture; rather, it seems that the cultural shift is broad and deep and would have occurred regardless of how many public schools retained prayer rituals.[9]

Spiritual socialism

The rhetoric attacking the Supreme Court is really nothing more than a transparent effort to shift the blame for declining morals and spirituality from families and churches to the public schools. If public schools are really responsible for the state of American spirituality and morality, then the churches have completely abdicated their responsibility. This sort of attack on public education by the "family values" crowd is, in actuality, a betrayal of the family and the church as the primary transmitters of faith and moral values. Indeed, it smacks of the sort of socialism that so many conservatives criticize in public and state programs—a sort of "spiritual socialism" that ascribes to public institutions responsibility for the transmission of spiritual and moral values.

In his final argument, Justice Black answered the contention that the Regents' prayer is constitutional because it doesn't establish a particular religion. Black argued that such a narrow reading of the First Amendment is inconsistent with the intent of the Framers, who denied the authority of government to establish religion either in general or in particular. In support, Black quoted James Madison: "It is proper to take alarm at the first experiment on our liberties. . . . Who does not see that the same authority which can establish Christianity, in exclusion of all other Religions, may establish with the same ease any particular sect of Christians, in exclusion of all other Sects? That the same authority which can force a citizen to contribute three pence only of his property for the support of any one establishment, may force him to conform to any other establishment in all cases whatsoever?"[10]

Sadly, many church leaders didn't bother to read Justice Black's opinion before publicly criticizing it and accusing the Court of kicking God and prayer out of public schools. This has led to an "experiment" in religious freedom that has produced an entire industry of revisionist history, which has ascribed to the First Amendment a much narrower scope than is clear from its language.[11]

The accusation that the Supreme Court removed God from public schools is not only a distortion of both law and history, it is theologically unsound. God doesn't answer to the Supreme Court and wouldn't submit to the Court's jurisdiction if it did attempt to banish Him from public-school classrooms. Biblically, God is said to dwell in the hearts of believers through His Spirit. God may therefore be seen to be present in public school whenever believers are in public schools. The charge that the Supreme Court eliminated prayer from public schools is equally false. The old quip says it all: "As long as there are math tests, there will be prayer in public school."

Does this mean there are no violations of student rights? Of course not. There have been repeated incidents of teachers and principals unfairly and unreasonably restricting private religious expression and practices even though these expressions are perfectly legal. Yet, such occasional restrictions haven't been given the force of law. By law, students are free to pray in school, to share their faith, to write about their faith in homework assignments, and also to form religion clubs. Students may bring their Bibles to school, say grace before lunch, and pray silently before a test. They may form a Bible-study club to pray with fellow students. It has long been clear that students don't leave their First Amendment rights at the school-house door in the morning. The public school simply is not the "religion-free zone" that critics have suggested.[12]

The attack on the school prayer decision was theologically unsound for another reason: It is doubtful that the Regents' prayer was an authentic form of prayer in the first place. Jesus' definitive teaching about prayer is recorded in Matthew 6. Before giving us the Lord's Prayer as an example, Jesus issued two specific warnings. He warned against "vain repetitions" and against public prayer. Jesus taught us to pray in private instead. One thoughtful religious writer put it this way: "Prayer is the opening of the heart to God, as to a friend."[13]

Edwin H. Tuller, testifying before Congress in 1964 for the National Council of Churches, astutely defined the theological problem in pragmatic terms: "Religious practices that are nonsectarian are too vague and generalized to have much meaning or effect for character development or moral motivation, whereas practices that are specific or demanding enough to effect character or motivation are unacceptable to some and therefore sectarian."[14]

There is a long tradition of formal public prayer—throughout much of Christian history, church and state have existed in a formal alliance. However, the history and tradition of formal public prayer cannot replace sound theology. The Hebrew Scriptures contain several examples of public prayer, but these were offered in the context of a unified believing community, not in a pluralistic environment that is supposed to welcome people of all faiths.[15]

Public-school prayer amendments

Majority religious practices upheld by force of law simply have no place in the American system of religious freedom. Congress considered public-school prayer amendments to the Constitution in the 1960s and again in the 1980s. Both times, our legislators wisely defeated the proposed amendments. While it would be well for public schools to require students to study the debates in Congress, a brief excerpt will have to suffice here. Constitutional law professor Norman Redlich testified on behalf of the American Jewish Congress in 1982. He said,

> I believe that this proposed amendment strikes at the very heart of the basic concepts of religious freedom in this country. I have been fortunate to grow up in a country where there are no preferred religions, where we are all equal before the law, where there are no prescribed religious faiths, or prescribed ceremonies that have the imprimatur of government.
>
> It is no accident that this country alone, among countries, has the kind of commitment that we do, to separation of church and State, and is at the same time the country where religious freedom flourishes as it does nowhere else on Earth.
>
> I do not want to be a religious stranger in this country, and I do not want my children or grandchildren to be religious strangers in this country.
>
> Permit school boards, whether in Brooklyn or in Utah, to adopt prayers of the majority, and have Mormon prayers in Utah, and Jewish prayers in New York, then whether they be Catholics or Protestants or Jews, in some parts of this country they will be religious strangers in their own home. There is no way that cannot be coercive.
>
> If the Establishment Clause was based on any values at all in our history, it was based on the value of neutrality, it was based on the value of no prescribed religious faith, and it was based on the value of no coercion. In those three essential respects, this proposed constitutional amendment violates some of the basic precepts of religious freedom in this country. . . .
>
> Every totalitarian government must do away with religious freedom, because religious freedom recognizes an authority that the government cannot control; that is why every totalitarian State either controls religion, subverts religion, or creates a State religion. It cannot put up with a religion that is free, and not controlled by the State.[16]

While Supreme Court critics have busied themselves demolishing the wall of separation between church and state and seeking to legislate majoritarian religious practices contrary to our nation's constitutional values, they have missed the real significance of the Supreme Court's prayer decision. When religion is separated from state support, it thrives. The Supreme Court gave a gift to the churches, to genuine spirituality, and to religion by refusing to approve state-sponsored religious exercises. Consider just one dramatic example of how this works in real life.

In Ecru, Mississippi, in the 1990s, Lisa Herdahl lent her name to a lawsuit challenging the practice of a devotional prayer and Bible reading at the start of school more than thirty years after the Supreme Court said this was illegal. A federal court issued an injunction halting the practice. In response, the community came up with a plan. They asked the court for permission to allow the students to meet on a voluntary basis in the school gym prior to the official start of the school day. The meeting would be supervised by teachers on a voluntary basis, but they would neither organize nor lead out in the service. The court agreed to permit this form of voluntary devotional activity.

The evangelical news magazine, *World,* ran a follow-up story. *World* reported that a spiritual revival had taken place in the school. Students admitted that when the devotional exercises were broadcast over the loudspeaker, they ignored them. Once it became a matter of personal choice and the students decided whether to participate, they took it seriously.[17] Consider this report:

> Two years after the judge's injunction, about 1,200 of North Pontotoc's 1,300 students are still meeting together to sing, pray, and share Scripture. The students' devotion to the meetings has surprised observers. Stacy Mattingly, a writer who covered the lawsuit and now lives in Ecru while doing research for a book about the proceedings, said, "A lot of people have been shocked by what these students have done. They think of typical American suburban kids and the idea of all that effort just to join together to pray seems unlikely." Jerry Horton, Pontotoc County school superintendent, shares that surprise: "Right at the time of the injunction, with all the media attention, it didn't really surprise me. There were rallies held by the community in support of school prayer where almost the entire community would show up. . . . But now, after all this time, they're still going strong. And you have to remember, it takes considerable effort on their part. Just try getting 1,200 kids to go

anywhere and do anything in an orderly fashion and you know what I mean." The school has divided into two groups for the meetings. The children in grades K–3 meet in one building and grades 4–12 meet in another. The meetings, which are completely led by student volunteers, include Bible readings, skits, readings from devotional books, and songs.[18]

The students in Ecru, Mississippi, can thank both Justice Hugo Black and James Madison for the opportunity to experience spiritual revival unfettered by state-sponsored religious mediocrity. When religion is truly voluntary, it can be genuine and alive. State-sponsored religion tends to be formal. Prior to Lisa Herdahl's lawsuit, students were responsible for planning and conducting the daily devotions. This didn't change. What the lawsuit changed was the nature of attendance: Instead of being compulsory, it became voluntary.

The push for school prayer is both majoritarian and coercive in character. It contradicts our constitutional tradition. The majority simply does not rule when it comes to individual rights. The Constitution protects the individual against the tyranny of the majority.

The compulsory flag salute

In 1943, a generation before the school-prayer case, the Supreme Court addressed a volatile and emotional issue during wartime: the compulsory flag salute. Three years earlier, the Supreme Court had upheld the punishment of Jehovah's Witness parents whose children were expelled from school for refusing, on religious grounds, to salute the flag. The religious objection to saluting the flag hadn't become more popular in the midst of World War II, but, in a swift and stunning reversal, the Court changed direction, declaring, "The very purpose of a Bill of Rights was to withdraw certain subjects from the vicissitudes of political controversy, to place them beyond the reach of majorities and officials and to establish them as legal principles to be applied by the courts. One's right to life, liberty, and property, to free speech, a free press, freedom of worship and assembly, and other fundamental rights may not be submitted to vote; they depend on the outcome of no elections."[19]

The Supreme Court rejected the notion that patriotism required trampling on the rights of individual religious freedom. The language of the Court's decision is inspiring and deserving of a careful read:

To believe that patriotism will not flourish if patriotic ceremonies are voluntary and spontaneous instead of a compulsory routine is to make an unflattering estimate of the appeal of our institutions to free minds. . . . Freedom to differ is not limited to things that do not matter much. That would be a mere shadow of freedom. The test of its substance is the right to differ as to things that touch the heart of the existing order.

If there is any fixed star in our constitutional constellation, it is that no official, high or petty, can prescribe what shall be orthodox in politics, nationalism, religion, or other matters of opinion or force citizens to confess by word or act their faith therein. If there are any circumstances which permit an exception, they do not now occur to us.[20]

Those who value religious freedom ought to jealously guard that freedom against state encroachment and ought to equally resist the temptation to align with the state to prop up religion. America has never subjected religion to majority vote, nor should it do so. Americans don't decide by popular vote whether Jesus is the Messiah, whether Islam is a religion of peace, or whether we should have prayer rituals in public school.

The wisdom of government neutrality to religion was reinforced in my mind by an article that appeared in the Raleigh, North Carolina, *News and Observer* in the 1980s. While attending law school and working with a professor on an article about the separation of church and state, I read a news report that a family had been run out of the nearby town of Dunn, North Carolina, for objecting to Bible teaching in the public school. Their home was destroyed by fire in an apparent arson attack after much public criticism of their "atheism." The newspaper reported that in the public schools in Dunn, the students were taught that each day of Creation was a thousand years. Although I was a stranger in the South, I knew that many if not most of the good citizens of that town didn't believe that each day of Creation was a thousand years. Many of those who protested the loudest would have been shocked and dismayed at what was actually being taught.

Whether they know it or not, those who criticize the Supreme Court's commitment to strict neutrality in religious matters are supporting a system of religious oppression. Tyranny can just as easily arise at the hands of a majority as in a dictatorship. This is why the founding generation insisted on a Bill of Rights. They didn't rely upon assurances that the Constitution provided for a federal government with only limited, delegated powers and no right to intrude on fundamental freedoms. They insisted on securing their freedoms in writing.[21]

The prophecy in the latter half of Revelation 13 says that someday the United States—which is represented in symbol in that chapter—will repudiate its "lamb-like" principles and speak like a dragon. This behavior is confusing. It is deceptive. Our national commitment to human rights and religious freedom is truly in harmony with the Spirit of Christ (i.e., "lamb-like"). It is the erosion of this commitment that will bear the character of the dragon. Sadly, this erosion is well underway.

This passage also warns against the infamous "mark of the beast." Three times the prophecy declares that those who don't conform to the worship enforced by law will be punished—even killed. Those who refuse the mark will be persecuted. The mark of the beast, then, is in principle, about coerced religion. Most Christians miss the warning because they assume the religion involved is distinctly un-Christian either in name or character. They associate it with an antichrist. They miss Jesus' own warning about end-time deceptions in the name of Christ (see Matthew 24:3–5, 11, 23–25). The mark of the beast anticipates a time when—contrary to the genius and character of the religion's Founder, Jesus Himself—popular Christianity is enforced by law.

Instead of seeking to employ the arm of the state to coerce students into practicing religious formality, those who believe in prayer would do well to direct their efforts to teaching the value of truly voluntary religion. Only in this way can we preserve our American legacy of religious freedom.

---

1. "Jimmy"—the author, Rabbi James Rudin—recounts this story in his book *The Baptizing of America: The Religious Rights' Plans for the Rest of Us* (New York: Thunder's Mouth Press, 2006), 23–27.

2. *Engel v. Vitale*, 370 U.S. 421 (1962) (school prayer); and *Abington Township School District v. Schempp*, 374 U.S. 203 (1963) (devotional Bible reading).

3. *Id.*

4. U.S. Congress, House Hearings, *School Prayers*, 1, 667, as cited by Robert S. Alley in *School Prayer: The Court, the Congress and the First Amendment* (Buffalo, N.Y.: Prometheus Books, 1994).

5. *Engel*, 432.

6. *Engel*, 436.

7. *Engel*, 432.

8. Alley, 129.

9. "Prayer rituals" is a better description for public-school religious practices, because they were not, in many if not most cases, consistent with biblical prayer.

10. *Engel*, 436, citing James Madison's "Memorial and Remonstrance."

11. The most scholarly representation of this industry is Robert L. Cord, *Separation of Church and State: Historical Fact and Current Fiction* (Grand Rapids, Mich.: Baker Books, 1988). The most popular may be David Barton, *The Myth of Separation: What Is the Correct Relationship Between Church and State?* (Aledo, Tex.: WallBuilder Press, 1992).

12. See "Religion in the Public Schools, A Joint Statement of Current Law." This document was signed onto by organizations across the religious and political spectrum and represents a true consensus about the law. It runs contrary to much of what people think they know.

13. Ellen G. White, *Steps to Christ* (Washington, D.C.: Review and Herald®, 1956), 93.

14. U.S. Congress, House Hearings, *School Prayers,* 656, 657; as cited in Alley.

15. See, e.g., Solomon's prayer upon the dedication of the temple, 2 Chronicles 6:12–42.

16. Alley, 254.

17. *World* 11, no. 36, February 15, 1997.

18. Ibid.

19. *West Virginia Board of Education v. Barnette,* 319 U.S. 624, 639 (1943).

20. *Id.,* 642, 643.

21. A lot of bad history and rhetoric is being tossed about regarding religious freedom and what our Founding Fathers really intended. The very best historical writing I have found on this topic includes: Edwin S. Gaustad, *Neither King Nor Prelate: Religion and the New Nation, 1776–1826* (Grand Rapids, Mich.: Wm. B. Eerdmans, 1993); Isaac Kramnick and R. Laurence Moore, *The Godless Constitution: A Moral Defense of the Secular State* (New York: W. W. Norton, 2005); Leonard W. Levy, *The Establishment Clause: Religion and the First Amendment,* 2d rev. ed. (Chapel Hill, N.C.: University of North Carolina Press, 1994); William Lee Miller, *The First Liberty: America's Foundation in Religious Freedom* (Washington, D.C.: Georgetown University Press, 2003).

Edwin S. Gaustad is one of the very best scholars on American religious history, and his book on Roger Williams, *Liberty of Conscience: Roger Williams in America,* is highly recommended to those wanting to understand where our First Amendment comes from. Kramnick and Moore are Cornell University scholars; their contribution is based on a sound analysis of colonial history. Leonard Levy's analysis of the origins and meaning of the Establishment Clause is unassailable. William Lee Miller is a University of Virginia scholar who first wrote this for the bicentennial of the Virginia Statute of Religious Freedom.

Barry W. Bussey

CHAPTER 9

The Marriage Debate: The Hidden Danger

For the Christian, the debate about marriage is not a political polemic. It is a debate about what it means to be human—about who we are, where we came from, and where we are going. Our comprehensive worldview begins with a Creator, the One who is the "I AM" and who is also holy, omniscient, omnipresent, and omnipotent. Our epistemology begins with the presupposition that there is "truth" and that one's life is a process of learning the depth and limits of truth. Truth is both revealed and hidden in the ancient text called the Bible and in nature. It is incumbent upon us to seek truth—including the truth about marriage. Marriage itself is a truth—one man, one woman, to the exclusion of all others.

The battle over marriage is one issue in a wider struggle over religious freedom. It involves a clash between the religious and secular individualist worldviews. These views collide in various ways. For example, when the gay community presses for an elementary school curriculum that teaches the equality of same-sex and traditional family structures, religious parents respond by insisting that public schools have no right to undermine and contradict the family's religious beliefs. So, from the Christian perspective, the battle is not simply whether gays and lesbians will be permitted to "marry." At issue is whether the Christian community can continue its religious belief and practice regarding marriage under a new orthodoxy. Of course, the gay community is equally concerned that the reaction against its push for marriage rights will deprive them of whatever gains and rights they have already achieved.

To many, the conflict over marriage appears to be a zero-sum game in which one orthodoxy must eventually prevail over the other. The critical question is whether a synthesis is possible—a coming together of a new ethic of civility among a diversity of views. While such a live-and-let-live approach would provide a welcome resolution to the conflict, if history is any indication, such a compromise is unlikely at best, if not downright impossible. However difficult the task may appear, it is urgent that those on both sides of this conflict extend respect for the opposing view and be satisfied to agree to disagree.

Human nature doesn't seem to tolerate tension between opposing views indefinitely. The pendulum of history tends to move from one extreme to another, as demonstrated by the French and Bolshevik revolutions. Could the antagonism over marriage result in persecution? The risk ought not to be dismissed lightly.

Roland Bainton's study on persecution of Catholics and Protestants[1] established three prerequisites for persecution: The persecutors must believe that they are right, that the issue is important, and that coercion will be effective.[2] In the marriage debate, both the gay-rights and the religious communities appear to possess at least the germ of all three.

In the past, the church has made the mistake of using the levers of state power to enforce doctrine. Today, many Christians perceive that the gay-rights movement seeks to manipulate the levers of state power to enforce their doctrine of rights in a manner that threatens the religious freedom of Christians. The student of prophecy, however, may understand that an even greater threat to religious freedom is described symbolically in Revelation 13. Here, the infamous "mark of the beast" passage describes the eventual enforcement of a religious orthodoxy—not a secular one—and the resulting loss of liberty. If the fulfillment of this prophecy emerges from the present culture warfare—including the battle over marriage—then it follows that the Christian view of marriage will prevail both culturally and legally. However, prophecy omits many details, including how far the secular agenda will swing before the pendulum reverses.

The present secular individualist worldview that supports gay rights is an outgrowth of classic liberalism. To better understand the present conflict over marriage, we must review the development of liberalism and its relationship to religion, assess liberalism's impact on the modern view of marriage, and finally, explore the relevance of Bainton's thesis regarding persecution.

From the ashes of persecution

The freedom of our age is an inheritance from our forefathers. Many of them were thinkers who fought against tyranny with the mighty pen. At first, the struggle was over matters of faith, since the church and monarchy established a symbiotic relationship that restricted individual freedom.

The Protestant Reformation emphasized the free individual conscience. It was "a grand act of emancipation from spiritual tyranny, and a vindication of the sacred rights of conscience in matters of religious belief."[3] Martin Luther proclaimed, " 'No one can command or ought to command the soul, except God, who alone can show it the way to heaven.' 'Belief,' " he said, " 'is a free thing which cannot be enforced.' "[4] Such radical concepts not only reverberated in matters of faith but also in politics. Reformation ideas spawned revolt against the existing order. Monarchs and bishops could no longer act with impunity. Increasingly, amidst persecution and the loss of life, their prerogatives were removed.

Liberal political theorists sought to protect civil society from the ravages of religious bigotry, persecution, and bloodshed that had unfolded during the Reformation era. The ensuing Enlightenment stressed that reason, not religion or superstition, provided the best course for the affairs of humankind.

Liberalism is "the principal philosophical tradition that underlies the Western concept of a liberal democracy."[5] It seeks to provide a basis for civil peace in a political cauldron bubbling with different ideas—allowing for the maximum participation of individuals in society. Charles Larmore describes it as a hope that we can live together without a rule of force even though we disagree about "matters of ultimate significance."[6]

The quest of liberal theory is the rational explanation for the most effective relationship between the individual and the state that permits the greatest potential for self-realization in an atmosphere of civil peace. The consistent application of liberal theory would require a peaceful compromise on the marriage question. Each side should respect the rights of the other, both in law and in public discourse. In the real world, of course, theory and reality often diverge.

The Age of the Enlightenment gave birth to liberalism. In his essay "What Is Enlightenment?" Immanuel Kant maintained, "Enlightenment is man's leaving his self-caused immaturity. Immaturity is the incapacity to use one's intelligence without the guidance of another. . . . Have the courage to use your own intelligence! is therefore the motto of the enlightenment."[7]

Liberalism is not comfortable with feelings or emotions; it distrusts tradition, mystery, and superstition. It is the language we most commonly associate today with science. Liberalism is at odds with religion. Anthony Cook points out that liberalism "sees questions of religious faith as a set of speculative assertions incapable of rational verification or disproof. Liberalism has, then, a structural bias against religious knowledge."[8]

Liberal rationalism has had a profound impact on society and the law. The religious "comprehensive view" is incompatible with an Enlightenment perspective. There is a shift from "the intellect (as a means of understanding the world) to the will (as a means of changing the world)."[9] Law, for the liberal theorist, is not a reflection of reality—what is—as the natural law theorists would have us believe. Rather, it is a means of creating a new world—what can be. Therefore, it becomes possible to use the law to re-create—for example, to change the institution of marriage to whatever configuration reason deems necessary.

Liberalism is primarily concerned with the individual. Liberal thinkers such as Michael Sandel use the term *the unencumbered self* to describe the individual. "We are separate, individual persons, each with our own aims, interests and conceptions of the good, and seek a framework of rights that will enable us to realize our capacity as free moral agents, consistent with a similar liberty for others."[10]

The individual must be free to make up his or her own mind about what constitutes the good life. Liberal thinkers insist that the state must not interfere with individual choice. Current liberal thought also contends that religious communities cannot interfere with individual choice—even if those individuals are volunteer members of such communities.[11]

The liberal envisions a state that is neutral on the issue of what constitutes the good life.[12] The state has no role when it comes to religion—it doesn't favor one religion over another nor does it promote religion. Liberalism sees itself "as a *procedural* theory; a mechanism or process for doing justice among individuals with differing conceptions of the good, rather than as a *substantive* conception of the good in its own right."[13]

Liberal theory seeks to marginalize the role of religion. "The learned have their superstitions, prominent among them a belief that superstition is evaporating," noted Garry Wills. "Since science has explained the world in secular terms, there is no more need for religion, which will wither away."[14] Religion is seen as the negation of the liberal rationalistic goal; the antagonist to the liberal quest.

Lucinda Peach gives three reasons why "religious lawmaking" or religious influence in public policy is problematic: (1) the coercive character of law—unbelievers are alienated and forced to act against their will, creating divisiveness; (2) the character of religion—only those of the faith understand it, and followers tend to be zealous, not respecting democracy, modern pluralism, or gender equality; and (3) the effect of the interaction of law and religion in a morally and religiously pluralistic polity is to favor the majority religious group at the expense of others.[15]

The liberal solution is to keep religion in the private sphere. Liberalism contends that religious arguments have no place in public policy. John Rawls maintained that "citizens realize that they cannot reach agreement or even approach mutual understanding on the basis of their irreconcilable comprehensive doctrines."[16] He advocates the use of "public reason"— "the basic moral and political values that are to determine a constitutional democratic government's relation to its citizens and their relation to one another."[17]

The prevailing view is that whatever justification is given for the public policy, it must be "reasonable"—in other words, rational and not subject to any religious or ideological argument.[18] It would be bad taste, according to Richard Rorty, "to bring religion into discussions of public policy."[19] "We shall not be able to keep a democratic political community going," he argues, "unless the religious believers remain willing to trade privatization for a guarantee of religious liberty."[20]

The net result is that religious people are free as long as they don't venture on the public stage. The problem is that over time, society changes its definition of *public*—it moves the goalposts. For some, as soon as religious communities get involved in such "public" areas as running a school or a hospital, then they must follow the values of society and not their own ethics. For example, in running a school, they argue, a church shouldn't be permitted to hire only members of its faith community to teach. The reasoning is that even though it is a private church school, the church is now working in the public sphere and it must be nondiscriminatory. When such reasoning is applied to the issue of same-sex marriage, it becomes clear why the gay community is so adamant that religious communities stay out of the "public" issue of marriage.

Having looked at liberalism and its view of the role of religion in society, we now turn our attention to liberalism's impact on the modern view of marriage.

The modern evolution of marriage

John Witte Jr. points out that the Western tradition of marriage received its foundation from two streams of thought—Christianity and the Enlightenment. These streams have provided us with four perspectives:

1. Marriage as a contract—as determined by the couple
2. Marriage as a spiritual association—subject to the teachings of the religious community
3. Marriage as a social estate—with laws of property and inheritance and expectations of the community
4. Marriage as a natural institution—subject to natural laws as understood by reason and conscience[21]

In Genesis, marriage is presented as a creation of God for man and woman to be fruitful and multiply, raising their children to love and serve God. Human intimacy in marriage reflects the image of God. After sin, and because of its presence, marriage also became a remedy for lust. Thus, marriage was of a natural origin.

Roman Catholicism emphasized marriage as a natural, contractual, and sacramental unit. As a sacrament, marriage represents the union of Christ and His church, and it confers sanctifying grace upon the two Christians. As a result, the church claimed sole jurisdiction over the institution—over its formation, maintenance, and dissolution. Though a sacrament, marriage was not considered the highest state. Celibacy took preeminence. The servants of the church, such as clerics, were to answer to a higher calling and forsake marriage. Witte notes that the Council of Trent in 1563 codified marriage law, including the solemnization of marriage that required parental consent, two witnesses, civil registration, and church consecration.[22]

Protestants rejected the notion of marriage as a sacrament. They perceived marriage from a practical perspective as a social institution for which the civil state was responsible. Clergy would act as state agents in solemnizing marriage. Celibacy had no virtue and led only to sexual perversions. In other respects, Protestants shared the Catholic understanding of marriage as a natural unit for procreation and mutual well-being and as a contractual arrangement of consenting parties of one man and one woman. Witte points out that Protestant Europe opened the door to divorce in the modern sense on the grounds of not only adultery but desertion, cruelty, or frigidity; with a right to remarry for the innocent party.[23]

Christianity made the most significant impact on the Western legal tradition regarding marriage. In America, jurists have looked back on the religious traditions to find the meaning of marriage. Jurist and legal historian Joseph Story noted:

> Marriage is treated by all civilized societies as a peculiar and favored contract. It is in its origin a contract of natural law. . . . It is the parent, and not the child of society; the source of civility and a sort of seminary of the republic. In civil society it becomes a civil contract, regulated and prescribed by law, and endowed with civil consequences. In most civilized countries, acting under a sense of the force of sacred obligations, it has had the sanctions of religion superadded. It then becomes a religious, as well as a natural and civil contract. . . . It is a great mistake to suppose that because it is the one, therefore it may not be the other.[24]

In the series of antipolygamy cases of the nineteenth century, the U.S. Supreme Court viewed marriage as more than a "mere contract." In *Maynard v. Hill* (1888) the Court declared:

> Whilst marriage is often termed . . . a civil contract, generally to indicate that it must be founded upon the agreement of the parties, and does not require any religious ceremony for its solemnization—it is something more than a mere contract. The consent of the parties is of course essential to its existence, but when the contract to marry is executed by marriage, a relation between the parties is created which they cannot change. Other contracts may be modified, restricted, or enlarged, or entirely released upon the consent of the parties. Not so with marriage. The relation once formed, the law steps in and holds the parties to various obligations and liabilities. It is an institution, in the maintenance of which in its purity the public is deeply interested, for it is the foundation of the family and society, without which there would be neither civilization nor progress.[25]

In the British tradition, the foundation of American common law, the situation is similar. In a polygamy case involving a marriage in the Utah Territory of the United States that became a matter of litigation in the United Kingdom, the House of Lords quoted the following with approval:

But marriage is one and the same thing substantially all the Christian world over. Our whole law of marriage assumes this; and it is important to observe that we regard it as a wholly different thing—a different status—from Turkish or other marriages among infidel nations, because we clearly should never recognise the plurality of wives, and consequent validity of second marriages, standing the first, which second marriages the laws of those countries authorise and validate. *This cannot be put on any rational ground, except our holding the infidel marriage to be something different from the Christian, and our also holding the Christian marriage to be the same everywhere.*[26]

Enlightenment thinkers rejected the theological basis of marriage. They regarded it as a "voluntary bargain struck between two married persons."[27] God, nature, and religion had nothing to do with it. Two individuals decided for themselves what the limits, expectations, and responsibilities were for their arrangement. In essence, it would be a pure contract with no religious significance.

Such thinking led to the different waves of reform over the last century. In the late nineteenth and early twentieth centuries, marriage laws were revised to provide women the right to own property. In the 1960s, reforms permitted no-fault divorce—allowing couples to dissolve their marriages without the usual rancor of having to establish adultery. No-fault divorce was meant to bring civility to contentious and often violent marriage breakdowns.

The extent to which the Enlightenment has transformed the legal definitions of marriage can be seen in Canada. That country, with its strong Christian heritage, has historically regarded marriage as involving one man and one woman. Now, however, through a series of judicial decisions, marriage has been defined as a union of "any two persons." It has concluded that modern legal thought entirely rejects the Christian norm of marriage. The Canadian Supreme Court was not impressed with the words "in Christendom"[28] that previous courts used to describe marriage:

The reference to "Christendom" is telling. *Hyde* spoke to a society of shared social values where marriage and religion were thought to be inseparable. This is no longer the case. Canada is a pluralistic society. Marriage, from the perspective of the state, is a civil institution. The "frozen concepts" reasoning runs contrary to one of the most fundamental principles of Canadian constitutional interpretation: that our Constitution is a living tree which, by way of progressive interpretation, accommodates and addresses the realities of modern life.[29]

Witte observed that marriage has taken the form of a Hegelian dialectic. Christian norms squared off against Enlightenment norms of private choice and contract, and the Enlightenment prevailed. "Thesis gave way to antithesis."[30] The question is whether this synthesis will be challenged by a new antithesis, such as marriage among more than two persons of whatever gender. There doesn't appear to be a logical basis for restricting marriage to two persons, hence the possibility of additional permutations can't be dismissed. If marriage is ultimately about contract and the notion of "committed love," it may be impossible to limit the number of parties who can enter into a contract and profess such love.

The debate about same-sex marriage is not an isolated one. It is the culmination of a long process of modernization—"the spread of technical rationality."[31] We are living in a time when society has focused on satisfying individual desires as efficiently as possible—much the same way a machine or a computer can perform its functions efficiently. The technological advances of our era have spawned the notion that our bodies are machines to be used in whatever capacity the imagination proposes. Each individual is the master of his or her own body and destiny. We don't have to be limited by the physical framework of the body, by societal mores, or by some metaphysical understanding as to how the body ought to be used. It is an age of hyperindividualism in which the individual has become the monarch of his or her domain.

The very existence of a public debate on redefining marriage is evidence of the potency of this new orthodoxy. For nearly two thousand years, the Christian marriage ethic stood unchallenged. Today, it has become an anachronism, at least in some circles. Tomorrow, it may be a heresy.

Modernity's pursuit of the triumph of science over religion, rationalizing all of life to the most efficient means of satisfying personal desire, is proving problematic with respect to marriage breakdown. Divorce has the greatest impact on the most vulnerable—women and children. Children today are more apt to be separated from their fathers than in any previous generation.[32]

Fractured family units also experience greater financial stress. The problem of divorce has led to a discussion of marriage renewal.

Don Browning contends that marriage needs to be renewed within the context of modernization.[33] He proposes a project that begins with Christianity's "seeds of excellence"[34] but also involves the "contributions of many faiths, many philosophies, many disciplines, and many sectors of society."[35] Backed by scientific, legal, and sociological analysis, participants from the groups that make up Western pluralist society would contribute from their traditions those elements most helpful for dealing with the problems of marriage. The goal would be to develop a new model of marriage grounded in the technical, rational enterprise of seeking the most efficient means to an end. Church and state would partner to implement this new model. State education would be required prior to entering into marriage, much like driver training is now compulsory for new drivers. Thus, the technical, rational enterprise of seeking the most efficient means to an end would be harnessed for a social good—the improvement of marriage.

Browning's proposal is easy to dismiss. It is difficult to imagine that in our individualistic age, people would accept advice from a state-sponsored authority on how to best live their lives—especially in such a sensitive institution as marriage. Consider, for example, the report from British Prime Minister Tony Blair's government on the family that suggested several state measures to support the traditional family, including a role in marriage education. The political pressure overwhelmed the government: "The British government has all but abandoned that position, acknowledging in a recent position paper that there were many alternatives to the classic family structure."[36]

Given the current climate, such a vision of marriage renewal seems remote. Yet, just as the RMS *Titanic* plowed through dark waters at full steam, blind to the danger ahead, our own society may be ignoring danger signs with respect to marriage.

The persecutor and the persecuted

Arguments about sexuality bring out the worst in people, observes Michael McConnell. He says, "Advocates lose their sense of balance and moderation. Self-righteousness abounds. Excessive attention is paid to the perceived sins of others. . . . Advocates on both sides are all too ready to seize the weapons of state power to stigmatize their foes and to inculcate their chosen positions in the children of the next generation."[37]

Because the marriage debate is so volatile, it is all the more necessary to guard against every attempt to seek conversion by means of state coercion. Roland Bainton's study of persecution between Catholics and Protestants has important lessons for the marriage conflict today. It appears that both the gay and religious communities display the essential prerequisites for persecution should either community gain sufficient power to enforce their view.[38] Emotionally charged controversies such as same-sex marriage tend to dim rational response. Ordinarily reasonable people are prone to taking irrational positions when they fear their entire sociological, religious, and cultural framework is threatened.

Many suppose that Western democracies couldn't succumb to extreme violations of human rights. Our society prides itself on its commitment to civility and justice.[39] However, people forget that Western liberal democracies are merely fragile experiments in human affairs that need protection. Any number of forces could sideline the niceties of civilization in the struggle for survival. Consider the aftermath of September 11, and the ease with which citizens yielded personal liberty and due process of law in the interest of fighting terrorism.

When law no longer has the support of the public at large, it becomes unenforceable. As Cass Sunstein observed, the United States Supreme Court could rule in *Lawrence v. Texas*[40] that antisodomy laws are unconstitutional because the law "had become hopelessly out of touch with existing social convictions."[41] Marriage laws that deny recognition to same-sex marriage will maintain legitimacy only as long as there is public support. Courts don't follow public opinion polls per se, but judges are members of society, and social changes tend to shift judges' views on anachronistic laws.[42] Obviously, such a position is not without its critics.[43]

The point is this: Eventually, the law will reflect whichever side of the marriage debate is consistent with the majority view. When the traditional religious view of marriage prevailed in society, homosexual conduct remained a criminal offense in some states. It wasn't until 2003 with the Supreme Court's decision in *Lawrence v. Texas* that the law changed to protect the right of same-sex adults to engage in consensual sexual activities. In other words, we are in the midst of the pendulum swing. If the gay-marriage position gains the same social acceptance as the religious view once had, the law may well treat traditional religious views of marriage as unlawfully discriminatory. It is by no means certain that a new majority will tolerate dissenting moral views of marriage from a religious minority, any more than the religious consensus tolerated homosexuality or gay marriage.

Wendy Becker and Mary Norton of Rhode Island went to Massachusetts to be married. They were denied a license because of a 1913 Massachusetts law that doesn't permit out-of-state couples to marry if the union would be "void if contracted" in their home state. They filed a court challenge. On September 29, 2006, Judge Thomas E. Connolly ruled that since Rhode Island has no law against same-sex marriage, the state of Massachusetts must issue marriage licenses to same-sex couples from Rhode Island. Speaking to reporters after the court decision was handed down, Becker, a social work professor, noted, "It's ridiculous that there's this incredibly important institution that some people can't be part of. That's so blatantly unfair."[44]

The Enlightenment prepared the philosophical foundation for the argument that marriage is merely a contract between two consenting persons. The gay community has seized upon this contractual approach to marriage. Adopting a secularist approach to law, gay-rights advocates contend that existing legal restraints on gay marriage unfairly restrict access to an important institution.

"I do happen to think," said Martha McCarthy, a prominent gay-rights lawyer in Canada, "that this is a subject where there isn't a grey area. You either agree that gay marriage is required as part of our commitment to equality or you're a bigot."[45]

"Bigotry laundered by religion and wedge politics," said Bill Kaufmann, speaking of Canadian Prime Minister Harper's call for a revote on the issue of marriage, "is a tough addiction to break."[46]

The gay community has effectively changed public opinion on the subject of equality. "Someone who thinks gays and lesbians are inferior human beings," says McCarthy, "[demonstrates] the same kind of thinking that put Rosa Parks at the back of the bus. There's no difference."[47]

Harvey Cox argued that as long as religion is kept private and in its place, then secularization will have "no serious interest in persecuting religion. Secularization simply bypasses and undercuts religion and goes on to other things. It has relativized religious world-views and thus rendered them innocuous."[48]

However, same-sex marriage, more than any other issue in recent times, has galvanized the religious community. In fact, members of that community reject the privatization of religion in return for "religious freedom," considering such a social contract a "pact with the devil." They see their absence from public policy as an important factor in the moral decline of society that led to the demand for same-sex marriage.

"Evil has a way of overreaching," noted influential religious leader James Dobson, "and that appears to have happened regarding the blatant lawless attack on marriage and biblical morality. In a strange way, the threats we are facing today could be the vehicle for a revitalized church. It is an exciting thing to watch."[49]

The religious community is not impressed with arguments that marriage is a civil contract in which any two people may participate regardless of gender. For the religious, there is a historical reality spanning millennia that has said otherwise. Part of that reality is the sacred text that teaches that marriage has a divine origin.

The Genesis account of Creation has God making human beings in His image and says that He made them male and female. Jesus endorsed the biblical view of marriage, teaching that a man could not divorce his wife except on grounds of adultery. The Bible establishes a clear sexual ethic, restricting sexual intimacy to marriage and forbidding extramarital relations of all kinds, including homosexual practices.

For the religious community, any deviance from the ideal only courts disaster. The taunts and jeers that they are bigoted, while unwelcome, are seen within the larger context of human history. Jeff Jacoby, in a *Boston Globe* editorial, noted, "It is not bigotry to try to learn from history, or to point out that some institutions have stood the test of time because they are the only ones that *can* stand the test of time."[50]

In the 1960s, it was a common assumption that secularization would eliminate the need for religious belief. Human beings would control their own destiny without the aid of the metaphysical. That assumption appears premature. Religious belief is more important than ever. Consider, for example, the effect of gay marriage on politics. According to Geoffrey Layman, moral issues such as gay marriage have polarized the Republican and Democratic parties and are key to understanding the split of religious voters. Now, the religious voter is more apt to support the Republican than the Democratic party.[51]

Both the gay community and the religious community are fully convinced that they are on the right side of the debate, that their position is the *only* position. This fulfills Bainton's first prerequisite for persecution with respect to both communities.

The second of Bainton's prerequisites for persecution pertains to the importance of the issue. Marriage is of paramount importance to both communities. The religious community believes that the very survival of civilization is at stake; while the gay community is fighting for equal status with the heterosexual majority.

Despite this apparent conflict of values, David Corbett insists that "there is no true 'collision of values' between religion and sexual orientation." Instead,

> there is a struggle to protect our public policy from being infused with religious ideals for the purpose of denying a particular and disapproved group their equal place within Canadian society. The conflict is real, of course—but it is not a conflict between lesbians and gay men and various religions. It is a conflict between the fundamental principles of our secular state—the Rule of Law, the principle of equality, and the primacy of the Constitution on the one hand, and a religiously based negative animus against homosexuality on the other. On the basis of first principles, the resolution of this conflict is a simple matter in law. The real question is whether we have the political will to defend our fundamental principles when to do so will be unpopular in some quarters.[52]

Corbett asserts two contradictory propositions. He insists that "public policy" shouldn't take sides in debates between religions, between those who are religious and those who are not. Instead public policy must "preclude attacks on some groups for religious reasons."[53] Yet, he violates this very premise by demanding that "public policy" take sides to defend what he regards as the "fundamental secular values of our society." He insists that "the state and the courts have a duty to take sides to defend the basic principles of our society."[54] In so doing, he demonizes those with a religious view of marriage as enemies of the fundamental principles of the secular state.

In a brief to the Massachusetts Supreme Court on a question concerning the *Goodridge v. Department of Public Health*[55] decision, the Gay and Lesbian Advocate and Defenders (GLAD) argued that it was only by allowing the plaintiffs access to marriage that they will "be understood to share the love and commitment of spouses, and all the protections, benefits and obligations that flow from that culturally unique status."[56]

The secularist presumption that all religious values must be expunged from public policy to gain that elusive goal of equality, as Corbett appears to advocate, is unworkable. Even John Rawls recognizes an "overlapping consensus" between "fundamental secular values" and religious values that public policy ought to defend, such as honesty and integrity. To deny a place in law or public policy to any value with a religious basis would negate much of existing law.[57]

Consider the notion of human dignity, which is the underlying basis for equality claims. Professor Lorne Sossin observes that respecting human dignity requires a "leap of faith" because it is subjective and nonrational in origin and cannot be measured, weighed, or counted.[58] Nevertheless, concepts of human dignity have made a tremendous contribution to our understanding of human rights. Secularist advocates of human dignity tend to overlook its religious origins: "Love thy neighbour as thyself," and "Do unto others what you would have others do unto you." Human dignity and equality are values shared equally by secular human-rights advocates and those with a foundation in religious faith.

If there is to be any solution to the conflict over marriage short of a winner-take-all approach, it must be based on achieving mutual respect between the religious and secularist perspectives. The gay community claims that as the basic principle in the issue of marriage, equality is of utmost importance. It is a value that the state must protect.

The religious community approaches the issue differently. "To put it succinctly," argues James Dobson, "the institution of marriage represents the very foundation of human social order. Everything of value sits on that base. . . . When it is weakened or undermined, the entire superstructure begins to wobble."[59] The religious community vilified the Massachusetts Supreme Court decision regarding gay marriage. "This decision," said Brian Fahling, senior trial attorney for the American Family Association Center for Law & Policy, "is on an order of magnitude that is beyond the capacity of words. The court has tampered with society's DNA, and the consequent mutation will reap unimaginable consequences for Massachusetts and our nation."[60]

The courts have felt the brunt of religious criticism on the rise of gay rights. For example, commenting on a Canadian case upholding the inclusion in elementary school curriculum of instruction about gay families, Father Alphonse de Valk proclaimed, "The judiciary has divided the country more than ever. Those who think that the Christian community and even other religious communities in this country will ever accept the sodomite lifestyle as normal and legitimate are pursuing an illusion. Just as the Catholic community cannot, and will not, accept the legitimacy of killing the unborn, so, too, it cannot and will not condone sodomy. The courts are alienating many Canadians and providing them with new reasons for a complete overhaul of law and politics."[61] Bainton's second prerequisite for persecution is that the issue must be sufficiently important. Clearly, both communities regard the issue of marriage as supremely important.

His third and final prerequisite for the development of persecution is that it prove to be effective. Recent and ongoing legal skirmishes demonstrate that both sides look to the law to enforce their own values regarding marriage. The gay community has already felt the sting of legal prohibition and intends to gain full legal acceptance. The religious community fears that such legal acceptance will result in secular persecution.

Law professor Bruce MacDougall argues that there is a three-step process for a marginalized group, such as the gay community, to obtain full equality—compassion, condonation, and celebration.[62] If any of those elements are missing, the group might have partial equality but not complete legal equality.

The process begins with the growing belief in society at large that members of the group shouldn't be discriminated against. In other words, they must begin to feel compassion. Condonation involves the extension of legal benefits to members of the group. The final step in the group's social assimilation is celebration. In this final step, the group is allowed to flourish in society as a benefit to the whole because its legal status is fully protected. The gay community believes that this step will be achieved only when gay marriage is permitted.

The gay community takes exception to those who aren't willing to "celebrate" their presence. Equating the discrimination they suffer to racial discrimination, they urge the adoption of laws not only to protect their rights but also to re-educate society on the need to value their inclusion. Reforming public-school curriculum is therefore of great importance to the gay community.

"Although religious individuals may find it hard to put their religious beliefs aside when they enter the public sphere, . . ." Professor Robert Wintemute observed, "a liberal democracy cannot function in any other way. This also means that religious individuals who accept employment in the public sector cannot insist on being exempted from serving LGBT individuals or same-sex couples, whether this involves selling them stamps, teaching them, or a few years from now, marrying them."[63]

Professor MacDougall stated, "Religious ideology cannot be used to determine what people who are not of that religion can do or how they should lead their lives."[64] The problem, of course, is that in a pluralistic society religious ideology ought to be given the same right as any other ideology in advancing a position in the public discourse, because it is in that process of deliberative democracy that society is able to establish its norms.

However, MacDougall doesn't end there. He goes on to say, "In my opinion, it should not even be used to judge those who are of that religious persuasion. Even children being raised in a particular religious tradition should not be exposed to ideology that excludes and refuses to accommodate homosexuality in their education. The state has an interest in all education of the young, and this ideal should prevail."[65]

The recent Joint Committee on Human Rights report of the British parliament appears to agree with that sentiment. The report argued that religious objections to school curriculum dealing with homosexuality shouldn't be recognized. There is increasing political pressure for religious schools to be forced to adopt the new curriculum.[66] The reform effort doesn't stop with religious schools. Even the everyday language used by various professional groups is being challenged. In Scotland, health professionals are being admonished not to use the homophobic language of "husband" and "wife," nor, when talking to children, to use the terms of "mother" or "father."[67]

In their search for wider acceptance in the community, the gay community sees as very positive any kind of government support meant to bring about societal change—whether through the judiciary or government agencies. For many it is a matter of proper education: As the lifestyle becomes more familiar, it becomes more acceptable to society at large. For example, studies show that individuals are more likely to support gay rights if they know someone who is openly lesbian or gay.[68] The more they and their positions are known, the less discrimination they suffer. As Carlos A. Ball noted, "The national debate engendered by the same-sex marriage cases has contributed to progress in all of these areas because the marriage issue has increased the visibility of lesbians and gay men in ways that no other gay rights issue had done before. The cases have, in effect, helped to humanize lesbians and gay men by encouraging (at least some) skeptical

Americans to better understand the full lives of those with a same-gender sexual orientation."[69]

So, the gay community sees the use of state action as a very effective tool for educating the citizenry as to their plight—even if that means education for those who don't want to be educated.

The religious community sees the debate over gay marriage as a part of the larger gay-rights movement, including the issue of adoption by gays. Extending rights to gays is believed to threaten the breakdown of the traditional family. The Catholic bishop of the Scottish diocese of Paisley wrote a pastoral letter concerning the British government's decision not to exempt Catholic adoption agencies from the sexual orientation regulations that allow for gay adoption. "Something sinister" is happening in Britain, he maintained. "For the first time in the modern era in this country, the Catholic Church is facing the prospect of being forced to act against her faith and against her convictions, or else face legal challenge and possible prosecution."[70] And Bishop Elio Sgreccia, president of the Pontifical Academy for Life, stated, "Affluence, prosperity, aspiration and a pervasive spirit of relativism may tempt some to set aside the principles and values of the Catholic faith and life. . . . This unfortunate episode may well herald the beginning of a new and uncertain time for the Catholic Church in the United Kingdom."[71]

Stanley Fish argues that the secular liberal and the religious person are both rational but start from different presuppositions. Says Fish, "While two persons proceeding within opposing faiths might perform identical operations of logical entailment, they will end up in completely different places because it is from different (substantive) places that they began."[72] He continues, "The religious person should not seek an accommodation with liberalism; he should seek to rout it from the field, to extirpate it, root and branch."[73]

Many observers have noted the impact the religious community has had on the Bush administration and its policy. For example, President Bush was strongly influenced by the religious community to support the constitutional amendment prohibiting gay marriage.[74] The ire of the Religious Right is often directed at the judiciary, seeing the courts as a greater threat than terrorist groups. Kevin Phillips quotes James Dobson: "Very few people know this, that the Congress can simply disenfranchise a court. They don't have to fire anybody or impeach them or go through that battle. All they have to do is say the Ninth Circuit doesn't exist anymore, and it's gone."[75]

The twentieth century is not without its "Hall of Shame" of religious communities in the West supporting government policy. One extreme example is that of the bishop of London, A. F. Winnington-Ingram, who called the British role in World War I against Germany "a great crusade." In speaking to *The Guardian,* he said, "You ask for my advice in a sentence as to what the church is to do. I answer MOBILIZE THE NATION FOR A HOLY WAR."[76]

Obviously, such a position is extreme. There is no group or individual in the religious mainstream in the West that is even contemplating the idea of violent revolution to advance a religious position against the secularization of our society and turning back to traditional marriage. However, there are voices raising some very serious accusations about our democratic institutions. Robert P. George, for example, has criticized secularization and "the judicial usurpation of politics" wherein equality-in-dignity of all human beings[77] is not being supported: "It weakens the citizens' reasons for giving their loyalty or allegiance to the regime. In a word, it *weakens,* even if it does not destroy, a regime's *legitimacy.*"[78]

There is a hidden danger in the marriage debate that arises from the profound sense of alienation experienced by both the gay and religious communities. This alienation can result in an escalation of the conflict over marriage. The prerequisites that Bainton identified appear to be in place for one group or another to gain the upper hand and introduce persecution either by legal means or by using violence as a means to support their cause.

Conclusion

The marriage debate may be the most contentious issue in public policy today. Traditional marriage is being buffeted by the claims of secular liberal thought that each person has the capacity to decide for himself or herself what marriage will be. Neither church nor state has the authority or legitimacy to define marriage for the modern individual. Of course, such logic doesn't rest upon the recognition of gay marriage alone, as former Senator Rick Santorum publicly observed—only to be vilified for stating the obvious.[79] If the state cannot define marriage, than any combination of persons of any age must attain legal status.

An added problem with this logic is the willingness to use the state to enforce a secular liberal definition of marriage on all of society—even on religious communities that do not hold such views. It is clear that secularists are willing to build upon the logic of a United States Supreme Court decision denying tax-exempt status to Bob Jones University because its policies forbidding students from dating interracially conflicted with the values of civil rights and equality.[80] If and when advocates of a secularist approach to marriage win the battle, a similar claim to the preeminence of equality will be employed to deprive the clergy of the right to refuse to perform marriages that conflict with their religious beliefs. Churches that continue to teach doctrines that conflict with the new legal and moral consensus will also be deprived of their privileges, beginning with tax exemption. Respect for equality will demand that all conform to the new orthodoxy.

So, it is no wonder that the religious community has fought against this trend, multiplying marriage amendments to state constitutions and a federal Defense of Marriage Act as well.[81] The effort is intended to preserve intact the definition of marriage as between one man and one woman.

Ironically, if a compromise is achieved, liberal theory will have to make a substantial contribution: It must contribute the principle that the law must respect every individual's rights to his or her own beliefs—even those that differ deeply from those of much of the rest of society. The contours of such a compromise, however improbable, can be readily discerned. It would begin with the recognition that marriage is not a creature of the state but is first and foremost a religious institution. As such, the state doesn't have the authority to change its definition. To do so would be to intrude on the realm of religion and place the state on holy ground, where it doesn't belong. While the state has no right to change the definition of marriage, however, it does have an obligation to provide legal protection to all its citizens.

The church, on the other hand, would publicly defend the right of gays to participate in religious wedding services and to receive a legal status for those relationships, although not as "marriage." By taking the moral high ground in advocating for the rights of conscience, it has the potential to create a much stronger legal basis for protecting its own freedom. It is equally true that the secularist agenda can establish a much stronger basis for gay rights by recognizing that all rights are interconnected and that it cannot build up the rights of gays by tearing down the right of religious freedom. If the secularists would publicly advocate the rights of conscience and respect for the "Christian heresy" that opposes gay marriage, they would seize the moral high ground and create a stronger climate to legitimize their own position.

In the end, it is unlikely that moderation will prevail in either camp. Neither side seems ready to recognize that liberty of conscience cannot be secured for one group alone. The risk remains that the veneer of civility could be swiftly peeled back to reveal the persecuting spirit of those who know they are right, believe their issue is critical, and are convinced that coercion is worth the risk.

---

1. Roland H. Bainton, *The Travail of Religious Liberty* (New York: Harper, 1958).

2. Bainton, 17, quoted in Barry G. Hankins, "Religious Coercion in a Postmodern Age," *Journal of Church and State* 1 (1997): 5.

3. Philip Schaff, *History of the Christian Church: Modern Christianity: The German Reformation*, vol. 7, 2d ed. (New York: Charles Scribner's Sons, 1910), 50.

4. Schaff, 59.

5. Rex Ahdar and Ian Leigh, *Religious Freedom in the Liberal State* (Oxford: Oxford University Press, 2005), 38.

6. Charles Larmore, "Political Liberalism," *Political Theory* 18 (1990): 339, 357; as quoted in Ahdar and Leigh, 39.

7. Immanuel Kant, "What Is the Enlightenment?" as quoted in A. J. Conyers, *The Long Truce: How Toleration Made the World Safe for Power and Profit* (Dallas: Spence Publishing, 2001), 174.

8. Anthony Cook, "God-Talk in a Secular World," *Yale J Law & Hum* 6 (1994): 435, 436; as quoted in Ahdar and Leigh, 41.

9. Conyers, 173.

10. Michael Sandel, ed., *Liberalism and Its Critics* (New York: NYU Press, 1985), 4, 5; as quoted in Ahdar and Leigh, 40.

11. Quoted in Ahdar and Leigh, 51.

12. Ronald Dworkin, "Liberalism," in Stuart Hampshire, ed., *Public and Private Morality* (Cambridge: Cambridge University Press, 1977), 127; as quoted in Ahdar and Leigh, 42: "Government must be neutral on what might be called the question of the good life; . . . political decisions must be, so far as is possible, independent of any particular conception of the good life, or of what gives value to life. Since the citizens of a society differ in their conceptions, the government does not treat them as equals if it prefers one conception to another, either because the officials believe that one is intrinsically superior, or because it is held by the more numerous or more powerful group."

13. Quoted in Ahdar and Leigh, 43.

14. Garry Wills, *Under God: Religion and American Politics* (New York: Simon & Schuster, 1990), 15.

15. See Lucinda Peach, *Legislating Morality: Pluralism and Religious Identity in Lawmaking* (Oxford: Oxford University Press, 2002), 16–36.

16. John Rawls, "The Idea of Public Reason Revisited," *University of Chicago Law Review* 64 (Summer 1997): 765, 766.

17. Rawls, 766.

18. Rawls, *Political Liberalism* (New York: Columbia University Press, 2005), 224, 225: "On matters of constitutional essentials and basic justice, the basic structure and its public policies are to be justifiable to all citizens, as the principle of political legitimacy

requires. We add to this that in making these justifications we are to appeal only to presently accepted general beliefs and forms of reasoning found in common sense, and the methods and conclusions of science when these are not controversial. . . . As far as possible, the knowledge and ways of reasoning that ground our affirming the principles of justice . . . are to rest on the plain truths now widely accepted, or available, to citizens generally."

19. Richard Rorty, *Philosophy and Social Hope* (London: Penguin, 2000), 169; as quoted in Jonathan Chaplin, "Beyond Liberal Restraint: Defending Religiously Based Arguments in Law and Public Policy," *University of British Columbia Law Review* 33, no. 2 (2000): 626.

20. Ibid., 627.

21. John Witte Jr., "Retrieving and Reconstructing Law, Religion, and Marriage in the Western Tradition," in Steven M. Tipton and John Witte Jr., eds., *Family Transformed: Religion, Values, and Society in American Life* (Washington, D.C.: Georgetown University Press, 2005), 244.

22. Ibid., 247.

23. Ibid., 249.

24. Joseph Story, *Commentaries on the Conflict of Laws, Foreign and Domestic: In Regard to Contracts, Rights, and Remedies and Especially in Regard to Marriages, Divorces, Wills, Successions, and Judgements,* 2d ed. (Boston: Hillard Gray and Co., 1834), §. 108; as paraphrased in Tipton and Witte, 252.

25. *Maynard v. Hill,* 125 U.S. 190, 210, 211; as quoted in Tipton and Witte, 253.

26. *Hyde v. Hyde and Woodmansee* (1866) All E.R. Rep. Div. 175, at 17; emphasis added.

27. Tipton and Witte, 254.

28. *Hyde,* L.R. 1 P. & D. 130, at 133: "What, then, is the nature of this institution as understood in Christendom? Its incidents may vary in different countries, but what are its essential elements and invariable features? If it be of common acceptance and existence, it must needs (however varied in different countries in its minor incidents) have some pervading identity and universal basis. I conceive that marriage, as understood in Christendom, may for this purpose be defined as the voluntary union for life of one man and one woman, to the exclusion of all others."

29. *Reference re Same-Sex Marriage,* [2004] 3 S.C.R. 698, SCC 79 at ¶ 21, 22.

30. Tipton and Witte, 261.

31. Don Browning and Elizabeth Marquardt, "What About the Children? Liberal Cautions on Same-Sex Marriage," in Robert P. George and Jean Bethke Elshtain, eds., *The Meaning of Marriage: Family, State, Market, & Morals* (Dallas: Spence Publishing Company, 2006), 30—referring to the work of Max Weber and Jurgen Habermas.

32. David Blankenhorn, *Fatherless America* (New York: BasicBooks, 1995).

33. Don S. Browning, *Marriage and Modernization: How Globalization Threatens Marriage and What to Do about It* (Grand Rapids: Eerdmans, 2003).

34. Browning, 24.

35. Browning, xi.

36. Sarah Lyall, "For Europeans, Love, Yes; Marriage, Maybe," *New York Times,* March 24, 2002; as quoted in Browning, 17.

37. Michael W. McConnell, "What Would It Mean to Have a 'First Amendment' for Sexual Orientation?" as quoted in Saul M. Olyan and Martha C. Nussbaum, eds., *Sexual Orientation and Human Rights in American Religious Discourse* (New York: Oxford Uni-

versity Press, 1998), 256.

38. Bainton, 17. Barry G. Hankins, "Religious Coercion in a Postmodern Age," *Journal of Church and State* 1 (1997): 5.

39. The shallow veneer of civilization was the subject of *Lord of the Flies,* by William Golding, which has become required reading in many high schools.

40. *Lawrence v. Texas,* 123 S. Ct. 2472 (2003).

41. Cass R. Sunstein, "What Did *Lawrence* Hold? Of Autonomy, Desuetude, Sexuality, and Marriage," (John M. Olin Law & Economics Working Paper No. 196 2d Series), University of Chicago, Chicago, 2003, 2; http://www.law.uchicago.edu/lawecon/index.html.

42. Sunstein outlines this argument further on page 5: "*Lawrence* was possible not because the Court reached, all on its own, an ambitious and novel view of the nature of constitutional liberty, or because it attempted to read a controversial view of autonomy into the due process clause. The decision was possible only because of the ludicrously poor fit between the sodomy prohibition and the society in which the justices live. And if I am correct, *Lawrence* will have broad implications only if and to the extent that those broad implications receive general public support. For example, the Supreme Court may or may not read *Lawrence* to require state to recognize gay and lesbian marriages. But if it does so, it will be following public opinion, not leading it. Political and social change was a precondition for *Lawrence*, whose future reach will depend on the nature and extent of that change."

43. Consider the sharp dissent of Justice Antonin Scalia in *Lawrence.*

44. Mary Vallis, "Gay-marriage Loophole Raises Alarm," *National Post,* October 4, 2006, A19.

45. Ellen Vanstone, "Redefining the family," *Canadian Lawyer* (February 2005): 23.

46. Bill Kaufmann, "Some Promises Better Broken: Marriage Vote Turns Back Clock on Rights," *The Calgary Sun,* October 23, 2006.

47. Vanstone, 23.

48. Harvey Cox, *The Secular City: Secularization and Urbanization in Theological Perspective* (New York: Macmillan, 1965), 2.

49. James Dobson, *Marriage Under Fire: Why We Must Win This Battle* (Sisters, Ore.: Multnomah, 2004), 23.

50. Jeff Jacoby, "Gay Marriage Would Change Society's Ideal," *Boston Globe,* July 6, 2003, H11; as quoted in Dobson, 22.

51. Kevin Phillips, *American Theocracy: The Peril and Politics of Radical Religion, Oil, and Borrowed Money in the 21st Century* (New York: Viking, 2006), 192, 193.

52. David L. Corbett, "Freedom From Discrimination on the Basis of Sexual Orientation Under Section 15 of the *Charter*: An Historical Review and Appraisal," in Debra M. McAllister and Adam M. Dodek, eds., *The Charter at Twenty: Law and Practice 2002* (Toronto: Ontario Bar Association, 2002), 415.

53. Ibid.

54. Ibid.

55. *Goodridge v. Department of Public Health,* 798 N.E. 2d 941 (Mass. 2003).

56. Brief of Interested Party/Amicus Curiae, Gay & Lesbian Advocates & Defenders, 4, 5; In re Request for an Advisory Opinion from the President of the Senate, 802 N.E. 2d 565 (Mass. 2004) (no. 09163); as quoted in Carlos A. Ball, "The Backlash Thesis and Same-sex Marriage: Learning From *Brown v. Board of Education* and Its Aftermath," *William & Mary Bill of Rights Journal* 14 (April 2006): 12.

57. Rawls, 765.

58. Lorne Sossin, "The 'Supremacy of God,' Human Dignity and the *Charter of Rights and Freedoms*," *University of New Brunswick Law Journal* 52 (2003): 227.

59. Dobson, 9.

60. Elisabeth Mehren, "Mass. High Court Backs Gay Marriage," *Los Angeles Times,* Nov. 19, 2003; as quoted in Marci A. Hamilton, *God vs. the Gavel: Religion and the Rule of Law* (Cambridge: Cambridge University Press, 2005), 52.

61. Fr. Alphonse de Valk, C.S.B., "Chief Justice McLachlin Overthrows Parental Rights," *Catholic Insight,* March 2003, 3.

62. Bruce MacDougall, "The Celebration of Same-Sex Marriage," *Ottawa Law Review* 32 (Spring 2001): 252.

63. Robert Wintemute, "Religion vs. Sexual Orientation: A Clash of Human Rights?" *University of Toronto Journal of Law & Equality* 1 (2002): 125.

64. MacDougall, 235–237.

65. Ibid.

66. House of Lords, House of Commons Joint Committee on Human Rights, *Legislative Scrutiny: Sexual Orientation Regulations,* Sixth Report of Session 2006-07, HL Paper 58, HC 350, February 28, 2007, 21, 22: "In our view the Regulations prohibiting sexual orientation discrimination should clearly apply to the curriculum, so that homosexual pupils are not subjected to teaching, as part of the religious education or other curriculum, that their sexual orientation is sinful or morally wrong. Applying the Regulations to the curriculum would not prevent pupils from being taught as part of their religious education the fact that certain religions view homosexuality as sinful. In our view there is an important difference between this factual information being imparted in a descriptive way as part of a wide-ranging syllabus about different religions, and a curriculum which teaches a particular religion's doctrinal beliefs as if they were objectively true. The latter is likely to lead to unjustifiable discrimination against homosexual pupils."

67. Scotland's National Health Service, "Fair For All—The Wider Challenge Good LGBT Practice in the NHS," http://www.lgbthealthscotland.org.uk/documents/Good _LGBT_Practice_NHS.pdf: "Using the terms 'husband,' 'wife' and 'marriage' assumes opposite sex relationships only and will automatically exclude all LGB people. Using the terms 'partner' and 'they/them' to refer to the partner will avoid this problem. This is also inclusive of all heterosexual couples, regardless of their marital status. Many people hold a mistaken belief that 'next of kin' must be a married partner or blood relation. In order to avoid this confusion it may be advisable to use 'partner, close friend or close relative.' This allows the patient to identify and choose who is important to them. . . .

"*Parenting*

"LGBT people can and do have children; sexual orientation or gender identity has nothing to do with good parenting or good child care. According to a Scottish wide survey, one fifth of LGBT people have children. Some children will have been born or adopted into heterosexual relationships before a parent had 'come out' and some are born into same-sex relationships or adopted by an LGB individual. Individual circumstances lead to varied family structures and parenting arrangements. It is important to be aware of this. When talking to children, consider using 'parents,' 'carers' or 'guardians' rather than 'mother' or 'father.' "

68. Ball, 36, referring to Gregory M. Herek and John P. Capitanio, " 'Some of My Best Friends': Intergroup Contact, Concealable Stigma, and Heterosexuals' Attitudes Toward Gay Men and Lesbians," *Personality & Social Psychology Bulletin* 22 (1996): 412;

Gregory M. Herek and Eric K. Glunt, "Interpersonal Contact and Heterosexuals' Attitudes Towards Gay Men: Results from a National Survey," *Journal of Sex Research* 30 (1993): 239; Joseph Shapiro et al., "Straight Talk About Gays," *U. S. News & World Report* (June 27, 1993), 42.

69. Ball, 43, 44.

70. Hilary White, "Vatican and Scottish Bishop Slam Britain for Equality Act's 'Violation of Religious Liberty,'" LifeSiteNews.com, February 22, 2007, http://www.lifesite.net/ldn/2007/feb/07022208.html.

71. Ibid.

72. Stanley Fish, "Stanley Fish replies to Richard John Neuhaus," *First Things,* February 1996, 35.

73. Stanley Fish, "Why We Can't All Just Get Along," *First Things,* February 1996, 21.

74. Phillips, 242.

75. Phillips, 245.

76. Niall Ferguson, *The Pity of War* (New York: Basic Books, 1999), 208, 209; as quoted in Phillips, 245.

77. He was speaking in the context of the courts' failure to protect the unborn child in abortion.

78. Robert P. George, *The Clash of Orthodoxies: Law, Religion, and Morality in Crisis* (Wilmington: ISI, 2001), 147.

79. Santorum's comments to The Associated Press in April 2003 found at: http://www.usatoday.com/news/washington/2003-04-23-santorum-excerpt_x.htm: "If the Supreme Court says that you have the right to consensual sex within your home, then you have the right to bigamy, you have the right to polygamy, you have the right to incest, you have the right to adultery. You have the right to anything. Does that undermine the fabric of our society? I would argue yes, it does." See also the comments of Charles Colson and Anne Morse, "Sowing Confusion," *Christianity Today,* October 1, 2003, http://www.ctlibrary.com/ct/2003/october/32.156.html.

80. *Bob Jones University v. United States,* 461 U.S. 574 (1983).

81. Defense of Marriage Act, Pub. L. No. 104–199, 110 Stat. 2419 (Sept. 21, 1996) and codified at 1 U.S.C. § 7 and 28 U.S.C. § 1738C.

Michael D. Peabody

CHAPTER 10

The Battle for the Supreme Court

Shortly after announcing her retirement from the Supreme Court in July 2005, Justice Sandra Day O'Connor said, "In all of the years of my life, I don't think I've ever seen relations as strained as they are now between the judiciary and some members of Congress. It makes me very sad to see it." The reserved Supreme Court justice then issued an uncharacteristically ominous warning: "The present climate is such that I worry about the future of the federal judiciary."[1]

When President George W. Bush attempted to replace the retiring O'Connor with a conservative nominee, Senate Democrats organized a filibuster to stop the appointment. In response, conservative Family Research Council president Tony Perkins cast the battle over the Supreme Court nominee as spiritual warfare: "For years activist courts, aided by liberal interest groups like the American Civil Liberties Union (ACLU), have been quietly working under the veil of the judiciary, like thieves in the night, to rob us of our Christian heritage and our religious freedoms."[2] In a series of *Justice Sunday* events, a coalition of Christian leaders, including James Dobson, Jerry Falwell, and D. James Kennedy, called for an end to the "activist" judiciary that they claimed had existed since the Supreme Court issued rulings recognizing the separation of church and state in 1947.[3]

"For 60 years this court has forced its will on the American people," James Dobson announced to a packed auditorium in Philadelphia on the eve of Samuel Alito's Senate confirmation hearings. "The decisions that have been made about religious concerns have not been chosen by the American people. They have been forced on the American people and it's time to put it to an end! . . . Catholics and evangelicals have come together. We understand the stakes. Our culture is going south and we must rescue it, we're all going down together."[4]

Jerry Falwell then took the podium. "What we've worked on for 30 years—to mobilize people of faith and values in this country . . . is coming to culmination, to consumeation [sic] right now. . . . And now we're looking at what we really stated over 30 years ago—a reconstruction of a court system gone awry."[5]

The federal judiciary has become a politically charged tool of the American culture wars. To understand why this is significant and how it happened, it is useful to step back from the immediate issues and see the bigger picture. The United States was established by people who drafted a document—a constitution—and pledged to uphold that writing as the ultimate legal authority. In an age of powerful monarchs, the democratic election of governing officials and their subordination to mere words on a piece of paper was revolutionary.

The Constitution's endurance as the legal standard for more than two centuries may be remarkable, yet interpretation of the Constitution has been anything but stable. Today, powerful conservative[6] critics of the federal courts insist that the courts have given Americans too much freedom. Although conservatives have failed to secure constitutional amendments, they continue to seek to limit the jurisdiction of the federal courts.

In a sense, this battle for the Supreme Court and the lower federal courts is a continuation of the American Civil War. It pits states' rights against a national unity enforced by the federal judiciary. The stakes are very high. If federal jurisdiction can be effectively curtailed, real power can be returned to state legislatures, which are subject to popular majorities. Then unpopular Supreme Court decisions can be overturned state by state. If a popularly elected president and Congress succeed in such efforts to reduce the jurisdiction of the federal courts, America may well return to an age when the Bill of Rights was little more than an undelivered promise.

Empowering the judiciary

According to Article III of the Constitution, the federal court system is the institution most responsible for interpreting the Constitution.[7] The judicial branch of government is the only one that is not popularly elected. It doesn't have the power to enforce its own decisions; instead, it relies on the other branches to ensure that its rulings are carried out. Its members, who serve for life so long as they maintain "good behavior," can outlast their sponsors and, through their decisions, can influence the course of the nation for decades. Thus, the judiciary is placed at natural enmity with the other two branches, providing a system of checks and balances on their power.

The powerful Supreme Court as we know it today wasn't a foregone conclusion in the first decades of the American Republic. In 1800, as President John Adams and Thomas Jefferson locked horns in a bitterly contested presidential election campaign,[8] the first chief justice of the Supreme Court, John Jay, resigned. Jay was one of the authors of the Federalist Papers, influential articles urging the ratification of the newly drafted Constitution. If anyone understood the new system of government created by the Constitution, surely Jay did. Yet he felt the Court wasn't respected enough to uphold the Constitution against brutal attacks from the very people who had created it. When President Adams urged Jay to return to the Supreme Court, he replied, " 'I left the Bench . . . perfectly convinced that under a system so defective it would not obtain the energy, weight, and dignity which was essential to its affording due support to the national government; nor acquire the public confidence and respect which, as the last resort of the nation, it should possess.' "[9]

Despite Jay's misgivings about the structural impotence of the Supreme Court, his successor, John Marshall, quickly figured out how to develop the Court's power, position, and prestige. Marshall seized on a political conflict well-known to students of American history as the case of *Marbury v. Madison.*

With the presidential election decided on February 17, 1801, the Republicans were slated to take control on March 4. In an attempt to mitigate the effect of the incoming Republican majority, lame-duck President John Adams and the Federalists in Congress worked quickly to pass the Judiciary Act of 1801, expanding the courts and permitting the appointment of a new slate of judges and justices of the peace. On March 3, these commissions were approved by the Senate, but they wouldn't go into effect until they were delivered to the appointees. The responsibility for delivering the commissions fell to John Marshall, still secretary of state under President Adams, though under appointment to become chief justice of the Supreme Court.

Marshall wasn't able to deliver all the commissions before the deadline. But he expected that Jefferson's new secretary of state, James Madison, would deliver the remaining commissions, including that of William Marbury, who had been appointed to a position as a justice of the peace. Instead, the Republican Congress repealed the Judiciary Act of 1801 and abolished the new commissions.

However, William Marbury, wanted the commission to which he had been appointed. In an effort to secure it, he went directly to the Supreme Court, where John Marshall now served as chief justice. Marbury sought a court order to enforce his appointment. He argued that Congress had violated the Constitution in repealing the Judiciary Act and denying him his commission.

Marshall certainly wanted to rule in Marbury's favor and uphold the Federalist court-packing scheme. However, he knew that this would have been an exercise in futility because the Supreme Court had no power to compel the Republicans to deliver the commissions to the Federalist appointees. The Court appeared to be at the mercy of the newly elected Republicans.

Marshall brilliantly found a way to turn the situation to the Supreme Court's advantage. His opinion ruled that the Judiciary Act of 1801 that established the new commissions was unconstitutional.[10] While this denied Marbury his commission, it assumed for the Supreme Court the authority to serve as the final judge of whether or not acts of Congress are constitutional. The Founding Fathers had vigorously debated this principle of "judicial review," but the debate had never been conclusively resolved. Now Marshall decided the issue by asserting the power of judicial review on behalf of the federal courts.[11] He insisted that acts of Congress that disagree with the Constitution are not law and that courts must interpret and apply the Constitution as the supreme law of the land. If the courts deferred to Congress when it violated the Constitution, there would be no point in having a constitution at all: "To what purpose are powers limited, and to what purpose is that limitation committed to writing; if these limits may, at any time, be passed by those intended to be restrained?"[12]

Marshall further reasoned that "those then who controvert the principle that the constitution is to be considered, in court, as a paramount law, are reduced to the necessity of maintaining that courts must close their eyes on the constitution, and see only the law [e.g., the statute or treaty]. This doctrine would subvert the very foundation of all written constitutions."[13]

Although the Supreme Court's assumption of the power of judicial review was controversial at the time, it has stood for two centuries. Members of Congress are frequently forced to choose between fidelity to the Constitution or to the political desires of their constituents. It is often convenient for elected officials—pressured to vote on the basis of politics rather than constitutional principle—to defer constitutional decisions to unelected judges. Of course, Congress also retains the ability to reverse unpopular

Supreme Court decisions either by proposing constitutional amendments or, where statutory interpretation is involved, by amending the statute.

Although this system of checks and balances was designed to preserve individual liberties, there have been some grave inconsistencies, especially with the perpetuation of the institution of slavery.

The Constitution's flaw

In the Declaration of Independence, American revolutionaries had confidently announced that "all men are created equal." And Article V of the Bill of Rights provided that citizens couldn't be deprived of their rights without due process of law. Nevertheless, legal recognition of the principle of equal treatment under the law remained elusive.[14] While the federal government was restrained from taking private property without just compensation and from convicting those accused of a felony without a jury trial, no government was compelled to treat everyone equally. This was especially evident in the denial of voting rights to women and in the institution of slavery.

The Founding Fathers, in asserting their independence, invoked the principle that our rights come from the hand of the Creator, and they denied that King George had authority to usurp these rights. Yet a very different political expediency was at work when the Bill of Rights was debated. James Madison proposed an amendment that would have prohibited the states from abridging the rights guaranteed in the Bill of Rights. His "No State shall . . ." amendment passed in the House of Representatives but failed in the Senate. Madison had considered this amendment the "most valuable amendment in the whole list."[15] Without it, states were free to trample on rights such as free expression, freedom of religion, and the right to a jury trial. Southern advocates of states' rights in the Senate defeated this amendment for one principal reason: to prevent any interference with slavery. If the Bill of Rights were applied to the states, all slaves would be afforded these rights as well. So, despite the noble rhetoric that rights emanate from God, only the federal government would be required to respect those rights. States were free to forge their own approach to American liberties.

While the Bill of Rights hobbled through its formative years, the states ran roughshod over the great principles enunciated by the Framers. State religious establishments continued, lasting as late as 1833 in Massachusetts. Beginning in the 1830s, some Southern states banned abolitionist literature. In *Barron v. Mayor of Baltimore* (1833), the Supreme Court ruled that the Bill of Rights provided "security against the apprehended encroachments of the general government—not against those of the local governments."[16] For most Americans, the notion of national equal justice under law remained nothing but a quaint twinkle in Madison's eye.

Schoolchildren often regard 1776 as the year when Americans secured their liberty. A better date would be fourscore and seven years later—when, on a blood-soaked battlefield in Gettysburg, Pennsylvania, Abraham Lincoln called for a "a new birth of freedom."[17] Ever since the Revolution, the Civil War had been brewing as a battle of states' rights versus the authority of the federal government. In a sense, the Civil War was a continuation of Madison's effort to include a "No State shall . . ." amendment in the Bill of Rights.

Reconstruction

Following the Civil War, Congress quickly moved to enact a series of three amendments. The Thirteenth Amendment, ratified in 1865, ended slavery forever. The Fourteenth Amendment, ratified in 1868, made all persons born in America full and equal citizens. And the Fifteenth Amendment, ratified in 1870, guaranteed black men the right to vote.

The Fourteenth Amendment guaranteed "equal protection of the laws" to all persons, and it required the states, for the first time, to respect the rights guaranteed under the Constitution. This shifted the balance of power from the states to the national government, making it clear that all Americans were citizens of the nation first and enjoyed all the rights affirmed in the Constitution.[18] In order to ensure that the Southern states had learned their lesson, Congress required them to ratify the Fourteenth Amendment as a condition of postwar readmission to the Union.[19]

The importance of the Fourteenth Amendment cannot be overestimated, as it has formed the basis for most civil rights legislation ever since. It has also come under vigorous attack by advocates of states' rights. Some have challenged the validity of the three post–Civil War amendments on the basis that they were "passed at gunpoint."[20] Others criticize the idea that the Fourteenth Amendment intended to "incorporate" liberties protected under the Bill of Rights and apply them to the states.[21] Supreme Court Justice Clarence Thomas has written, for example, that states should be permitted to display the Ten Commandments because the First Amendment's prohibition against religious establishments was never intended to apply to the states and shouldn't have been applied through the Fourteenth Amendment.[22] The Civil War may have ended on the military battlefield more than a century ago, but the battle over states' rights continues to rage.

However, though the three Reconstruction amendments promised civil rights, the fulfillment of the promise was delayed till the next century—until a second Reconstruction known as the civil rights movement. They didn't, for instance, end state-sponsored racial discrimination. In 1896, in *Plessy v. Ferguson*,[23] the Supreme Court issued a decision that upheld Louisiana's requirement that railroad cars provide separate accommodations for whites and nonwhites despite obvious differences in quality. It was here that the Court announced the infamous doctrine of "separate but equal" accommodations.

In *Plessy*, Justice John Marshall Harlan wrote an eloquent dissent, advancing a principle of racial equality that wouldn't be recognized in law for nearly six more decades: "Slavery, as an institution tolerated by law would, it is true, have disappeared from our country, but there would remain a power in the States, by sinister legislation, to interfere with the full enjoyment of the blessings of freedom; to regulate civil rights, common to all citizens, upon the basis of race; and to place in a condition of legal inferiority a large body of American citizens."[24]

So, the principle that the Fourteenth Amendment "incorporated" rights contained in the first ten amendments and applied them to the states may have been secured in the nineteenth century, but the application of that principle proceeded rather slowly. The Supreme Court didn't begin extending the Bill of Rights to protect citizens from abuses at the state and local level until the twentieth century. The first such cases involved freedom of speech in *Gitlow v. New York* (1925)[25] and the free exercise of religion in *Hamilton v. Regents of the University of California* (1934).[26]

The second Reconstruction

It wasn't until 1954 that the Supreme Court outlawed public-school segregation (*Brown v. Board of Education*).[27] African-American school children in several states—including Kansas, South Carolina, Virginia, and Delaware—who were denied admission to white public schools sued the school districts claiming they had been denied equal protection of the law under the Fourteenth Amendment. The lower court relied on the "separate but equal" doctrine of *Plessy v. Ferguson* to deny them admission. Chief Justice Earl Warren could have attacked *Plessy* directly but chose not to. By moderating the tone of the decision, Warren was able to obtain a unanimous vote in favor of desegregating the nation's schools.

The civil rights movement of the 1950s and 1960s has commanded the much-deserved spotlight. At the same time that the Fourteenth Amendment was being invoked to protect the equal rights of blacks, it was also relied upon by those wanting to ensure that the religious liberty promises of the First Amendment would protect those of minority faiths. By incorporating fundamental freedoms expressed in the Bill of Rights and guaranteeing them against abridgement by the states, the Fourteenth Amendment created a platform for the federal courts to develop concepts of nonestablishment and free exercise of religion.

The American philosophy of rights is that rights derive from "the Laws of Nature and of Nature's God," a phrase taken from the Declaration of Independence. To the Framers of the Constitution, religious freedom was paramount. Yale law professor Akhil Reed Amar has observed that the First Amendment "declared certain pre-existing principles of liberty and self-governance."[28] Rather than aggregating and then dispensing these rights, Congress simply recognized its obligation not to interfere with the rights that already existed, such as "*the* free exercise" of religion and "*the* freedom of speech." This has given rise to a principle of government neutrality with respect to religion. Americans are entitled to worship God and adhere to religious beliefs without government interference and control.

Increasingly, however, religious conservatives are offended not only by the constitutional obligation of government to remain neutral toward religion but also by what they charge is the Supreme Court's fostering of official state hostility toward religion through its interpretation of the First Amendment's Establishment Clause. And front and center in the battle over the Supreme Court has been the future of the relationship between church and state.

The Supreme Court had no occasion to interpret the First Amendment religion clauses before the twentieth century, because religious freedom was subject to state law. In fact, in an 1845 decision, the Supreme Court specifically denied that the Free Exercise Clause applied to the states.[29] In 1875, following the Reconstruction amendments, Congressman James Blaine introduced a constitutional amendment to address immigration and prohibit public aid to Catholic schools. His amendment provided that "no State shall make any law respecting an establishment of religion or prohibiting the free exercise thereof."[30] The amendment failed in the Senate, ending Blaine's effort to require states to respect the Establishment Clause.

James Madison had wanted to end state religious establishments in his day; however, it wasn't until 1947 that the Supreme Court finally applied the Establishment Clause to the states. Justice Hugo Black wrote in *Everson v. Board of Education* that "the First Amendment has erected a wall between

156 • Politics and Prophecy

church and state. That wall must be kept high and impregnable. We could not approve the slightest breach."[31] Ironically, although Justice Black was well-known as a textual literalist, his view of the Establishment Clause has been widely criticized by those who insist the Framers intended the First Amendment to prevent only the establishment of a national church. Actually, these critics conveniently ignore the fact that their cherished view was considered and rejected by the Founding Fathers.[32] Chief Justice William Rehnquist was among those who later criticized *Everson* for introducing the phrase "the separation of church and state," which Black borrowed from Thomas Jefferson's letter to the Danbury Baptists.[33]

Subsequent Supreme Court decisions prohibited public schools from requiring nondenominational prayers[34] and from mandating devotional Bible reading.[35] In 1971, in *Lemon v. Kurtzman,* the Supreme Court refined its approach to interpreting the Establishment Clause by adopting a three-pronged analysis. Since government has no authority to act either to promote or to restrict religion, the primary purpose and effect of all laws and government actions must be secular. These are the first two prongs of the *Lemon* test—the secular purpose and secular effects tests. The final test is that state laws and actions cannot unduly entangle church and state.[36] By 1980, when the Supreme Court considered a Kentucky law requiring public elementary school classrooms to display a copy of the Ten Commandments, it had a solid legal framework to rely upon. It could readily see that both the purpose and effect of requiring the display of the Ten Commandments in public-school classrooms were religious rather than secular.[37]

The threat of a third Reconstruction

As the Supreme Court began to address the intrusion of religious practices into public schools and to require strict governmental neutrality toward religion, Christian conservatives became increasingly uncomfortable. Liberal interest groups such as the ACLU fueled this irritation to a fever pitch by filing lawsuits against cities and counties challenging the public display of religious symbols such as Christmas displays of Baby Jesus in the manger and crosses on government-owned hilltops and on government seals. Many of these suits succeeded.

Unsuccessful attempts to scrape "In God We Trust" off coins and to remove "under God" from the Pledge of Allegiance confirmed in the minds of many that not only were cherished symbols threatened but their faith itself was under attack. At the same time, many Christians interpreted the growing prevalence of sexual immorality, abortion, drug abuse, and crime as evidence that God's grace was being withdrawn from this favored land—for which it became easy to blame atheists and secular humanists. They were the ones who argued that ethics and justice should be based on reason, not religion.[38] Since the federal courts appeared to be responsive to liberals' attempts to remove religion from public life, religious conservatives began to see the urgency of "reforming" the entire judiciary. In 1982, Dr. Francis Schaeffer, a patron intellectual of the Christian Right, said that the federal courts "are not subject to the people's thinking, nor their will, either by election or by re-election. Consequently the courts have been the vehicle used to bring [secular humanism] and force it on our total population."[39]

Throughout the 1980s and the 1990s, conservative religious groups recognized the difficulty of reversing the Supreme Court's Establishment Clause holdings unless they could completely transform the makeup of the Court or reform the Constitution itself. Before a proposed amendment becomes part of the Constitution, it must be approved by two-thirds of the members of both houses of Congress and then ratified by majority vote of three-fourths of the state legislatures. In the early days, Congress placed no time limit on when states could ratify these bills, but now Congress typically allows about seven years for ratification.[40] Despite the difficulty of amending the Constitution, the Religious Right has made several attempts to do so in order to protect expression of religion on public property.

A school-prayer amendment was debated in Congress in the 1960s and again in the 1980s, when a Reagan-era House actually voted in favor of such an amendment, although it failed to achieve the needed two-thirds majority.[41] Throughout the 1990s, Rep. Ernest Istook (R-OK) repeatedly introduced an amendment that stated, "Nothing in this Constitution shall be construed to prohibit individual or group prayer in public schools or other public institutions. No person shall be required by the United States or by any state to participate in prayer. Neither the United States nor any state shall compose the words of any prayer to be said in public schools." Ironically, these prayer amendments expressly agree with the Supreme Court, which struck down the use of a prayer written by the New York State Board of Regents.[42]

Rep. Istook also introduced a broader effort called the Religious Equality Amendment: "To secure the people's rights to acknowledge God according to the dictates of conscience: Neither the United States nor any State shall establish any official religion, but the people's right to pray and to recognize their religious beliefs, heritage, or traditions on public property, including schools, shall not be infringed."[43] This was the more dangerous constitutional amendment since its relationship to the First Amendment's Establishment Clause prohibitions was so uncertain. Would this amendment effectively nullify the entire Establishment Clause or merely supersede part of it? What did the amendment mean by protecting the "people's rights"? Did it mean to permit government officials to actively engage in promoting and requiring religious activities? The language is fraught with mischief. This amendment never came close to passage.

Efforts to limit jurisdiction

After various attempts to amend the Constitution failed, religious conservatives changed course and began to focus on efforts to limit the jurisdiction of the federal courts. In 1996, Christian conservative David Barton published a small book titled *Impeachment: Restraining an Overactive Judiciary.* Publication was timed to coincide with a bill introduced by Rep. Tom DeLay (R-TX) to give Congress the ability to impeach judges. "The judges need to be intimidated," said DeLay.[44]

Attempts by Congress and the executive branch to control the federal courts are nothing new. The Judiciary Act of 1801, which gave rise to *Marbury,* dealt with that very issue. Even President Franklin D. Roosevelt tried to advance his New Deal agenda in the 1930s by packing the Supreme Court with additional justices.

In recent years, attempts to control the courts have begun to focus on limiting their jurisdiction. Some of these efforts have been successful. For instance, in 1996, Congress enacted the Illegal Immigration Reform and Immigrant Responsibility Act, giving the Immigration and Naturalization Service (INS) the exclusive authority to determine asylum status without the right of appeal to the courts.[45] After the terrorist attacks of September 11, Congress enacted the Antiterrorism and Effective Death Penalty Act, which limited the number of habeas corpus petitions that inmates could make to the federal courts.[46] These successes have emboldened Congress and led to additional efforts to rein in the jurisdiction of federal courts.

In July 2004, the House of Representatives passed the Marriage Protection Act (MPA) to limit the power of courts to review the constitutionality of the Defense of Marriage Act. Rep. Jim McGovern (D-MA) criticized supporters of the Act: "They couldn't amend the Constitution last week, so they're trying to desecrate and circumvent the Constitution this week."[47] Georgetown University law professor Chai Feldblum said that the MPA represented the first time that Congress had restricted the federal courts from hearing cases with constitutional questions since 1868, when Congress passed an act preventing the federal courts from hearing challenges to the Reconstruction amendments. Feldblum wrote, " 'When legislators rail that "unelected judges" are finding legislative acts unconstitutional, they are attacking the very structure of our democracy.' "[48]

In 2004, Alabama Senator Richard Shelby introduced the Constitution Restoration Act (CRA) in the U.S. Senate.[49] An identical bill was proposed in the House of Representatives.[50] Nearly identical bills were proposed again in 2005. The bill's central effect is stated: "The Supreme Court shall not have jurisdiction to review, by appeal, writ of certiorari, or otherwise, any matter to the extent that relief is sought against an entity of Federal, State, or local government, or against an officer or agent of Federal, State, or local government (whether or not acting in official or personal capacity), concerning that entity's, officer's, or agent's acknowledgment of God as the sovereign source of law, liberty, or government."

In other words, the bill would limit the power of the federal judiciary in a group of religious liberty cases. The bill also states that judges or other court officials who violate this prohibition are subject to impeachment. More than forty-four members of Congress endorsed the Constitution Restoration Act, which was based on the premise that Article III of the Constitution gives Congress the power to tell the federal courts what cases they can hear.

This bill was drafted by attorney and law professor Herb Titus. He had represented former Alabama Supreme Court Chief Justice Roy Moore in his failed defense of the Ten Commandments monument that he had placed in the rotunda of the Alabama Supreme Court building in 2003. Moore claimed that the Ten Commandments monument was his way of acknowledging God. The Constitution Restoration Act was an effort to prevent courts from interfering with future attempts to acknowledge God.

In an interview, Justice Roy Moore explained what the bill is designed to do:

> The purpose of the CRA is to restrict the appellate jurisdiction of the United States Supreme Court and all lower federal courts to that jurisdiction permitted them by the Constitution of the United States. The acknowledgment of God as the sovereign source of law, liberty, and government is contained within the Declaration of Independence which is cited as the "organic law" of our Country by

United States Code Annotated. The constitution of every state of the Union acknowledges God and His sovereignty, as do three branches of the federal government. The acknowledgment of God is not a legitimate subject of review by federal courts.[51]

Attempts such as the Constitution Restoration Act are frontal assaults on the principle of government neutrality toward religion. In place of neutrality, the Act asserts the right and power of government officials to acknowledge God and restrains courts from interfering. If the principle of neutrality is to be replaced, what will replace it? Although the Act seems blatantly inconsistent with established First Amendment precedent regarding the separation of church and state, a new conservative Supreme Court majority may reject this precedent in favor of a new approach to the Establishment Clause. Justices Scalia and Thomas have been vocal critics of the existing Establishment Clause precedent.

The Court limits its own jurisdiction

In addition to attempts by Congress to limit the jurisdiction of the federal courts, the recently reconstituted Supreme Court has taken unprecedented steps toward limiting the jurisdiction of cases which it can hear. In *Hein v. Freedom from Religion Foundation,*[52] in which a group of atheists sued the executive branch, alleging that the president's "faith-based initiative" violated the Establishment Clause, the United States Supreme Court ruled by a 5–4 decision that individual taxpayers don't have the right to challenge the constitutionality of executive branch expenditures on religion. Pat Robertson's American Center for Law and Justice hailed the decision, stating, "It will now be more difficult for separationists to claim special privileges to sue as taxpayers without showing that a law or government activity actually injured them in any way."[53]

This decision overturned the portion of *Flast v. Cohen,*[54] which for more than forty years had protected the right of taxpayers to bring suit for injunction against congressional use of taxpayer funds that violates the Establishment Clause. The *Flast* Court recognized that when a taxpayer's money is spent in violation of the Constitution, a direct harm has occurred. Prior to *Hein,* the Court recognized that the taxpayer who files suit is actually a proxy for the many other taxpayers who are likewise harmed.[55] The Court further recognized that the "Establishment Clause was designed as a specific bulwark against such potential abuses of governmental power and . . . operates as a specific constitutional limitation upon . . . the taxing and spending power."[56]

The *Flast* Court further noted that "our history vividly illustrates that one of the specific evils feared by those who drafted the Establishment Clause and fought for its adoption was that the taxing and spending power would be used to favor one religion over another or to support religion in general."[57]

Although some might be concerned that the taxpayer standing recognized in *Flast* would have opened the floodgates of litigation on any number of constitutional issues, this standing was limited to cases involving the Establishment Clause because, as indicated above, it provides the only clear limit available within the Constitution on the ability of Congress to tax and spend.[58] In fact, the federal courts have routinely dismissed claims of taxpayer standing on other issues.[59]

When the Supreme Court overturned the availability of taxpayer standing in *Hein* to file suit for violations of the Establishment Clause, it held that the executive branch is not answerable to the public for violations of the separation of church and state. Although this ruling didn't involve Congress, in defending the interests of the executive branch, Solicitor General Paul D. Clement said that he believed that taxpayer standing should likewise be unavailable to sue Congress for violating the Clause.[60] It is conceivable that the Court will depend on *Hein* to remove taxpayer standing to sue for acts of Congress as well.

In his dissent, Justice David Souter wrote that removing executive branch decisions from judicial review was dangerous. He said that the majority decision

> points to the separation of powers to explain its distinction between legislative and executive spending decisions . . . but there is no difference on that point of view between a Judicial Branch review of an executive decision and a judicial evaluation of a congressional one. We owe respect to each of the other branches, no more to the former than to the latter, and no one has suggested that the Establishment Clause lacks applicability to executive uses of money. It would surely violate the Establishment Clause for the Department of Health and Human Services to draw on a general appropriation to build a chapel for weekly church services (no less than if a statute required it), and for good reason: if the Executive could accomplish through the exercise of discretion exactly what Congress cannot do through legislation, Establishment Clause protection would melt away.[61]

It appears that Congress and the executive branch are free to concoct a variety of schemes to divert tax dollars to religion. Although the Supreme Court didn't say so directly, it now appears that so long as a congressional appropriation is "facially neutral" with respect to religion, the executive branch is free to expend those funds on religion without any fear of judicial restraint or constitutional limitation.

The danger of circumventing the courts

Congressional efforts to circumvent the courts and the Supreme Court's own complicity in this are dangerous. In 2004, the task force of the Courts Initiative of the Constitution Project unanimously concluded " 'that the Constitution's structure would be compromised if Congress could enact a law and immunize that law from constitutional judicial review.' " The Constitution Restoration Act failed in both 2004 and 2005, but the war on federal jurisdiction continues.

The immediate danger that Congress would approve legislation to restrict the courts from hearing religion cases is restrained by the Democrats' majority in Congress since the Democrats generally favor the separation of church and state. Should such bills succeed in the future, however, there are various legal challenges that can be raised. Despite vigorous arguments to the contrary, the Constitution simply does not give Congress the power to select the issues that an Article III court can adjudicate. Moreover, the courts themselves have the ultimate authority to settle the matter of interpreting Article III and have self-interested reasons for resisting efforts to restrict their jurisdiction.

Threats to impeach federal judges and efforts to restrict federal court jurisdiction are transparent attempts by Congress to coerce the courts to render favorable decisions. In large part, the Constitution grants federal judges life tenure to immunize them from political pressures. Attacks on the courts are rather sophomoric attempts to short-circuit that principle.

What if these efforts succeeded, and Congress somehow rolled back the Fourteenth Amendment and negated federal jurisdiction over the states with respect to individual rights? State courts would have the final authority to determine the scope of religious freedom, free speech, racial equality, and every other individual right. The result would be utter chaos. Each state would become a law unto itself. American citizens' basic rights would depend on where they lived. Some states would become more permissive, while others would become more restrictive. In states like Alabama, where judges are popularly elected, individual rights would increasingly depend on public popularity. Unwittingly, perhaps, not only would federal courts lose the power to interpret or defend individual rights from encroachment by the states, so would Congress. The relationship between church and state, for example, would be wholly controlled by the legislative and judicial power of each state. If Utah wished to declare itself a Mormon state, it would be free to do so. If Alabama wished to require that all public-school children be indoctrinated into the fundamentals of the Christian faith, the federal courts and Congress would be powerless to interfere.

Congressional antipathy toward federal judges continues, and pressure is mounting.

After a judge was killed by a defendant in a rape case in an Atlanta courtroom and another was assassinated in Chicago after he dismissed a lawsuit, conservative Senator John Cornyn offered a unique perspective on the floor of the U.S. Senate:

> I don't know if there is a cause-and-effect connection, but we have seen some recent episodes of courthouse violence in this country. . . . I wonder whether there may be some connection between the perception in some quarters, on some occasions, where judges are making political decisions yet are unaccountable to the public, that it builds up and builds up and builds up to the point where some people engage in, engage in violence. Certainly without any justification, but a concern that I have.[62]

Although staffers dismissed what Senator Cornyn said as an off-the-cuff remark to a nearly empty chamber, the sentiment still caused shivers to reverberate down the spines of court watchers.

In 1801, John Jay left his position on the Supreme Court because he felt that owing to excessive influence from the executive and legislative branches, the system had become so muddled that it no longer had the public confidence and respect to be the last resort of the nation. Two centuries later, it is clear that John Jay has been proven wrong. John Marshall established the power of the courts to be the final judge of the law, and the courts have served that role ever since. Today, this role is under vigorous assault. Congressional conservatives wish to exchange the mostly successful system of checks and balances for power over the federal courts. Such mischief would shift the balance of power away from the Constitution's protection of individual rights against the tyranny of legislative or popular majorities to whatever the political winds might blow in.

Americans must not permit our national birthright of religious freedom and the separation of powers to be exchanged for such a chaotic stew.

---

1. Blaine Harden, "O'Connor Bemoans Hill Rancor at Judges," *Washington Post,* July 22, 2005, A15.

2. Charles Babington, "Frist to Participate in Anti-Filibuster Telecast," *Washington Post,* April 16, 2005, A06.

3. Christian activists often reference *Everson v. Board of Education* 330 U.S. 1 (1947) as the beginning of the separation of church and state. The fallacies with this argument will be discussed below.

4. James Dobson, "Proclaim Liberty Throughout the Land" *Justice Sunday III* transcript from January 8, 2006; available at http://www.frc.org/get.cfm?i-LH06A11.

5. Jerry Falwell, "Proclaim Liberty Throughout the Land" *Justice Sunday III* transcript from January 8, 2006; available at http:://www.frc.org/get.cfm?i-LH06A11.

6. The term "conservative" has come to mean something very different than in previous generations. A conservative used to value individual liberty and the rule of law as superior to the exercise of governmental authority. Today's conservatives appear to favor the consolidation of power at either the state or federal level at the expense of individual liberty.

7. A careful review of Article III is consistent with the purpose of this chapter; the reader is directed to Appendix A: Article III of the U.S. Constitution.

8. For a detailed treatment of the election of 1800, read John Ferling, *Adams vs. Jefferson: The Tumultuous Election of 1800* (New York: Oxford University Press, 2004).

9. To President Adams, Jan. 2, 1801, Jay *MSS,* as quoted in George Pellew, *American Statesman: John Jay* (Boston: Houghton, Mifflin and Company, 1890), 337, 338.

10. For a thorough treatment of the political issues surrounding *Marbury v. Madison,* see David F. Forte, *Marbury's Travail: Federalist Politics and William Marbury's Appointment as Justice of the Peace,* 45 Cath. U. L. Rev. 349 (1996).

11. *Marbury v. Madison,* 5 U.S. (1 Cranch) 137 (1803).

12. *Id.,* at 176.

13. *Id.,* at 178.

14. While the Fifth Amendment includes a due process clause, it doesn't include—as the post–Civil War Fourteenth Amendment does—an *equal protection* clause, and the Fourteenth Amendment applied only against the states. It wasn't until *Bolling v. Sharpe,* 347 U.S. 497 (1954) (concerning desegregation of public schools—often considered a companion case to *Brown v. Board of Education,* 347 U.S. 483 [1954]) that the Supreme Court recognized the absurdity of the idea that the Constitution could deny the states the power to abridge equal protection of the laws yet permit Congress to deny equal protection. "The concepts of equal protection and due process, both stemming from our American ideal of fairness, are not mutually exclusive," wrote Chief Justice Earl Warren. The *Bolling* Court interpreted the Fifth Amendment's due process clause to include an equal protection element but continues to hold that there is a difference between due process and equal protection.

15. See *Annals of Congress,* 1st Cong., 1st sess., June 8 and Aug. 17, 1789, 452–455, 784; See also *Senate Journal,* 1st Cong., 1st sess., Aug. 24, 1789, 64.

16. *Barron v. Mayor of Baltimore,* 32 U.S. (7 Pet.) 243 (1833). (Holding that the Fifth Amendment's guarantee that the government provide just compensation when it

takes property belonging to a private individual for public use didn't apply to a person whose wharf was rendered unusable by the City of Baltimore.)

17. Abraham Lincoln, "Gettysburg Address" (November 19, 1863).

18. See Akhil Amar, *America's Constitution* (New York: Random House, 2005), 381.

19. Douglas Kmiec and Stephen Presser, *The American Constitutional Order* (Cincinnati: Anderson Publishing Company, 1998).

20. Kmiec, 1186; see also Amar, 365. Yale Law professor Bruce Ackerman has been making the argument that the Reconstruction amendments are of suspect validity because Congress forced the Southern states to accept these amendments.

21. See Kmiec, 1186.

22. In his concurring opinion in *Van Orden v. Perry,* Thomas said, "The [Establishment] Clause's text and history 'resis[t] incorporation' against the States." 545 U.S. 677, 693 (2005).

23. 163 U.S. 537 (1896).

24. *Id.*

25. 268 U.S. 652 (1925). The Court reversed *Barron v. Baltimore* (see endnote 6) and said the Bill of Rights applied through the Fourteenth Amendment to a New York bill that said it was a crime to advocate for the violent overthrow of the government. Although a major victory for the Bill of Rights, Mr. Gitlow's conviction of criminal anarchy for advocating unlawful overthrow of the government was upheld.

26. 293 U.S. 245 (1934). (Holding the right of California to force its university students to take classes in military training even if they object on religious grounds. However, the Court did say that the Bill of Rights applied here through the Fourteenth Amendment.)

27. 347 U.S. 483 (1954).

28. Amar, 316.

29. *Permioli v. First Municipality,* 44 U.S. (3 How.) 589, 610 (1856).

30. 44th Cong., 1st sess., *Congressional Record* 205 (1875).

31. 330 U.S. 1 (1947). Despite the large amount of opposition to the dicta, the Court had actually ruled that the State of New Jersey had not violated the Establishment Clause when it spent tax-raised funds to pay the bus fares of parochial-school students as part of a general program that paid bus fares for students attending public and private schools.

32. See Leonard Levy, *The Establishment Clause: Religion and the First Amendment* (Chapel Hill, N.C.: University of North Carolina Press, 1994) for an excellent overview of the congressional debates on the issue of disestablishment.

33. See also, *Wallace v. Jaffree,* 472 U.S. 38, 106 (1985) (Rehnquist, J., dissenting).

34. *Engle v. Vitale,* 370 U.S. 421 (1962). (Holding it is unconstitutional for state officials to compose an official school prayer and require its recitation in public schools.)

35. *Abington School District v. Schempp,* 374 U.S. 203 (1963).

36. 403 U.S. 602 (1971). (Holding that Pennsylvania's program that allowed for public reimbursement of parochial teachers' salaries, textbooks, and other instructional materials violated the Establishment Clause.)

37. *Stone v. Graham,* 449 U.S. 39 (1980).

38. Secular humanists and atheists annoyed Christians who resented the idea that secularism could be taught in public schools with impunity while Christianity was prohibited, particularly since Secular Humanism was a complete philosophy, albeit void of the supernatural, and Justice Hugo Black had identified it along with non-Christian religious groups in a footnote to *Torcaso v. Watkins,* 367 U.S. 488 (1961). (Reaffirming that the Constitution prohibited states from requiring any religious tests for public office.)

39. Francis Schaeffer, *A Christian Manifesto* (Wheaton, Ill.: Crossways Books, 2005), 110.

40. The Twenty-seventh Amendment to the Constitution, which deals with compensation of members of Congress, took more than two hundred years to ratify. It was introduced in 1789 and was not added to the Constitution until it was finally ratified by three-fourths of the states in 1992.

41. Elizabeth Ann Oldmixon, *Uncompromising Positions: God, Sex, and the U.S. House of Representatives* (Washington, D.C.: Georgetown University Press, 2005), 106–108.

42. "Prayer in Public Schools Polls Show Support, but Passage of an Amendment Could Prove Difficult," *The Virginian-Pilot,* December 5, 1994, A1.

43. H.J.Res. 78.

44. Cited in Max Blumenthal, "In Contempt of Courts," *The Nation,* April 25, 2005.

45. This was challenged unsuccessfully in *Reno v. American Arab Anti-Discrimination Committee,* 525 U.S. 471 (1999).

46. The Antiterrorism and Effective Death Penalty Act of 1996 (also known as AEDPA) is a series of laws in the United States signed into law on April 24, 1996, to "deter terrorism, provide justice for victims, provide for an effective death penalty, and for other purposes."

47. Mary Fitzgerald and Alan Cooperman, "Marriage Protection Act Passes," *Washington Post,* July 23, 2004, A04.

48. Ibid.

49. S 520, 109th Cong., 1st Session,

50. HR 1070, 109th Cong., 1st Session.

51. "Judge Roy Moore Introduces Constitution Restoration Act of 2004," *WAFF News,* February 13, 2004; available online at http://www.waff.com/Global/story .asp?S=1644862. The CRA also protects and preserves the Constitution of the United States by restricting federal courts from recognizing the laws of foreign jurisdictions and international law as the supreme law of our land.

52. 127 S. Ct. 2553, 75 USLW 4560, June 25, 2007.

53. "Justice Alito: A Promise Kept," *Notebook,* American Center for Law and Justice, July 12, 2007; available online at http://www.aclj.org/TrialNotebook/Read.aspx?id=509.

54. *Flast v. Cohen,* 392 U.S. 83 (1968). This case was confirmed by the Supreme Court as recently as 2006 in *DaimlerChrysler Corp.* v. *Cuno,* 126 S. Ct. 1854 (2006).

55. See *Frothingham v. Mellon,* 262 U.S. 447, 485, 486 (1923).

56. See *Flast* at 104.

57. *Id.* at 103.

58. *Id.,* at 102, 103.

59. Examples of federal courts' refusal to grant taxpayer standing on other issues are found in *Kurtz* v. *Baker,* 829 F.2d 1133 (D.C. Cir. 1987) and *Langendorf v. Administrators of Tulane Educational Fund,* 528 F.2d 1076 (5th Cir. 1976). These cases were dismissed at the lower level and not considered by the Supreme Court.

60. Oral Arguments in the Supreme Court of the United States, *Hein v. Freedom from Religion Foundation.*

61. See Souter dissent in *Hein v. Freedom from Religion Foundation.*

62. See Charles Babington, "Senator Links Violence to 'Political' Decisions; Unaccountable Judiciary Raises Ire," *Washington Post,* April 5, 2005, A07.

Timothy G. Standish

CHAPTER 11

The Battle Over Origins

The United States Supreme Court has twice ruled that creation science is religion and cannot be taught in public-school science classes. In recent years, a new approach to origins has developed known as intelligent design. To its critics, intelligent design is simply a disguise for creationism, is equally religious, and consequently, is out of place in the public-school science curriculum. Advocates contend that intelligent design is genuine science and that it doesn't delve into the theological implications of its theory—namely, the nature or character of the intelligent creator. To date, intelligent design hasn't fared well in the courts. In a prominent case, a federal judge in Dover, Pennsylvania, ejected intelligent design from county schools.

If you listen to Darwin's defenders, intelligent design is a religious theory and must be censored out of the science curriculum. Design advocates respond that Darwinists have exalted Darwin's theory to the status of religious belief and have virtually established the religion of scientific materialism as a state religion, at least for purposes of public education. They insist that the principles of free inquiry require that both theories be fairly presented and evaluated using the same scientific methods.

Long before the time of Christ, theories abounded about the origin of all things. Much as some modern-day cosmologists believed the universe was eternal before the big bang theory was developed, some of the ancients believed the universe was eternal and that there was no creation. The Epicureans believed that everything resulted from the unguided interaction of atoms, reminding us of modern materialists, who believe essentially the same thing. Cicero tells us, " 'For he [Epicurus] who taught us all the rest has also taught us that the world was made by nature, without needing an artificer to construct it, and that the act of creation, which according to you cannot be performed without divine skill, is so easy, that nature will create, is creating, and has created worlds without number. You on the contrary cannot see how nature can achieve all this without the aid of some intelligence.' "[1]

Epicurean materialism leads fairly consistently to a theory of origins that closely resembles modern Darwinian views. The Roman Epicurean poet Titus Lucretius Carus demonstrated this in his *De Rerum Natura* (*On the Nature of Things*):

> The atoms did not intend to intelligently place themselves in orderly arrangement, nor did they negotiate the motions they would have, but many atoms struck each other in numerous ways, carried along by their own momentum from infinitely long ago to the present. Moving and meeting in numerous ways, all combinations were tried which could be tried, and it was from this process over huge space and vast time that these combining and recombining atoms eventually produced great things, including the earth, sea, and sky, and the generation of living creatures.[2]

Here Lucretius outlines the basic formula for Darwinian evolution: Given a large enough universe and plenty of time, everything, including living things, comes about via random interactions and natural laws. In more recent times, the Darwinist apologist Richard Dawkins put it this way: "Given infinite time, or infinite opportunities, anything is possible. The large numbers proverbially furnished by astronomy, and the large time spans characteristic of geology, combine to turn topsy-turvy our everyday estimates of what is expected and what is miraculous."[3]

Willingly ignorant

The question of whether the Creator God is responsible for creation or whether the universe and life as we know it came about via some other means independent of an intelligent agent has been controversial for a long time. Prophecies related to this question are common in the Old and New Testaments. For example, the apostle Peter wrote, "There shall come in the last days scoffers, walking after their own lusts, And saying, Where is the promise of his coming? for since the fathers fell asleep, all things continue as *they were* from the beginning of the creation. For this they willingly are ignorant of, that by the word of God the heavens were of old, and the earth standing out of the water and in the water" (2 Peter 3:3–5; emphasis added).[4]

Peter's prophecy about the end of time seems to be related to one of the great prophecies of Revelation. In chapter 14 of that book, an angel described as having the "everlasting gospel" to preach to everyone on earth, proclaims, "Fear God, and give glory to him; for the hour of his judgment is come: and worship him that made heaven, and earth, and the sea, and the fountains of waters" (verses 6, 7).

The reference to judgment places this pronouncement at the end of earth's history. Why would Christians need special urging to worship the Creator during the end-time judgment when the Ten Commandments already tell believers to "remember"[5] to do this? There must be something special about the end time that requires this additional reminder to the faithful.

Clearly, arguments against creation haven't changed substantially over time. It is a myth that Charles Darwin came up with the idea of natural selection and that this component of his theory of evolution changed everything. The idea of natural selection was published well before Darwin's day.[6] The sensation caused by his *Origin of Species* occurred because he substituted natural selection for the role of God as an agent in the empirical world and particularly in the creation of the life we now see on earth. However, Darwinian thinking was prevalent in the pagan world before the time of Christ. Ironically, many of the ancient arguments used by the Epicureans against creation are still heard today. For example, in recent times, Stephen J. Gould (and many others) have triumphantly proclaimed that "imperfection carries the day for evolution,"[7] while more than two thousand years ago Lucretius argued, "The world was certainly not made for us by divine power: so great are the faults with which it stands endowed."[8] Solomon was correct when he said, "There is no new thing under the sun" (Ecclesiastes 1:9)!

Perhaps the clearest explanation of why the creation aspect of the gospel is worthy of special emphasis at the end of the world is hinted at by the Old Testament prophet Daniel, who, when referring to the time of the end, predicted that "knowledge shall be increased" (Daniel 12:4). Some might argue that this only suggests knowledge of Daniel's prophecies, but the text doesn't seem to require this or even suggest that he is thinking about anything less than knowledge in general. This would include both knowledge of the creation and knowledge of prophecies related to it. If the time that we live in is the time of the end or the judgment time, then we should be seeing a fulfillment of this prophecy, and no reasonable argument can be made against the assertion that knowledge of the creation, if not the Creator, has increased dramatically in recent times.

What does this have to do with the call to worship the Creator during the time of judgment? It is ironic that as our understanding of the workings of nature is exploding, the knowledge is released through a "Darwinian filter."[9] The apostle Paul seems to be describing a situation like this in his second letter to the believers in Thessalonica. He starts out by referring to the "mystery of iniquity" (2 Thessalonians 2:7) that was already at work when he was writing.[10] As a Jew and a scholar, Paul would have been aware of Epicurean arguments used against the existence of a Creator God and would have considered these iniquitous. In fact, the Bible specifically tells us that Paul met with Epicurean philosophers in Athens (see Acts 17:18, 19) and attempted to convince them of the Creator God's existence. Perhaps the evolutionary arguments they used against God are what he had in mind when he went on to write to the Thessalonians about God sending a "strong delusion, that they should believe a lie: That they all might be damned who believed not the truth, but had pleasure in unrighteousness" (2 Thessalonians 2:11, 12).

It isn't unreasonable to suspect that the "strong delusion" Paul was referring to is the Darwinian "universal acid: it eats through just about every traditional concept, and leaves in its wake a revolutionized world-view."[11] As Richard Dawkins put it, "Darwin made it possible to be an intellectually fulfilled atheist." Dawkins is clearly a brilliant man and occupies a unique position of authority in the academic establishment as Charles Simonyi Professor for the Public Understanding of Science at Oxford University, Fellow of New College, and Fellow of the Royal Society. The power of the delusion is such that it works on the brilliant and the dull, the powerful and the weak.

Filtering out the beauty

The great difference between the time when Paul lived and the present is that our understanding of how nature works is clearly more complete both in scope and resolution. Given this increased knowledge predicted by Daniel, fresh opportunities present themselves to make the logical inference from design in nature to some intelligent cause for life and the universe. Yet while each new discovery reveals to us more of nature's elegant design, when we view it through a Darwinian filter, we miss the beauty of the design.

Take the following recent example, which requires a basic understanding of photosynthesis—the process in which plants use light energy to combine atmospheric carbon dioxide and water into sugars while at the same time releasing oxygen into the atmosphere. A microscopic protein machine (an enzyme) called Rubisco (Ribulose diphosphate carboxylase) catalyzes the step at which carbon dioxide from the atmosphere is attached to an organic molecule that ultimately is made into sugar. Without Rubisco, life as we know it couldn't exist.

As long as carbon dioxide concentrations are high and oxygen concentrations are low, Rubisco works like a well-oiled machine. However, on hot, dry days, the leaves of many plants close the little pores on their surface, allowing internal carbon dioxide levels to fall and oxygen levels to rise. Under these circumstances, instead of incorporating carbon dioxide, Rubisco starts joining oxygen into organic molecules, a phenomenon referred to as photorespiration. This process appears to be wasteful because ultimately the product is broken down to carbon dioxide and water, which is exactly the opposite of what photosynthesis is supposed to do. As a result of photorespiration, a quarter of the carbon harvested in photosynthesis goes back into the atmosphere. Some plants, like those that live in deserts, have special adaptations to reduce the problem, but none of these entirely eliminate photorespiration.

This raises the question of why Rubisco would be so poorly designed that it can wastefully incorporate oxygen instead of carbon dioxide. A standard textbook explanation has been that the Rubisco maladaptation reflects the earth's evolutionary history: The ancient atmosphere must have had lower oxygen concentrations and higher carbon dioxide concentrations, and thus there was little selective pressure to choose more discriminating forms of Rubisco.[12] This is just the kind of poor design that Gould and Lucretius argue disproves divine creation. However, the recent discovery that photorespiration is essential for amino-acid production in plants calls into question the evolutionary explanation.[13] Amino acids are the nitrogen-containing molecules used as building blocks to make proteins. Because Rubisco is made out of protein, it appears Rubisco is necessary to make the building blocks of more proteins so that more Rubisco—not to mention other proteins—can be made. Rather than being leftover evolutionary baggage, photorespiration now appears vital for plant growth and survival.

One would think that our better understanding of Rubisco and its elegant design would raise doubts about the utility of Darwinian explanations of Rubisco's origin, but this is only the case for those not already burned by the "universal acid." A Darwinian apologist might argue that the design now apparent in Rubisco is exactly what one would expect in such a crucial and ubiquitous protein—especially given evidence interpreted to mean that the first Rubisco evolved over 3.8 billion years ago, providing plenty of time to be refined by natural selection.[14] Evolutionary explanations have just such an infinitely plastic nature: On the one hand, poor design is exactly what evolution would predict; and on the other hand, well-adapted designs are exactly what evolution would predict. In reality, Darwinism appears to offer little insight into why nature exhibits good or bad design, but it does provide endless explanations that make a Creator God superfluous.

Bible-believing Christians now find themselves in a particularly awkward position. On the one hand, nature appears increasingly likely to be a product of intelligence, the Logos referred to by John the Evangelist. On the other hand, a well-established theory, Darwinism, dominates academic thought, apparently blinding those who are studying nature from seeing the logical inference to intelligent cause that their discoveries suggest. This appears to fit very well with the prophetic picture of the end times laid out in the Bible: the increase in knowledge prophesied by Daniel, the powerful delusion predicted by Paul, and the Revelation 14:7 reminder to the faithful during the judgment time to worship the Creator God.

What kind of recent knowledge points toward an intelligent cause in nature? In physics, two sets of very precise numbers seem to suggest either incredible luck or an intelligent cause. The first set deals with constants like the strength of gravity and the force that holds atoms together. These numbers have to be exact if the universe is going to be capable of maintaining conditions in which life can exist. The second set of constants has to do with production of materials that would be necessary to move from an initial big bang creation to the kind of universe that has elements like carbon in sufficient quantities for life to exist. In both sets of constants, some of which overlap, it seems that extreme precision is required. Sometimes this is referred to as "cosmic fine-tuning" or the "anthropomorphic principle."

Impediments to the evidence

A second set of discoveries has to do with life itself. Before and during Darwin's time, cells—the fundamental building blocks of life—were thought of as relatively simple, "primitive protoplasm" made up of "inorganic nitrocarbonates."[15] They were thought of as having prime potential for evolving. Today, we know that cells are incredibly complex structures that incorporate both information and information-processing systems, as well as numerous minute machines that operate within specified tolerances. Information encoded in DNA and the machines for which that DNA contains blueprints may constitute only a subset of all the phenomena within cells that suggest an intelligent cause for life, but information and machines comprise an obvious logical inference to intelligence. There is no evidence that either natural laws or even natural selection can produce information, although the latter may act as an "editor" of already existing information. We know that information is a product of intelligent causes. The same is true of machines, whether macroscopic or microscopic.

It seems almost ironic that at the very time when the evidence—from both nature and the prophetic writings in the Scriptures—points most logically to the Creator God and the need to worship Him, the greatest impediments are in place to prevent people from seeing that evidence and responding with worship. Unfortunately, institutions of higher learning are at the forefront of promoting Darwinism, and many policymakers view this quasi-scientific[16] theory as religiously neutral. This is particularly unfortunate as evolution is clearly religiously loaded.[17] The designations "religious" and "secular" have become tools for manipulation of public opinion and policy to restrict teaching about apparent intelligence behind nature and to promote a delusion—Darwinism.

Abusing temporal power to advance a religious agenda is repugnant within a Christian worldview, particularly given Jesus Christ's clear statement that His "kingdom is not of this world" (John 18:36). And the fact is that Christians do live in the empirical world, not in a separate reality; they don't worship an imaginary god or look forward to an imaginary kingdom of heaven. Nor do they live their lives focusing on questions such as the length of a Sabbath day's journey or how many angels fit on the head of a pin. When confronted with very real delusions about the nature of reality, those wishing to worship the Creator God who "made heaven, and earth, and the sea, and the fountains of waters" (Revelation 14:7) aren't called to ignore those delusions. Whether in public life or in private, Christians honor and seek truth, not to keep it to themselves but in order to be "the light of the world" (Matthew 5:14). It seems axiomatic that the more closely one's beliefs are grounded in reality, the better off one is likely to be. The same is true of public policy.

This is not a warrant to rush in and attempt to make policies that won't withstand legal challenges or to restrict the God-given rights of others or to attempt to impose Christianity on anyone. The recent *Kitzmiller v. Dover Area School District* case[18] in Dover, Pennsylvania, illustrates the baleful consequences of misguided attempts at public policy in this area. The defendants, the Dover Area School District Board, decided to enact a policy requiring teachers to read a statement in front of high school biology classes that pointed out the theoretical nature of Darwinism and that cited the existence of other theories about life's origins, including intelligent design.[19] While this may seem reasonable on the surface, it provided an opportunity to advance the agenda of those who wish to make classrooms a closed shop for Darwinism. The defendants were advised by fellow Christians with expertise in these matters not to pursue the case,[20] but they chose to defend the policy instead.

The result was predictable—the school district lost in court, resulting in a poorly reasoned decision endorsing Darwinian orthodoxy and dismissing its critics in scornful terms. It was a significant setback for critics of public education's treatment of origins and for the school district, which had to pay a million dollars to the American Civil Liberties Union (ACLU) for its role as legal counsel to the plaintiffs.[21] At the next election, the Dover School Board was ejected, and other school boards now must operate in fear of similar outcomes if they implement anything other than unquestioned Darwinian orthodoxy. Christians aren't advised to rush in where angels fear to tread in these cases, but instead to be "wise as serpents, and harmless as doves" (Matthew 10:16).

Misuse of the First Amendment

When public policies restrict either the free exercise of conscience or free inquiry into the nature of reality, they are in clear tension with Christian beliefs. This is precisely the case with teaching about origins in the United States and some other countries. Ironically, the First Amendment to the United States Constitution, which was designed to protect religions and religious beliefs from government interference, is used as a justification for enforcing a Darwinian hegemony on science education. This is expressed clearly in Judge Jones's ruling in *Kitzmiller*. "To preserve the separation of church and state mandated by the Establishment Clause of the First Amendment to the United States Constitution, and Art. I, § 3 of the Pennsylvania Constitution, we will enter an order permanently enjoining Defendants from maintaining the ID Policy[22] in any school within the Dover Area School District, from requiring teachers to denigrate or disparage the scientific theory of evolution, and from requiring teachers to refer to a religious alternative theory known as ID."[23] Thus the principle banning state "establishment of religion, or prohibiting the free exercise thereof"[24] enshrined in the United States Constitution is used as a justification for providing Darwinism, a theory about origins, with special state protection while forbidding exposing children to alternative views.

The logic of the *Kitzmiller* decision seems to do injustice to the Constitution, which clearly doesn't say that just because some religious viewpoints agree with a given idea they must be untrue or can't be taught in public schools. The Bible does describe creation, but it also describes the water cycle and even attributes it to God's activity (see Job 36:27, 28). It hardly seems reasonable to demand that children not be taught about the water cycle just because it is found in the Bible or that banning teaching about it or any number of other natural phenomena would somehow prevent establishment of a state religion. The same principle that applies to the water cycle applies in public life when it comes to evidence of an Intelligent Cause for life. It is hardly the place of government to forcibly support an orthodoxy (Darwinism) that demands a specific answer that impinges on the nature of God just because that answer goes against Christian beliefs as well as the beliefs of some other faiths, not to mention the preponderance of empirical evidence. In fact, this seems to be the very kind of government meddling that the First Amendment was designed to prevent and turns on its head the idea that separation of church and state will help maintain both the free exercise of religion, free inquiry, and free speech.

Speaking about the end of time, Jesus Christ prophesied, "This gospel of the kingdom shall be preached in all the world for a witness unto all nations; and then shall the end come" (Matthew 24:14). The angel of Revelation 14:6, 7 tells us that worship of the Creator God is a central part of the gospel. Given the current state of affairs, it shouldn't surprise us to discover that every possible means—including the state in some cases—is being employed to prevent the gospel from being heard and taking root. No one said that the work of Christians living at the end of time would be easy. In fact, Christ prophesied exactly the opposite (see Matthew 24:4–13). But it is the work of Christians both in sunshine and in rain to "demolish arguments and every pretension that sets itself up against the knowledge of God" and "take captive every thought to make it obedient to Christ" (2 Corinthians

10:5, NIV)—not through demagoguery but by using the methods of Christ Himself in an open marketplace of ideas.

When public policies, academic hierarchies, or other coercive means are used to prevent this openness, they stand in direct opposition to the Christian faith and good public policy. A proper and healthy separation of church and state is not in conflict with the genuine pursuit of knowledge. An open marketplace of ideas is one of those things that is both good public policy and consistent with Christian views, just as are laws against murder and theft. Wise policies designed to allow an unfettered discussion of ideas in the public square, public institutions, and public schools—both those that Christians embrace and those, like Darwinism, that they reject—deserve the active support of all Christians.

---

1. Marcus Tullius Cicero, *De Natura Deorum,* http://www.epicurus.net/en/deorum.html.

2. This is my own translation of the original Latin as printed in Titus Lucretius Carus, *De Rerum Natura,* Book 5, lines 416–431 (c. 55 B.C.); see *Lucretius: On the Nature of Things,* W. H. D. Rouse, Martin F. Smith, trans. (Cambridge, Mass: Harvard University Press, 1992).

3. Richard Dawkins, *The Blind Watchmaker: Why the Evidence of Evolution Reveals a Universe Without Design* (New York: W. W. Norton and Co., 1989), 139.

4. Except where otherwise noted, all Scripture quotations are from the King James Version.

5. In the words of Exodus 20:8, "Remember the sabbath day, to keep it holy."

6. Edward Blythe wrote quite detailed descriptions of natural selection during the 1830s. For a discussion of this, see L. Eiseley, "Charles Darwin, Edward Blyth, and the Theory of Natural Selection," *Proceedings of the American Philosophical Society* 103, no. 1 (1959): 94–114.

7. Stephen J. Gould, *The Panda's Thumb: More Reflections on Natural History* (New York: W. W. Norton, 1980), 37.

8. Carus, lines 198, 199; as quoted in Rouse and Smith.

9. By this I mean that at the time of their publication, most discoveries are explained in Darwinian terms whether or not they are consistent with Darwinian theory.

10. Note that I am not arguing for this interpretation of the "mystery of iniquity" to the exclusion of all other interpretations. It seems reasonable to view this entity as multifaceted and thus manifested in multiple ways, one of which may be what we now call Darwinism. The unifying characteristic of the "mystery of iniquity" seems to be that it stands in opposition to the true worship of the Creator God.

11. D. C. Dennett, *Darwin's Dangerous Idea: Evolution and the Meanings of Life* (New York: Simon & Schuster, 1995), 63.

12. For examples, see N. A. Campbell, J. B. Reece, and L. G. Mitchell, *Biology,* 5th ed. (San Francisco: Benjamin Cummings, 2002), 182, 183; and D. Voet and J. G. Voet, *Biochemistry* (New York: John Whiley and Sons, 1990), 613.

13. S. Rachmilevitch, A. B. Cousins, and A. J. Bloom, "Nitrate Assimilation in Plant Shoots Depends on Photorespiration," *Proceedings of the National Academy of Sciences* 101, no 31 (2004): 11506–11510.

14. S. J. Mojzsis et al., "Evidence for Life on Earth Before 3,800 Million Years Ago," *Nature* 384 (Nov. 7, 1996): 55–59. Note that I do not endorse these dates.

15. E. Haeckel, *The Riddle of the Universe at the Close of the Nineteenth Century* (New York and London: Harper and Brothers Publishers, 1900), 369.

16. By "quasi-scientific" I mean that the theory is rooted more in the tradition of rationalism and lacks the empirical basis on which the best scientific theories are built. In addition, I agree with Daniel Dennett that Darwinism is a belief system that transcends science and impacts almost all other fields of human knowledge. In other words, Darwinism is a theory of everything, not just a scientific theory.

17. As Michael Ruse put it, "Evolution is promoted by its practitioners as more than mere science. Evolution is promulgated as an ideology, a secular religion—a full-fledged alternative to Christianity, with meaning and morality. . . . Evolution is a religion. This was true of evolution in the beginning, and it is true of evolution still today." Michael Ruse, "How Evolution Became a Religion," *The National Post Online*, Saturday, May 13, 2000 (www.nationalpost.com/artslife.asp?f=000513/288424).

18. *Kitzmiller v. Dover Area School District*, 400 F. Supp. 2d 707 (M.D. Pa. 2005).

19. The text of the statement is available at numerous locations on the Internet. The version that follows was taken from http://www.discovery.org/scripts/viewDB/index.php?command=view&id=3633&program=CSC%20-%20Views%20and%20News:

"The Pennsylvania Academic Standards require students to learn about Darwin's Theory of Evolution and eventually to take a standardized test of which evolution is a part. Because Darwin's Theory is a theory, it continues to be tested as new evidence is discovered. The Theory is not a fact. Gaps in the Theory exist for which there is no evidence. A theory is defined as a well-tested explanation that unifies a broad range of observations.

"Intelligent Design is an explanation of the origin of life that differs from Darwin's view. The reference book Of Pandas and People is available for students who might be interested in gaining an understanding of what Intelligent Design actually involves.

"With respect to any theory, students are encouraged to keep an open mind. The school leaves the discussion of the Origins of Life to individual students and their families. As a Standards-driven district, class instruction focuses upon preparing students to achieve proficiency on Standards-based assessments."

20. See, for example, the statement of the Discovery Institute, who advised the Dover school board against going ahead with their policy: http://www.discovery.org/scripts/viewDB/index.php?command=view&id=2847.

21. For a detailed analysis of the judgment, see http://www.discovery.org/scripts/viewDB/index.php?command=view&id=2879. See also D. K. DeWolf et al., *Traipsing Into Evolution: Intelligent Design and the Kitzmiller vs. Dover Decision* (Seattle, Wash.: Discovery Institute Press, 2006), 124.

22. By "ID Policy," Judge Jones was referring to the policy of reading the statement in endnote 19 to ninth-grade students in Dover Area public schools.

23. Jones III JE. 2005 Memorandum Opinion Case Number 04cv2688 Tammy Kitzmiller *et al.* plaintiffs v. Dover Area School District *et al.* defendants United States District Court for the Middle District of Pennsylvania, December 20, 2005, 138.

24. First Amendment to the Constitution of the United States of America.

Alan J. Reinach

CHAPTER 12

The Battle for the Ten Commandments

People came to Montgomery, Alabama, from all over the country. They gathered at the courthouse, praying and singing, to defend God from the latest assault by the federal courts. Inside, a 5,280-pound slab of Vermont granite occupied the central rotunda. It was etched with a Protestant rendition of the Ten Commandments, along with historical references to God. Citizens waited for the inevitable day when federal marshals would remove Roy's Rock, as the monument was affectionately known, by federal court order.

After the monument was removed, the cameras disappeared and the story vanished from the media. But Roy's Rock has become an itinerant preacher for God and country, accompanying former Alabama Chief Justice Roy Moore as he campaigns around the country, speaking to churches, pastors, and anyone who will listen, about America's Christian heritage and the nation's obligation to acknowledge God according to the first commandment. The monument travels on the back of a flatbed truck with its own twenty-three-foot tall crane.[1]

The drama surrounding the removal of the monument, complete with television cameras, protestors singing and crying, and federal marshals in uniform carrying out their orders, was in stark contrast to the monument's origin. Justice Moore had secretly installed the monument in the middle of the night. He intended to make a simple point: America is a Christian nation, and under the first commandment, it has an obligation to acknowledge God.[2] Moore rejects the constitutional interpretation that holds the state to strict neutrality in matters of religion. He made no pretense of installing the monument as a secular or historical symbol of Western law. His was an overtly religious act.

Moore's boldness made the federal courts' job much simpler, and it deprived Moore of the Supreme Court precedent that he sought—eventually it refused to hear his appeal. Later, however, the Supreme Court took cases involving Ten Commandments displays in Texas and Kentucky. Its rulings in these cases (in 2005), permitted one Ten Commandments display to remain intact but ordered the removal of the other. These rulings have not slowed the pace of litigation in courts around the country over local displays of the Ten Commandments.

Those who object to the displays contend that the state has no business meddling with religion and promoting an overtly religious symbol. They say that the official preference for this religious symbol sends a message to those who don't adhere to this faith that they are outsiders, second-class citizens, guests but not "real" Americans. To those who support the public displays, the Ten Commandments are a symbol of America's moral and spiritual health. To remove the commandments is to offend God and to risk His wrath and judgment. Displays of the commandments are thought to honor God and to ensure for America an increased measure of His blessing.

The battle over the Ten Commandments isn't just a fight over a symbol. There are important spiritual and even prophetic issues at stake. How American churches relate to God's law is central to our understanding of the gospel of Jesus Christ and to the nation's spiritual health. Recovery of a genuine gospel experience has profound implications not only for the improvement of public morals and the social good in general but also for the future of American freedom. In order to grasp the spiritual dimension of the conflict, we must see the legal and historical context.

Ten Commandments monuments

In 1956, Cecil B. DeMille released his blockbuster movie *The Ten Commandments,* starring Charlton Heston. In order to promote the movie, he secured the cooperation of a national service organization, the Fraternal Order of Eagles, who sponsored Ten Commandments monuments throughout the country. DeMille and Heston appeared for many of the unveiling ceremonies and attracted considerable media attention. The promotion was an extremely successful one.

Some forty years later, the American Civil Liberties Union (ACLU) challenged one of those monuments—one that was located on the grounds of the Texas State capitol in Austin. It was one of seventeen monuments and twenty-one historical markers scattered throughout the grounds. This case went to the Supreme Court as *Van Orden v. Perry.*

Meanwhile, in the summer of 1999, two Kentucky counties placed framed Ten Commandments displays in their county courthouses. The ACLU challenged these displays in court too. A federal court issued an injunction—a court order requiring that the displays be removed. The county legislatures responded by authorizing a new display entitled "Foundations of American Law and Government." This included the Ten Commandments displays but added to them nine other documents referencing God, such as the Declaration of Independence's "endowed by our Creator" phrase and "The Star-Spangled Banner." The Ten Commandments display was modified to include the entire text of the commandments in the King James Version of the Bible and an explanation about the historical and legal significance of the commandments. Challenged again by the ACLU, this case was decided by the Supreme Court as *McCreary County v. American Civil Liberties Union of Kentucky*.

The Supreme Court was sharply divided, upholding the Texas display while striking down the one in Kentucky—both in 5–4 decisions. Although widely criticized as inconsistent and incomprehensible, the decisions are much more logical and reasonable than many realize.[3]

The late chief justice, William Rehnquist, wrote the opinion in the Texas case. Early in his career he had famously criticized the Supreme Court's interpretation of the Establishment Clause, declaring, "The 'wall of separation between church and State' is a metaphor based on bad history, a metaphor which has proved useless as a guide to judging. It should be frankly and explicitly abandoned."[4] By the end of his career, when he was serving as the chief justice, Rehnquist displayed a much more moderate tone and considerable respect for precedent. Advocates urged the reversal of *Stone v. Graham*, a prior case striking down the display of the Ten Commandments in a public-school classroom. But Rehnquist refused to criticize *Stone*. Instead, he distinguished the coercive effects of an overtly religious Ten Commandments display in a public school from the Texas monument, which was one of many historical monuments in a public park. As one of seventeen monuments representing various "strands in the State's political and legal history," Rehnquist found the monument acceptable. He didn't downplay the religious nature of either the Ten Commandments or the monument, but he held that they were constitutional because of the context.

The decisive swing vote was cast by Justice Stephen Breyer. His vote struck down the Kentucky display and upheld the Texas monument. Breyer explicitly applied the Supreme Court's historic Establishment Clause test, the *Lemon* test, which asked whether a state action is performed for a secular purpose and effect, whether the action unduly entangles church and state, and whether the entanglement with religion is unduly divisive. For Breyer, context was decisive—the fact that the Texas monument was one religious reference in a sea of historical monuments and markers meant that the state was not simply endorsing a religious message. Breyer also focused on the absence of controversy in the first forty years of the monument's history as evidence that it could remain without causing civil strife.

The principle that emerges from Breyer's decision, and indeed, from all of the opinions taken together, is that under the American constitutional system, religious symbols may be included in public life but they cannot be singled out too prominently in ways that would convey the impression of special state endorsement and promotion. Visitors to the Texas State capitol would be unlikely to infer state endorsement of religion by the inclusion of the Ten Commandments monument among the many monuments exhibited.

The Kentucky case was dramatically different. In the Kentucky county courthouses, the commandments were the lone display at first. After the display was challenged in court, the commandments were accompanied by secular documents chosen for their references to God. To the lower federal courts, there was no mistaking the legislative intent to highlight the religious origins and commitments of the nation. The displays unambiguously endorsed the religious content of the Ten Commandments.

Justice Souter's opinion striking down this display emphasized the constitutional requirement that government act for fundamentally secular purposes, not religious ones. This principle has sound historical support. Even before the Bill of Rights was adopted, defenders of the newly proposed federal Constitution insisted that the federal government was given only limited, delegated powers. They argued that the federal government had no power to infringe on fundamental freedoms of speech, press, and religion. Several states insisted that they wouldn't approve the proposed Constitution unless those freedoms were made explicit in a bill of rights. The Bill of Rights didn't grant Congress power to act for religious purposes that it never had under the Constitution itself. To the contrary, the Establishment Clause specifically precludes Congress from pursuing religion as an aim of government.

A Christian nation?

From a legal perspective, the argument over Ten Commandments displays invokes a larger issue: Is America a Christian nation, and if so, can government support and promote the majority Christian faith? The Supreme Court declined to support this proposition in either case, but it came close.

Justice Scalia, writing in dissent in the Kentucky case, insisted that Ten Commandments displays were a valid expression of the 97.7 percent of Americans who belonged to one of the Abrahamic faiths that regarded the text as sacred. Joined by Justices Rehnquist and Thomas, Scalia rejected the principle of government neutrality toward religion.[5] He wrote approvingly of state efforts to encourage religion.

Scalia's approach to the religion clauses is essentially majoritarian. He considers the wishes of the 97.7 percent as more important than the Bill of Rights. So long as enough people want governmental recognition of a sacred text, it is majority will and might that makes right. In principle, this means that legislatures can provide and support whatever religious monuments, displays, invocations, exercises, or practices that are approved by the majority of the population.

This principle isn't a new one for Scalia. In *Employment Division v. Smith,* he severely eroded the Free Exercise Clause by adopting a similar majoritarian principle. Americans may no longer object to a law that infringes on their religious freedom so long as the law is "facially neutral." As long as legislators mask legal restrictions on religious activities in "neutral" language that doesn't identify the target as religious, the law will be immune from constitutional attack. The majority now rules in matters of religion—at least it does as far as the Free Exercise Clause is concerned. If the new conservative Supreme Court majority follows Scalia's leadership, the same majoritarian principle may well destroy the Establishment Clause, freeing the state to enact religious legislation.

This majoritarian principle is, at its core, a complete repudiation of the Bill of Rights. The Bill of Rights was intended to protect the rights of individuals from being trampled on by the government. The executive and legislative branches of government are essentially majoritarian in that their representatives are elected and consequently represent the majority of the people. The courts are fundamentally different. They exist to protect individual rights secured by the Constitution against abuse by the other branches of government. No right is an island. The legal theories that uphold one right are frequently invoked in support of another.[6] To grant the majority power to infringe individual rights, as Scalia does, is tantamount to saying that the majority can enact laws making it a crime to root for the New York

Yankees in public.[7] If that seems too absurd, consider a more dangerous approach to censorship: A conservative-dominated Congress and presidency could equate criticism of the war in Iraq with treason and punish outspoken critics with prison sentences.[8]

This eventuality seems unthinkable in the United States. Yet, such censorship has become all too common in totalitarian nations.[9] It would be foolish, therefore, to discount the possibility that, given the proper legal framework, a political majority would take undue advantage of the opportunity to abuse its power. The purpose of this discussion isn't to advance intemperate predictions of totalitarian doom. Rather, it is to make sense of where majoritarian power may lead. The Founding Fathers established a republican form of government with checks and balances to protect against the accumulation of power by any branch. James Madison reasoned that the multiplicity of religious sects would prevent the accumulation of power by any particular church or denomination—an idea that later became known as "the tyranny of the majority."[10]

Today, the "original intent" of the Founding Fathers is invoked to support a radical reinterpretation of the Constitution they bequeathed to us. This radical revision of the Constitution turns the principles of freedom upside down. Instead of the rights of the individual being supreme because they are given by God, the rights of the majority now reign supreme. In effect, it enables the majority to say, "We have every right to display our sacred text of the Ten Commandments because this is our nation, a Christian nation, and those who don't like it can leave!" Advocates of Ten Commandments displays repeatedly voice this sentiment. Little do they realize that they are trading their own sacred rights for ones that the majority chooses for them.

Majority rule in matters of religion may have appeal as long as you are in the majority. Baptists or Pentecostals in the Bible Belt of the United States may find majority rule quite convenient until they go somewhere else. Bible Belt Christians who venture into Utah or Hawaii will find another religion dominant and may take a different view of majority rule in religious affairs. Indeed, this highlights the very danger our Founding Fathers sought to avoid. They didn't want the nation splintered along religious lines—divided by sect from town to town, state to state. They didn't want the nation "ethnically cleansed" along religious lines.

Justice Sandra Day O'Connor, now retired, expressed the principle clearly in her concurring opinion in the Kentucky case:

Reasonable minds can disagree about how to apply the Religion Clauses in a given case. But the goal of the Clauses is clear: to carry out the Founders' plan of preserving religious liberty to the fullest extent possible in a pluralistic society. By enforcing the Clauses, we have kept religion a matter for the individual conscience, not for the prosecutor or bureaucrat. At a time when we see around the world the violent consequences of the assumption of religious authority by government, Americans may count themselves fortunate: Our regard for constitutional boundaries has protected us from similar travails, while allowing private religious exercise to flourish.[11]

O'Connor rejected Scalia's premise that the majority may determine what religious beliefs and texts will be approved. She declared,

It is true that many Americans find the Commandments in accord with their personal beliefs. But we do not count heads before enforcing the First Amendment. See *West Virginia Bd. of Ed.* v. *Barnette,* 319 U.S. 624, 638 (1943). ("The very purpose of a Bill of Rights was to withdraw certain subjects from the vicissitudes of political controversy, to place them beyond the reach of majorities and officials and to establish them as legal principles to be applied by the courts.") Nor can we accept the theory that Americans who do not accept the Commandments' validity are outside the First Amendment's protections. There is no list of approved and disapproved beliefs appended to the First Amendment—and the Amendment's broad terms ("free exercise," "establishment," "religion") do not admit of such a cramped reading.[12]

A peculiar irony

A peculiar irony arose in the Supreme Court Ten Commandments cases. Opponents of the public display of the Ten Commandments argued that the government couldn't display them because they are religious. According to this argument, the state can't endorse and promote a sacred text. Supporters of the displays, supposedly taking the Christian perspective, contended that the displays were permitted because of their historic and legal significance as foundations of Western law. Recall that in Kentucky, after the courts rejected the display of the Ten Commandments text by itself, the legislatures adopted a new approach that involved multiple documents styled as "Foundations of American Law and Government." The Christians downplayed the religious significance of the text while the liberals and atheists emphasized its sacredness!

At a minimum, such an argument by the Christian supporters of the Ten Commandments is disingenuous. Christians didn't fight all the way to the Supreme Court merely to defend historic displays. Many of them share Roy Moore's religious zeal. The Ten Commandments are a battleground because of their sacred significance, not because of their legal or historic meaning. So, the Christian organizations and their attorneys who contended for the secular significance of the Ten Commandments displays may well have compromised their integrity in the process—ironically, violating the commandment against bearing false witness.

This only hints at the deeper problems. The Ten Commandments are a profound symbol. To supporters, they symbolize everything that is right with America. They represent that our national greatness may be rooted in our faith in God. So, to them, the removal of crosses from hillsides and Ten Commandments displays from public schools is symbolic of the moral and spiritual decline of the nation. And conversely, the return of such symbols to American public life is thought to signify a return of God's blessing. At its heart, then, the battle is really a spiritual conflict over the soul of America.[13]

Sadly, the culture war is being fought primarily in terms of public policy and politics. Countless political skirmishes have been fought over gay-rights bills, abortion bills, and other policies. Despite Congress being in conservative hands for more than a decade and the nation having a conservative president for the past six years, little progress has been made on the "social agenda." Meanwhile, school killings continue to remind Americans that something has gone desperately wrong. Hollywood has intensified the pace of violence and nudity in movies in an effort to satisfy our unquenchable thirst for shock value in entertainment. Meanwhile, Christians are looking for cultural renewal in all the wrong places—in Washington, D.C., for example.

Moral, spiritual, and cultural renewal may truly be found in only one place—before God. Genuine spiritual revival is the only real hope for America. The first of the three angels who give warning messages in Revelation 14 proclaims the need to return to true worship of the Creator. Such worship is said to be the "everlasting gospel" and suggests the need to recover from moral and spiritual decline. Today, American Christians seek to serve multiple masters. Our secular gods are many—mammon, yes, but also cars, clothes, sex, and sports.

The movement to display the Ten Commandments publicly represents a false theology. It is decidedly "old covenant." This is the second great irony of the battle for the Ten Commandments—allegedly new covenant Christians are returning to God's law in an old covenant manner.

Christians today have a distorted view of the new covenant, which is commonly understood to emphasize salvation by grace. While it is true that salvation is by grace, few understand the biblical definition of the covenants. This, in turn, leads to the unseemly distortion of approaching God's law in the wrong way. One need not be a theologian to grasp the theological confusion.

On the eve of the giving of the Ten Commandments, Moses climbed Mount Sinai and received a message from the Almighty: "Moses went up to God, and the LORD called to him from the mountain, saying, 'Thus you shall say to the house of Jacob, and tell the children of Israel: "You have seen what I did to the Egyptians, and how I bore you on eagles' wings and brought you to Myself. Now therefore, if you will indeed obey My voice and keep My covenant, then you shall be a special treasure to Me above all people; for all the earth is Mine. And you shall be to Me a kingdom of priests and a holy nation." These are the words which you shall speak to the children of Israel' " (Exodus 19:3–6, NKJV).

So Moses climbed down the mountain, called the elders of the people together, and reported what God had said. They responded appropriately and declared, " 'We will do everything the Lord has said' " (Exodus 19:8). Thus Israel entered the old covenant. The covenant, or agreement, was founded on the human promise to obey God. This is a promise that people can't keep. Israel had been in captivity in Egypt. Perhaps, having just been released from slavery, the Jewish leaders felt that transferring their obedience from Pharaoh and their Egyptian taskmasters to the God who had delivered them would be a simple task. It wasn't. They didn't have an adequate grasp of the human condition. They couldn't obey God in their own strength.

Later, when Moses penned the book of Deuteronomy, he reminded the nation that it wasn't enough to have the law written externally—the love of God must be in the human heart (see Deuteronomy 6:4–10). This lesson was repeated by Jeremiah, who made the new covenant explicit. The new covenant is based on God's promise to write the law in the human heart and mind (see Jeremiah 31:31–34). When Paul discussed the new covenant in Hebrews, he observed that it is based on "better promises" (Hebrews 8:6). Then he quoted what Jeremiah said about God writing the law on the human heart.

The key to understanding the covenants then, is not time. The difference between the old and new covenants is our response. When we are under the old covenant, we believe that we can bring our performance in-line with God's expectations—that we can obey in our human strength. When we enter the new covenant, it is with the recognition that we require an inner spiritual transformation and that only God can bring this about.

A modern power play

The Ten Commandments have become part of a modern political power play. The renewed emphasis on God's law has much less to do with rendering the obedience due to our Creator and much more with cultural renewal through political action. While Americans have every right to seek to change the laws in order to change the culture, from a theological perspective, this is the wrong approach. It is old covenant—which is a metaphor for external measures as contrasted with inner spiritual renewal.

We hear a great deal about America being a Christian nation and about our right to acknowledge God publicly and to display the Ten Commandments publicly. It is easy to give lip service to God but much harder to live a life of faithful obedience, dependence upon God, and full submission to His will. Declaring that America is a Christian nation and that we need to display God's law publicly does a grave disservice to the gospel of Christ.

The heart of the matter is the human heart. This is where cultural and spiritual renewal must take place. Placing the emphasis on changing laws or on public displays is a diversion. Americans need the law of God written in the heart. As long as the American church is fixated on politics and civil law and on God's law as an external symbol, this nation will never experience genuine spiritual revival.

We cannot separate the law of God from the gospel of Jesus Christ. Jesus died to pay the penalty for the sins of the human race. These sins are defined by God's law—defined as transgressions of the law (see 1 John 3:4). Jesus died not only to forgive people but also to transform them from the inside out, to restore them to their full humanity as free men and women in Christ. This is the gospel. It is freedom from both the penalty and power of sin. Today, many American preachers emphasize the forgiveness freely offered but fail to adequately present both the opportunity and necessity of inner change. In doing so, they deny the gospel its power.

In such a climate, God's law is rarely presented as the normative standard of human conduct—as God's reasonable requirement for all people. Instead, it is more often presented as a standard for society to enforce. Such an emphasis on the social, political, or public relevance of the Ten Commandments is distinctly old covenant. In the new covenant, it is not the nation but the human heart that requires the transformation that God—and only God—can produce when He writes His law there.

What does it mean for the law of God to be written in the human heart? It means an entire change of the inner life. The heart and mind are symbolic of one's thoughts and attitudes, one's motives and values. The governing principles of a person's life must be totally changed. Paul declared, "If any man is in Christ, he is a new creation; old things have passed away, behold, all things are become new." This is the emphasis that is lacking in many modern discussions of the Ten Commandments. This is the new covenant.

America is facing both a spiritual crisis and an opportunity, depending on how Americans approach God's law. The public display of the Ten Commandments has become a symbol for the desired moral, spiritual, and cultural renewal. Such renewal is definitely needed, but it can be achieved only if Americans pursue a new covenant experience. Instead of invoking God as some sort of national tribal deity who will bless America if we will only acknowledge Him publicly, Americans need to return to the Lord in a genuine way—not publicly, but on our knees. We must recover an authentic gospel and place the law of God where it belongs—in our hearts.

Those who advocate "saving America" by political means deprive the gospel of its true power. Spiritual revival has transformed culture in the past, and it can again. The American Revolution was profoundly shaped by the First Great Awakening, just as the abolitionist movement and the Civil War were influenced by the Second Great Awakening. The civil rights movement of the twentieth century was likewise dependent on spiritual principles and leadership for its power. Many of America's most profound problems simply cannot be solved by political panaceas. They are matters of the heart. Homosexuality won't disappear because Christians want to outlaw it. Neither will abortion.

If Americans return to God's law in a truly new covenant way, they can rediscover the power of God. This has real capacity to transform individual lives and families, and by extension, communities, states, and the nation. Failing this, it is possible, even probable, that Americans will continue to pursue God's law in an old covenant manner and seek to enact laws to compel people to obey God.

While many have heard of the prophecy of the infamous "mark of the beast," few comprehend that this prophecy describes a time when worship is compelled by force of law. Those who receive the mark are those who worship in the approved manner; while those who are faithful to God refuse to accept the mark and consequently are subject to intense persecution. Revelation 13:11–17 says that those who don't worship the beast will be subject to severe penalties, including the death penalty. Legislated worship ought to be listed among the greatest of oxymorons, for if there is one thing the law cannot command, it is genuine worship of the Almighty. This is the lesson of Revelation 13. It is a lesson that we learn too late at our peril.

The battle for the Ten Commandments isn't just symbolic. It is a real battle, and the stakes are high. This battle is being fought in the courts, on the airwaves of talk radio, and even at the ballot box.[14] Like the war on terrorism, the battle for the Ten Commandments is unlikely to end anytime soon. It has all the staying power of issues like abortion and school prayer. It raises strong emotions and has proven to be effective when used in fund-raising appeals—Americans will open their checkbooks generously to defend the Ten Commandments. Should time endure, it is likely that future generations will still be fighting over the role of God's law in American public life.

The Ten Commandments deserve a better fate. God didn't etch them on tablets of stone merely to have them become a political or cultural football. True fans of the Ten Commandments will take them to heart themselves and teach them to their children. When they do, they will be preserving both their faith and their freedom.

---

1. Joshua Green, "Roy and His Rock," *Atlantic Monthly,* October 2005.

2. Roy Moore, *So Help Me God: The Ten Commandments, Judicial Tyranny, and the Battle for Religious Freedom* (Nashville: Broadman & Holman, 2005).

3. The Supreme Court's split decision, a sort of "divide the baby" approach, was expected and even sought by some within the community of religious liberty activists, including this author.

4. *Wallace v. Jaffree,* 472 U.S. 38 (1985) at 107.

5. Scalia's hypocrisy is matched only by his consistency in attacking religious freedom. In *Employment Division v. Smith,* Scalia advanced a false theory of government "neutrality" toward religion in order to eviscerate the Free Exercise Clause and practically eliminate the clause as an effective guardian of religious freedom. Here, Scalia does the opposite to the Establishment Clause, rejecting state neutrality and again, undermining religious freedom by giving to the majority the power to advance religion to the detriment of the minority.

6. Alan J. Reinach, "No Right Is an Island," *Liberty,* March/April 2002.

7. I became a New York Mets fan after being crushed by the Yankees' loss to the St. Louis Cardinals in the 1964 World Series, so the prospect of punishing Yankees fans holds more than a little amusement for me.

8. Our political discourse has already degenerated to the point where those who criticize American foreign policy are regularly accused of being unpatriotic, against the American military, and worse. The demonization is already prevalent. Should the demonizers gain sufficient power, it would be a simple matter to criminalize the political views of their opponents. This is a familiar course of political disintegration.

9. According to Freedom House's 2006 survey (www.freedomhouse.org), 43 percent of nations are "not free" regarding press freedom, and only 17 percent are identified as free. In Iran, for example, publishing antigovernment "propaganda," a term that is undefined, can result in a prison sentence. Publishing something regarded as "an insult to religion" is punishable by death.

10. According to Wikipedia, James Madison referenced the concept but not the phrase in Federalist No. 10, the phrase being attributed alternately to Alexis de Tocqueville and John Stuart Mill. In his famous essay "On Liberty" (1859), Mill discussed the problem of the tyranny of the majority:

> Like other tyrannies, the tyranny of the majority was at first, and is still vulgarly, held in dread, chiefly as operating through the acts of the public authorities. But reflecting persons perceived that when society is itself the tyrant— society collectively over the separate individuals who compose it—its means of tyrannizing are not restricted to the acts which it may do by the hands of its political functionaries. Society can and does execute its own mandates: and if it issues wrong mandates instead of right, or any mandates at all in things with which it ought not to meddle, it practices a social tyranny more formidable than many kinds of political oppression, since, though not usually upheld by such extreme penalties, it leaves fewer means of escape, penetrating much more deeply into the details of life, and enslaving the soul itself. Protection, therefore, against the tyranny of the magistrate is not enough: there needs protection also against the tyranny of the prevailing opinion and feeling; against the tendency of society to impose, by other means than civil penalties, its own ideas and practices as rules of conduct on those who dissent from them; to fetter the development and, if possible, prevent the formation of any individuality not in harmony with its ways, and compel all characters to fashion themselves upon the model of its own. There is a limit to the legitimate interference of collective opinion with individual independence: and to find that limit, and maintain it against encroachment, is as indispensable to a good condition of human affairs as protection against political despotism.

John Stuart Mills, *On Liberty*, The Library of Liberal Arts ed. (Charlottesville, Va.: Michie Co., 1999), 7.

11. *McCreary County v. American Civil Liberties Union of Kentucky*, 545 U.S. 844 (2005), O'Connor, J. concurring.

12. *Id.*

13. This is exactly what Pat Buchanan declared in his speech at the 1992 Republican National Convention when he announced a "cultural war" for the soul of America. For the text of his speech, see http://www.buchanan.org/pa-92-0817-rnc.html.

14. In November 2006, the citizens of Boise, Idaho, voted on whether to return a Ten Commandments monument to Julia Davis Park.

Appendix

Article III of the U.S. Constitution

Section 1. The judicial Power of the United States, shall be vested in one supreme Court, and in such inferior Courts as the Congress may from time to time ordain and establish. The Judges, both of the supreme and inferior Courts, shall hold their Offices during good Behaviour, and shall, at stated Times, receive for their Services, a Compensation, which shall not be diminished during their Continuance in Office.

Section 2. The judicial Power shall extend to all Cases, in Law and Equity, arising under this Constitution, the Laws of the United States, and Treaties made, or which shall be made, under their Authority;—to all Cases affecting Ambassadors, other public ministers and Consuls;—to all Cases of admiralty and maritime Jurisdiction;—to Controversies to which the United States shall be a Party;—to Controversies between two or more States;—between a State and Citizens of another State;—between Citizens of different States;—between Citizens of the same State claiming Lands under Grants of different States, and between a State, or the Citizens thereof, and foreign States, Citizens or Subjects.

In all Cases affecting Ambassadors, other public Ministers and Consuls, and those in which a State shall be Party, the supreme Court shall have original Jurisdiction. In all the other Cases before mentioned, the supreme Court shall have appellate Jurisdiction, both as to Law and Fact, with such Exceptions, and under such Regulations as the Congress shall make.

The Trial of all Crimes, except in Cases of Impeachment, shall be by Jury; and such Trial shall be held in the State where the said Crimes shall have been committed; but when not committed within any State, the Trial shall be at such Place or Places as the Congress may by Law have directed.

Section 3. Treason against the United States, shall consist only in levying War against them, or in adhering to their Enemies, giving them Aid and Comfort. No Person shall be convicted of Treason unless on the Testimony of two Witnesses to the same overt Act, or on Confession in open Court.

The Congress shall have Power to declare the Punishment of Treason, but no Attainder of Treason shall work Corruption of Blood, or Forfeiture except during the Life of the Person attainted.

If you've appreciated this book, you'll like these also.

No Peace for a Soldier
Walter C. Utt / Helen Pyke
Part One
The devout French Protestants of the seventeenth century combined faith and works in heroic proportions. During severe persecutions, while some abandoned their faith, others were martyred. Follow a Huguenot family and an army officer forced to choose between loyalty to the king or to God.

Part Two
The story continues with the exiles in Holland after the Edict of Revocation eliminated the rights of non-Catholics in France. Follow Armand de Gandon, Madeleine Cortot, and Mathieu Bertrand as they each cope with exile in their own way.
Paperback, 256 pages.
ISBN 13: 978-0-8163-2172-8   ISBN 10: 0-8163-2172-8

Any Sacrifice but Conscience
Part One
This is the history of the "Glorious Return" of the Vaudois (Waldenses) to their valleys in southern France. Although their soldiers numbered less than a thousand, they fought the king of France and His Royal Highness the Duke of Savoy, and held their own against armies of 20,000 men. Miraculously they re-enter their ancestral lands and reestablish their worship of God which had been forbidden for three and a half years.

Part Two
The Vaudois were now free to return to their beloved valleys, but the Huguenots remained exiles abroad or a persecuted minority in France, forbidden to worship as their consciences dictated in a country which mandated religious uniformity. Adventure, tragedy, and hope await Armand de Gandon who makes a daring return to France to advance the Good Cause. Would these exiles ever be free to worship in their homeland again?
Paperback, 256 pages.
ISBN 13: 978-0-8163-2171-1   ISBN 10: 0-8163-2171-X

Three ways to order:
1. Local Adventist Book Center®
2. Call 1-800-765-6955
3. Shop AdventistBookCenter.com